The Algerian War, The Algeria

Natalya Vince

The Algerian War, The Algerian Revolution

palgrave
macmillan

Natalya Vince
School of Area Studies, History,
Politics and Literature
University of Portsmouth
Portsmouth, UK

ISBN 978-3-030-54263-4   ISBN 978-3-030-54264-1   (eBook)
https://doi.org/10.1007/978-3-030-54264-1

For Ali and Ally
Loughlin, El Hadj Mustapha and Clive

CONTENTS

About the Author

Natalya Vince is Reader in North African and French Studies at the University of Portsmouth, UK. She is the author of *Our Fighting Sisters, Nation, Memory and Gender in Algeria, 1954–2012* (2015), which was the winner of the 2016 Women's History Network Book Prize. The manuscript for *The Algerian War, The Algerian Revolution* was completed during a European Commission H2020 Marie Skłodowska-Curie Actions Global Fellowship (705763/STUSOCSTA).

ABBREVIATIONS

AGEA	General Association of Students of Algeria (Association générale des étudiants d'Algérie)
AJEMA	Association of Muslim Algerian Student Youth (Association de la jeunesse estudiantine musulmane algérienne)
AJIR	Association for Justice, Information and Reparation for *harkis* (Association justice, information et réparation pour les harkis)
ALN	National Liberation Army (Armée de libération nationale, jaysh al-tahrīr al-watani)
AML	Friends of the Manifesto and of Liberty (Amis du manifeste et de la liberté)
ANFANOMA	National Association of the French of North Africa, Overseas and their Friends (Association nationale des Français d'Afrique du Nord, d'outre-mer et de leurs amis)
ANP	National Popular Army (Armée nationale populaire)
ANPA	National Army of the Algerian People (Armée nationale du peuple algérien)
ASAF	Association to Support the French Army (Association soutien à l'armee française)
AUMA/AOMA	Association of Algerian Muslim 'Ulama (Association des 'ulama [sometimes transliterated oulémas] musulmans algériens/jam'iyyat al-'ulamā' al-muslimīn al-jazā'iriyyīn)
CCE	Coordination and Execution Committee (Comité de coordination et d'exécution)
CDL	Combatants of Liberation (Combattants de la libération)
CFLN	French Committee of National Liberation (Comité français de libération nationale)
CFMRAA	Confederation of French Muslims Repatriated from Algeria (Confédération des Français musulmans rapatriés d'Algérie)
CNRA	National Council of the Algerian Revolution (Conseil national de la révolution algérienne)
COM	Military Operational Committees (Comités opérationnels militaires)
COMINTERN	Communist International (Third International)

CRUA	Revolutionary Committee for Unity and Action (Comité révolutionnaire d'unité et d'action)
CSP	Committee of Public Safety (Comité de salut public)
DAF	Deserter from the French Army (Déserteur de l'armée française)
EEC	European Economic Community
EMG	Army General Staff (Etat major général)
EMSI	Itinerant Medical-Social Teams (Equipes médico-sociales itinérantes)
ENA	North African Star (Etoile nord africaine)
FF-FLN	French Federation of the FLN (Fédération de France du FLN)
FFS	Front for Socialist Forces (Front des forces socialistes)
FIS	Islamic Salvation Front (Front islamique du salut, al-jabha al-islamiyya lil-inqādh)
FLN	National Liberation Front (Front de libération nationale, jabhat al-taḥrīr al-watani)
FN	National Front (Front national)
FNACA	National Federation of Veterans of Algeria, Morocco and Tunisia (Fédération nationale des anciens combattants en Algérie, Maroc et Tunisie)
FPA	Auxiliary Police Force (Force de police auxiliaire)
FSNA	French of North African Origin (Français de souche nord africaine)
GPRA	Provisional Government of the Algerian Republic (Gouvernement provisoire de la République algérienne)
GPRF	Provisional Government of the French Republic (Gouvernement provisoire de la République française)
HCE	High Council of State (Haut conseil d'Etat)
LAI	League Against Imperialism and for National Independence
MNA	Algerian National Movement (Mouvement national algérien, al-haraka al-wataniyya al-jazā'iriyya)
MRAP	Movement against Racism and for Friendship between Peoples (Mouvement contre le racisme et pour l'amitié entre les peuples)
MTLD	Movement for the Triumph of Democratic Liberties (Mouvement pour le triomphe des libertés démocratiques)
NATO	North Atlantic Treaty Organisation
OAS	Secret Armed Organisation (Organisation armée secrète, sometimes translated as Secret Army Organisation)
OCRS	Common Organisation of the Saharan Regions (Organisation commune des régions sahariennes)
OS	Special Organisation (Organisation spéciale, OS)
PCA	Algerian Communist Party (Parti communiste algérien, al-hizb al-shuyū'ī al-jazā'iri)
PCF	French Communist Party (Parti communiste français)
PPA	Algerian People's Party (Parti du peuple algérien, hizb al-shāab al-jazā'iri)
RECOURS	Unitary Rally and Coordination for Repatriates and the Dispossessed (Rassemblement et coordination unitaires des rapatriés et spoliés)

SAS	Specialised Administrative Sections (Sections administratives spécialisées)
SAT-FMA	Technical Assistance Service for French Muslims of Algeria (Service d'assistance technique aux français musulmans d'Algérie)
SAU	Urban Administrative Sections (Sections administratives urbaines)
SFIO	French Section of the Workers' International (Section française de l'Internationale ouvrière, SFIO, the future Socialist Party)
SMA	Algerian Muslim Scouts (Scouts musulmans algériens, al-kashāfa al-islamiyya al-jazā'iriyya)
UDMA	Democratic Union of the Algerian Manifesto (Union démocratique du manifeste algérien)
UGEMA	General Union of Algerian Muslim Students (Union générale des étudiants musulmans algériens)
UIC	Intercolonial Union (Union intercoloniale)
UMP	Union for a Popular Movement (Union pour un mouvement populaire)
UN	United Nations
UNEF	National Union of Students of France (Union nationale des étudiants de France)
ZAA	Algiers Autonomous Zone (Zone autonome d'Alger)

LIST OF FIGURES

CHAPTER 1

Context and Historiography

Between 1954 and 1962, one of the most violent wars of decolonisation of the twentieth century took place. As French rule came to an end in Indochina in 1954, Morocco and Tunisia in 1956 and in West and Equatorial Africa in 1960, France clung on in Algeria, the oldest of its African colonial possessions. The Algerian National Liberation Front (Front de libération nationale, jabhat al-tahrīr al-watani, FLN) sought to chip away at French will to remain through rural and urban guerrilla warfare in both Algeria and mainland France, and by actively campaigning to persuade the international community that French rule in Algeria was illegitimate. In response, successive French governments sent a total of around two million soldiers, the vast majority of whom were conscripts, to fight a war through tactics which included aerial bombing, massive population displacement, army-led police operations and intensive propaganda efforts to 'win hearts and minds' within the local population.

The number of people killed during the war is subject to ongoing disagreement. French army losses are the least contentious as reliable records are available: they number around 25,000 men (Stora 2005, 23). European settler losses in Algeria have been evaluated at around 4000–4500 people (Stora 2005, 23), although some claim that many more European civilians were killed. The debate over this statistic is part of a wider controversy about what many former settlers see as the French state's 'abandonment' of them in 1962. Indeed, in 1961, hardliner settlers and army officers who refused to accept the end of 'French Algeria' formed a paramilitary organisation, the Secret Army Organisation (Organisation armée secrète, OAS), which waged a campaign of assassinations and bomb attacks targeting the French army, the FLN and the wider Algerian population. Even more contentious are debates surrounding the number of Algerians who served as either soldiers or auxiliaries in the French army (today generically referred to as *harkis*) who were killed at the end of the war by other Algerians as 'traitors'. *Harki* community activists have put

© The Author(s) 2020
N. Vince, *The Algerian War, The Algerian Revolution*,
https://doi.org/10.1007/978-3-030-54264-1_1

this figure as high as 150,000. Historians' estimates range from 15–30,000 people (Stora 2005, 24) to 60,000–75,000 people (Eldridge 2009, 92).

In Algeria, 'one and a half million martyrs' is the official number of Algerian combatants and civilians killed during the liberation struggle, and this figure has been central to the construction of Algerian national identity since 1962. Comparing different censuses before and after the war, researchers have calculated that 350,000–400,000 men, women and children were killed during the conflict, representing three per cent of the Algerian population at the time. Of these, up to 150,000 may have been combatants—in 1974, this was the number of pensions being paid by the Algerian state to families of soldiers killed in combat (Stora 2005, 24–25). Beyond a war of numbers, what these statistics immediately foreground is that this anti-colonial struggle was much more complex than a straightforward confrontation between 'the French' and 'the Algerians'.

There is also no consensus about what to call the conflict. For nearly four decades after the end of the war, the official term in France was 'operations in North Africa', which was used alongside other euphemistic expressions such as 'events', 'operations to maintain order' and 'pacification'. This 'war without a name' was only officially recognised as a war by the French state in 1999, when a law was passed to rename 'operations in North Africa' the 'Algerian War' (*Guerre d'Algérie*). Yet this is not a neutral term either: instead it reflects a French national perspective, in the same way that Americans talk about the 'Vietnam War' whilst the Vietnamese talk about the 'Resistance War against America' from the mid-1950s to 1973. More recently, the term 'French-Algerian War' has emerged, which is also unsatisfactory, as it suggests a symmetrical conflict between two similar powers, when in fact the war pitched one of the largest and best equipped armies in the world against rural and urban guerrillas operating within a civilian population.

In Algeria, the war is officially celebrated as the 'Algerian Revolution' (*al-thawra al-jazā'iriyya*), and often referred to as the 'War of National Liberation'. The terms 'revolution' and 'liberation' have been contested within and beyond Algeria, notably by those who question if a revolution took place after independence, and to what extent Algerians were liberated, given that colonial rule was followed by the creation of an authoritarian political system in which the only permitted political party was that of the FLN. Sylvie Thénault (2012, 14) has proposed the term 'Algerian War of Independence' as a neutral term which brings together different perspectives on the conflict. Todd Shepard (2015, 877) argues that this is too neat a package. For Shepard, the different terminology used to refer to the war should be used simultaneously to reflect the multiple ways in which the war has been understood and interpreted, both at the time and subsequently.

Debates about the origins, course and legacies of the war are inextricable from the wartime and post-independence politics of Algeria and France. The conflict is in many ways a textbook example of how interpretations of the past are shaped by the political demands of the present. In both France and Algeria, this past provides a seemingly endless source of easily accessible controversies, which reach far beyond the community of historians, and through which public debates can take place about pressing issues in the present such as political legitimacy, national identity and immigration. Whilst the Algerian War/ the Algerian Revolution, and French colonial rule in Algeria more generally, remains 'useful' in this way, there is little chance of it becoming a historical object that can be dispassionately discussed.

Understanding the underlying, and often unspoken, arguments about the present which loom behind ostensibly historical debates is a demanding task, notably for English-language readers new to Franco-Algerian history. The first challenge is to get to grips with the history of a country which has had relatively little visibility in the English-speaking world and on which the majority of research is not published in English—although one of the first overviews of the conflict, a vivid account titled *A Savage War of Peace: Algeria 1954–62* (1977), was written by a British journalist and historian, Alistair Horne. The second challenge is understanding how the history which has followed the period under examination has profoundly shaped the interpretations which we have at our disposal. This task is enriched but also made more difficult by the explosion in the quantity of internet content about the war in the past 20 years and the emergence of social media. This has created an online space for debates which are often even more virulent than those which take place in the local and national press, and on television and radio. Put 'Algerian War of Independence' (or one of its other names) into a search engine and millions of hits immediately appear. Some of these are balanced chronological overviews by trusted academic sources, others are in-depth and not always easy-to-understand research articles on specific aspects of the war, others still are personal accounts or forthright demands demanding recognition and reparation from the French or Algerian state for 'crimes against humanity'. The latter in particular contain, in differing doses, fascinating nuggets, highly partisan views and outright false information. This excess of information, and, in particular, this excess of information which rarely explicitly declares its political leanings, makes acquiring a broad overview of the topic, identifying a hierarchy of arguments and locating and analysing a source's biases more of a challenge.

The aim of this book, then, is twofold. Firstly, it aims to provide an overview of the key approaches to and debates about the events of the Algerian War/the Algerian Revolution. In particular, it focuses on how these debates have been revisited in the most recent scholarship. Secondly, it seeks to provide insights into the contexts in which these approaches have emerged—that is, how debates about the past are connected to present concerns—in order to provide readers with tools to navigate and decode the increasingly vast quantities of information available at their fingertips. This, then, is also a book about historiography, and its central importance in our supposedly globally connected information age, as hierarchies of knowledge production are both flattened and reinforced.

KEY FEATURES OF COLONIAL ALGERIA

Not a Colony But Départements *(Provinces) of France, a Large Settler Population, 'the Civilising Mission' and the Language and Lessons of 1789*

In order to understand the origins, course and legacies of the Algerian War / the Algerian Revolution, an understanding of some of the key features of colonial Algeria is essential. Algeria was part of the French empire from 1830 to 1962. At its highpoint in 1930, this empire spanned most of North, West and Equatorial Africa as well as Madagascar, Indochina (modern-day Vietnam, Cambodia and Laos), Syria and Lebanon (Fig. 1.1). Algeria had a unique status within this empire. Legally, from 1848 onwards, Algeria was not considered a colony. Instead, its north region constituted three *départements* (provinces) of France: the Oran region, the Algiers region and the Constantine region. Like all the other provinces in metropolitan France (see Glossary), these Algerian provinces came under the authority of the Ministry of the Interior not the Ministry for Colonies. The less populated territories of the south in the Sahara were under military rule. In the course of the Algerian War of Independence, the three *départements* of Oran, Algiers and Constantine were reorganised into smaller administrative regions, and the territories of the south were also departmentalised: thus in 1959, Algeria constituted 15 provinces of France.

The other distinct feature of Algeria was that it had a large number of settlers. These settlers came not only from metropolitan France, but from across Europe, notably Spain and Italy, but also Malta, Germany and Switzerland. By 1954, there were around one million 'Europeans' for 8.5 million 'French Muslims'—we will return to the significance of this terminology shortly. Some settlers came to seek their fortune, others were landless peasants trying to eke out an existence, others still were left-wing political exiles expelled from France after the failed Paris Commune in 1871. Some of them did acquire land and become rich, others formed a poor, urban working class. Through a mixture of informal settler land grab and legally sanctioned expropriation, many Algerian farmers were reduced to cultivating shrinking parcels of less fertile soil, or pushed off their lands altogether and denied access to previously communal forests. A symbol of both sovereignty and how much Algerians had lost to colonialism, 'recovering our land' was a central theme in Algerian nationalism.

It is not within the scope of this book to examine the various motivations for conquest and colonisation (see Sessions 2011; McDougall 2017), but it is important to note that one of the distinctive features of the French empire was the emphasis it placed on its 'civilising mission'. All European empires claimed to be 'civilising the natives' and often this involved converting them to Christianity. In the French case, the role of religion and religious missionaries coexisted alongside more secular missionaries. The origins of the French 'civilising mission' can be found in the idea dating from the late-eighteenth-century Enlightenment and the French Revolution of 1789 that all men (and

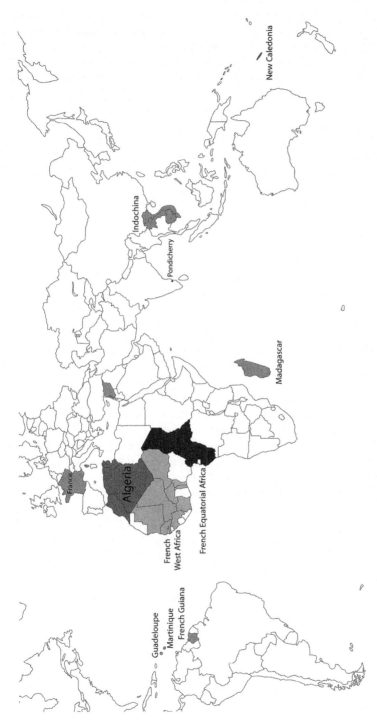

Fig. 1.1 Map of the French empire in 1930 (simplified)

this was very much all about men, not women) shared the same universal values and potential for improvement in order to ultimately become the same and equal. Intimately intertwined with this apparent promotion of equality were racist ideas about 'superior' and 'inferior' 'races', which supposedly explained current differences in levels of 'civilisation' between peoples around the world. Predictably, European (and more specifically, French) politics, economic models, society and culture were considered to be at the summit of civilisational development. Colonial conquest was presented as an act of generosity towards the childlike, irrational, barbarian 'natives' by incrementally assimilating them. Assimilation meant becoming culturally and legally French. The rhetoric of the civilising mission was particularly potent under the Third Republic (1870–1940), and much closer to the hearts of French Republicans from the left and centre than it was to anti-Republicans on the right. The latter, although not against imperial expansion, were much more likely to adhere to ideas about cultural immutability—that is, the 'natives' are so different from us that they can never be our equals, so there is no point trying to improve them.

Viewed from today, the 'civilising mission' might seem a cynical justification for subjugating peoples and exploiting their lands. However, some historians have argued that we should take seriously the sincerity of at least some of those colonial officials, teachers and doctors who claimed to be participating in a 'civilising mission', whilst recognising that it failed to live up to its own claims of improvement on the ground (Conklin 1997). Attachment to the idea that imperial rule could be a force for good is key to understanding many left and centre-left French politicians' policy pronouncements and much policy-making by civil servants in relation to Algeria right up into the late 1950s.

Whilst rejecting the idea that they were 'backwards' and needed to be 'civilised', many Algerian anti-colonial activists could also be inspired by the values of the French Revolution—liberty, equality and fraternity. In the 1920s and 1930s, the idea of 'Two Frances'—that is, that the 'France' in Algeria was an exploitative perversion of the 'true France' of 1789 and the Rights of Man—provided a powerful political language for some of Algeria's first anti-colonial campaigners, such as Ferhat Abbas (1899–1985), to articulate their demands (Stora 1989). In the 1950s, the lessons of the French Revolution, as understood by a new generation of Algerian nationalists, were less focused on the utopia of a 'true France' and instead foregrounded the legitimacy of taking up arms against a despotic political system which did not represent the people. Explaining why she joined the FLN in the 1950s, 17-year-old urban bomber Baya Hocine (1940–2000) declared: 'The history teaching I received at high school clearly showed me that nationalist and revolutionary movements were in no way subversive, on the contrary, all my textbooks spoke with admiration and respect of those who sought to shake off the yoke of foreign domination' (Vince 2015, 46).

The Importance of Law and the Creation of Categories in the Construction of Colonial Algeria and in Shaping Anti-colonial Struggles

Although Algeria was officially *not* a colony, its autochthonous inhabitants (see Glossary) undoubtedly lived in a colonial situation. This was built on exclusionary and discriminatory laws and practices which kept political, economic, social and cultural power in the hands of the settlers. At the heart of this system were laws on citizenship. The Sénatus-consulte of 14 July 1865 (a law voted by the French Senate) set out the boundaries of who in Algeria was entitled to full French citizenship. This was important because if Algeria really was an integral part of France, then all men in Algeria should have benefitted from the right to vote, as all men did in France. In reality, because the settler population in Algeria was in the numerical minority, universal male suffrage was unthinkable because they would be outvoted by the autochthonous population. The Sénatus-consulte of 14 July 1865 thus declared that the 'indigenous Muslim' was French and therefore obliged to carry out military service and was able to join the civil service, but that he could not gain the rights of full French citizenship through naturalisation unless he renounced his 'Muslim personal status' in matters of family law. This 'personal status' consisted of customs such as polygamy, the right of husbands' to unilaterally end their marriage (repudiation) and the privileging of male children over female children in inheritance which were considered by the French state to be incompatible with the French civil code and, therefore, made Muslim men impossible to assimilate into the French nation.

The 1865 law was not about the lack of rights, or supposed lack of rights, of Muslim women—in any case, French women in metropolitan France had few rights themselves in the mid-nineteenth century. Instead, this law was about using claims made about the 'too different' *culture* of colonised peoples as the basis for excluding them from accessing *political* rights. During the colonial period, only a very tiny number of 'indigenous Muslims' requested naturalisation, because renouncing one's personal status was considered apostasy (an abandonment of one's religion). Those who did try to renounce their personal status encountered administrative resistance. In the eyes of the French state and the colonial administration, being 'Muslim' was not just a set of religious and cultural practices that one chose to participate in, it was an inescapable ethnic-legal identity which was hard to relinquish, even if one wanted to do so, and which conferred a form of second-class citizenship (Weil 2008). In turn, for anti-colonial activists working in a context where colonialism had profoundly disrupted and reshaped Algeria's political structures, economy, society and culture, the Muslim personal status became a key marker of what distinguished 'us' from 'them'. It was the basis of an alternative collective identity to that of second-class French citizen.

Whilst it was made very difficult for 'Muslims' to become French citizens, the 'French' national identity of Algeria was strengthened through co-opting the autochthonous Jewish population as well as European migrants from countries other than France. Between 1865 and 1870, the 1865 Senatus-consulte also applied to the Jewish population of Algeria—full citizenship was only offered if the individual renounced Jewish family law. The 1870 Crémieux decree, passed under the Third Republic, naturalised en masse around 30,000 Jews in Algeria (excluding those living in the Sahara). Henceforth, these Jews were legally categorised as 'Europeans', even though a Jewish presence in Algeria long preceded French colonisation, dating back to the arrival of the Phoenicians between 1100 and 146 BC. This presence had been augmented by Jews expelled from Spain in the late fifteenth and early sixteenth century coming to North Africa alongside Muslims who had also been expelled. The Jewish population of Algeria was heterogeneous. Some naturalised Jews would seize the opportunities which citizenship presented to them and rise up the ranks of the colonial administration. Others would remain poor, living alongside and sharing in the same dress, music and cultural traditions as their Muslim neighbours. Whilst most of the Jews of Algeria were full French citizens, anti-Semitism was often even more virulent amongst the settler population than it was in mainland France. In 1889, in a bid to further reinforce the French identity of a settler population whose origins were in Spain and Italy as much as they were in mainland France, French nationality and full citizenship rights were automatically given to children born in Algeria whose parents were non-French Europeans.

Indeed, it was settlers of European origin who informally appropriated for themselves the term 'Algerian' ('Algérien') in the late nineteenth century, as a way to underline what they considered to be their distinctive virile, Mediterranean identity compared to effeminate mainland France. The majority of settlers considered that Algeria had been a 'blank space' before they arrived, and that they had 'made the desert bloom'. Throughout the colonial period, including during the War of Independence, relations between those living in mainland France and Europeans living in Algeria were nearly always distant, and often openly hostile.

The colonised population of Algeria was refused the title of 'Algerians' by the colonial power. They were variously labelled 'the indigenous' (*indigènes*) or 'Muslims', with the category of 'indigenous' sometimes further subdivided into 'Arabs' and 'Berbers'. The French often used 'Berbers' interchangeably with 'Kabyles', which was one Berber (Tamazight)-speaking region in northern Algeria, although there were other Berber-speaking regions, notably in the Aures (eastern Algeria) and the Sahara. This subdivision of 'Muslims' into 'Arabs' and 'Berbers' was based on nineteenth-century pseudo-scientific theories about the Berber-speaking minority of Algeria forming a different (and superior) 'race' to the Arabic-speaking majority, more likely to benefit from the 'civilising mission' and become loyal administrators. This was a classic case of a colonial attempt to divide-and-rule (Lorcin 1995), similar to how the Belgians privileged Tutsis over Hutus in Rwanda, and the British privileged Muslims over Hindus in India. In reality, in terms of ethnicity, the vast majority of the inhabitants of North Africa are likely to be Imazighen (Berbers). The Arab invasion of North Africa from the seventh century onwards involved relatively few men, and therefore it is probable that most Arabic speakers in Algeria are Arabic-speaking Berbers rather than descendants of those who came from the Arabian Peninsula (Temlali 2015; Meynier 2007). After the Second World War, the term 'French Muslims' became commonplace in French politicians' speeches and policy pronouncements. From 1958 onwards, when the Muslim-majority population finally acquired full French citizenship, 'French of North African Origin' (Français de souche nord africaine, FSNA) was frequently used.

Some historians still use 'Muslims', 'French Muslims' and so forth, as this was the language of the time. However, this does reproduce the colonial refusal to recognise an autochthonous Algerian identity. This book, therefore, will mainly usually use the term 'Algerians' to refer to the autochthonous population excluded from full French citizenship. The terms Europeans of Algeria or settlers will be used to refer to those who had full French citizenship, whilst recognising that within this group were subsumed a minority of Jews who were neither settlers nor of European origin. When specifically discussing the legal categories of 'Europeans' and 'Muslims', these terms will be used in inverted commas. Muslim without inverted commas will be used to refer to a religious identity, that is, a follower of Islam.

Discrimination: The Indigénat, Education and Religion

Between 1881 and 1944, the vast majority of Algerians—that is, those who were not citizens, i.e. 'Muslims'—were subject to the *indigénat* (indigenous code). This was a series of repressive measures which only applied to French subjects and not citizens. The *indigénat* made meeting without authorisation, disrespect to an agent of authority even when he was off duty and leaving the local area without authorisation all infractions punishable by fine or imprisonment, or indeed subject to collective punishments such as burning down a local forest.

Furthermore, flying in the face of the rhetoric of the 'civilising mission', in 1954, 86 per cent of men and 95 per cent of women were illiterate, with only 14.6 per cent of school age children having a place at school (Kateb 2005, 115 and 29). This was a decline in literacy in comparison with the pre-colonial era, when there was a developed educational system built around religious institutions (Benrabah 2013, 32). In the colonial period, Algerian students who had gone beyond a primary education were rare. Those who were literate tended to only read and write in French. It was from this small, French-educated Algerian elite that some of the early demands for reform to the colonial system would emerge from the early twentieth century onwards. Arabic was designated a foreign language in 1935. The colonial authorities closed a number of Arabic-language and Qur'anic recitation schools, suspecting them of being centres of sedition. The same logic of surveillance and control also explains why one of the guiding principles of French Republicanism—the 1905 law separating

Church and State (*laïcité*), with neither institution allowed to interfere in affairs of the other—was never applied to Algeria. On the contrary, colonial authorities wanted to keep control over mosques, who was running them and what they were saying, in order to prevent them becoming hotbeds of anti-colonial and/or nationalist sentiment.

The creation of a second-class citizenship, the *indigénat*, the non-application of the 1905 law… none of this necessarily demonstrates that Algeria was an 'exception' in the French Republic, a place where the usual rules did not apply. Rather, the case of Algeria can be more fruitfully understood as revealing the ways in which universalist Republican ideology was dependent on sustaining hierarchies of difference. At some undefined point in the future it was vaguely anticipated that Algerians would be 'ready' to appreciate the full benefits of French civilisation and citizenship—just not yet. The truth underpinning this vagueness—largely unspoken until the dying days of French rule—was that real political equality would mean the end of the colony and the end of the empire, because the very definition of an empire is a powerful centre dominating a geographically distant periphery.

Key Themes in the Recent Historiography

This list of the different forms of oppression to which Algerians were subjected is not provided in order to suggest that colonial rule was monolithic or repre-sented a coherent plan for domination—it was neither of these things. Indeed, one of the features of colonial rule is its ad hoc and contradictory nature. This background information is instead provided in order to understand what hap-pened next. As will by now be clear, locating the Algerian War/ the Algerian Revolution in a longer period than the eight years between 1954 and 1962 has been a major theme in the historiography in recent years. This book thus begins with the outbreak of the First World War in 1914 and ends in 2020. Within this timeframe, it engages with four interconnected themes which have provoked—and continue to provoke—debate amongst historians and the wider public. To facilitate more focused reading, pathways are suggested for each theme which flag some of the key sections to look at in order to understand these debates in the historiography. These thematic pathways are highlighted throughout in textboxes. In addition, within each chapter, arrows (<< or >>) indicate addi-tional pages to look at to deepen understanding and draw broader connections for readers dipping in and out of the book rather than reading it from begin-ning to end. These can be used in conjunction with the index, which also enables individual people and places to be tracked through the book.

Thematic Pathway 1: Connecting the Local, National, Transnational and Global

During the War of Independence, both the French state and the leadership of the Algerian National Liberation Front were intensely aware that the conflict was being played out on the world stage and its eventual outcome would, to a significant degree, be determined by each side's ability to operate within and leverage to its advantage the post-1945 world order (the Cold War, the emergence of international organisations such as the United Nations and decolonisation in Africa and Asia) (Fig. 1.2). After 1962, both French and Algerian national histories 'nationalised' the war, limiting it to a Franco-Algerian affair. According to the Algerian state, the war was won through the Algerian people's armed struggle and sacrifice. According to the French state, President Charles de Gaulle (1890–1970, president 1958–69) deftly manoeuvred Algeria, as well as France's other African colonies, to independence and a new era of bilateral Franco-African relations. In the last two decades, the importance of the international context and transnational (see Glossary) connections have been brought firmly back into the historiography of the origins, course and legacies of the conflict, initially by historians who were neither French nor Algerian (Connelly 2002; Byrne 2016). The historiographical challenge now is to connect this global and transnational history (often carried out by scholars in the Global North, who have the funds and visas to travel to archives scattered across the world) to the rich local histories of regions, prisons, villages and families produced by scholars in Algeria (often gathered through years of interviewing, based on local connections using local languages) which reveal everyday strategies of colonial domination, resistance, negotiation and survival (Adel 2019; Siari Tengour 2014; Zekkour 2011; Soufi 2000).

> **Thematic pathway 1 textboxes:** *Manoeuvring for change within the limits of the possible* (Chap. 2, p. 24), *African American soldiers on the streets of Algeria* (Chap. 2, p. 44), *Aït Ahmed's 1948 report* (Chap. 2, p. 53), *Why was Bandung significant?* (Chap. 3, p. 73), *Leveraging Cold War Rivalries* (Chap. 3, p. 76), *Launching the 'Battle of Algiers'* (Chap. 3, p. 92), *'Psychological action', 'modernisation' and their impacts* (Chap. 3, p. 101), *De-centring de Gaulle* (Chap. 3, p. 113), *Modernisation* (Chap. 3, p. 117), *An alternative framework for thinking about the legacies and memories of the Algerian War/the Algerian Revolution* (Chap. 4, p. 166), and *Transnational memory frames* (Chap. 4, p. 179).
>
> In addition, using the following key words in the Index will facilitate locating the origins, course and legacies of the Algerian War of Independence often told as a national story within a broader international history: Arab League, Atlantic Charter, Cold War, Comintern, EEC (European Economic Community), Eurafrique, First World War, *islah*, LAI (League Against Imperialism), propaganda, revolutionary warfare, Rif War, Second World War, self-determination, Suez Crisis, *tirailleurs sénégalais*, Third Worldism, UIC (Intercolonial Union), United Nations and the names of other countries (e.g. United States, Egypt, Tunisia, Morocco, USSR, etc.).

Fig. 1.2 Map of Africa and the Middle East, listing countries and cities referred to in this account of the Algerian War/Algerian Revolution

Thematic Pathway 2: Going Beyond 'Missed Opportunities' and 'Inevitable Violence': Re-examining the Relationship Between Politics and Violence

After 1962, two of the most dominant—and diametrically opposed—interpretations of the length, violence and destruction of the war were that (a) opportunities were missed for more peaceful solutions and (b) the turn to violence was inevitable. The theory of 'missed opportunities' was notably promoted by liberal French historians who blamed the intransigence of the European settler community and their inability to accept even the most modest reforms to the colonial system until it was too little, too late and mass bloodshed had already occurred. Charles-Robert Ageron (1923–2008) lived and taught in Algeria in 1947–57. In 1956–7, the middle of the war, he was part of a group of liberals who sought restart the discussion about reform, and non-violent steps to self-determination. He had little patience for settlers' bitter complaints that they had been 'abandoned' by de Gaulle and the French state in 1962. Writing in 1964, Ageron argued:

We shouldn't be seeking to point fingers at the 'person who sold out' French Algeria [i.e. de Gaulle]: whatever the political system in place, in the age of decolonisation, France never could have Frenchified Algeria through a war against Arab nationalism. Those who are truly to blame are those who, obstinately between 1919 and 1954, refused or sabotaged all reforms, and [yet] who, after 1958, preached integration [i.e. the extension of full political rights and socio-economic opportunities to Algerians] as a useful and dishonest alibi. (Quoted in Pervillé 2008, 375)

In a different spirit, but nevertheless connected vein, since the 1990s, a strand of liberal-leaning colonial nostalgia has emerged which has wondered aloud, albeit with little sensitivity to historical context, if a 'South African solution' might have been possible in Algeria. This is a reference to the end of white-minority rule without the departure of the white population in South Africa in 1994, an event which ended political and legal discrimination against black South Africans without overcoming racialised social and economic inequalities. The underlying assumption in the 'missed opportunities' approach is that Algeria could have remained part of France, an overseas department or territory like Reunion or French Polynesia are today. For Sylvie Thénault (2012, 21–22), the 'missed opportunity' approach is not only unrealistic about the prospect of reform, but it also writes from the perspective of the colonial state and settlers, largely ignoring whether or not Algerians wanted to remain part of France or become 'full' French citizens.

The opposite view—that a protracted, violent end to colonial rule was inevitable—has been promoted by actors of diverse political persuasions, for different reasons. In the dominant version of history promoted in independent Algeria, Algerian resistance to colonial rule began the moment French boots stepped onto Algerian soil in June 1830 and continued unwaveringly, in armed, political and cultural, but especially armed, forms, until 1962. In the words of Mohand Saïd Mazouz, an anti-colonial activist who spent 17 years in prison between 1945 and 1962, prefacing a book titled *Aux sources de novembre* [The Sources of November], published with the support of the Algerian Ministry of Culture to mark the fiftieth anniversary of independence, 'this country, so often attacked, has developed a kind of resistance atavism, to the point where one might demand if [resistance] is not passed down through our genes' (Chaalal and Haya 2013, 10).

There are various issues with such interpretations: firstly, not every Algerian resisted colonial rule all the time, some negotiated and compromised to survive (and in some cases, thrived), others accommodated the colonial system not to 'resist' or 'collaborate' but rather for social advancement or to settle a land dispute with their neighbour (Abbink et al. 2002). Secondly, such accounts of 1830–1954 as a long prelude to the War of Liberation give the FLN the starring role: it is presented as both the natural culmination of this continuous history of unwavering anti-colonial resistance and a necessary rupture with earlier, non-FLN, non-violent forms of action, which are ultimately dismissed as doomed to failure. Thirdly, the idea of a genetically transmitted prospensity for resistance hovers rather uncomfortably to essentialising views of Algerians as 'naturally' predisposed to violence. After the outbreak of civil violence in Algeria in the 1990s, which pitched armed Islamists against the Algerian state and army, the view that Algeria was locked in an interminable cycle of violence gained ground amongst journalists and some historians, both within and beyond Algeria. In this historically dubious interpretation, which still permeates many scholarly and popular accounts, the violence of colonial rule gave way to the violence of the liberation struggle which in turn gave birth to the civil violence of the 1990s (for criticisms of this approach see Benkhaled and Vince 2017; McDougall 2005).

In more recent years, a number of historians have fruitfully gone beyond both the counter-factual ('what if?') history of (a) and the overly deterministic approach of (b). Instead, they have closely considered the entangled relationship between politics and violence across a long period, from the First World War until 1962. Scholars have examined how Algerian political and cultural leaders, associations and parties adopted different arguments and strategies to get their point across and bring about change in a colonial situation which was repressive (and used censorship, banning and imprisonment) but not always repressive to the same degree all the time. James McDougall (2006, 64) underlines the 'endurance and perseverance of Algerians in seeking to find some means of accommodation with the inflexible autism of the colonial system'. Other historians have argued that some French politicians and civil servants were less rigid than the colonial system in which they were operating, and sought to reimagine a future, more equal French relationship with Algeria which did not involve France withdrawing to its European borders with a predominantly white European population (Shepard 2006). The question, then, was the possibility, or impossibility, of making one's political vision a reality without recourse to violence on a massive scale.

Thematic pathway 2 textboxes: *One interpretation of the Popular Front—a disappointment with far-ranging impact* (Chap. 2, p. 38), *Newer interpretations of the Popular Front—Marking the shift of mass politics to Algerian soil* (Chap. 2, p. 39), *Assessing the Brazzaville Conference* (Chap. 2, p. 46), *An inevitable turn to violence after Setif?* (Chap. 2, p. 50), *Aït Ahmed's 1948 report* (Chap. 2, p. 53), *One interpretation of 20 August 1955—a point of no return?* (Chap. 3, p. 79), *Another interpretation of 20 August 1955—not so significant?* (Chap. 3, p. 80), *Investment, reform and 'Special Powers'* (Chap. 3, p. 83), *Launching the 'Battle of Algiers'* (Chap. 3, p. 92), *What can we learn from* Centres sociaux, SAS *and* camps de regroupement *about French attempts to 'really' make Algeria French?* (Chap. 3, p. 103), *'Fraternisation' in 1958* (Chap. 3, p. 111), *Possible alternative ends to empire?* (Chap. 3, p. 129) and *Impossible alternative ends to empire?* (Chap. 3, p. 132).

Thematic Pathway 3: Debating the Nature of Algerian Nationalism:
From Asking 'What Was the National Liberation Front?'
to Examining 'Why Are There Arguments About What It Was?'

Given that the FLN was formally created just days before it carried out its first attacks on 1 November 1954, it is hardly surprising that its organisational and ideological roots have been much debated. For many historians, the FLN was an unideological marriage of convenience between a range of political tendencies, whose single unifying goal—national independence—would be its strength in 1954, and its weakness when independence finally came in 1962 (Meynier 2002). More recently, some historians have attempted to rehabilitate the political thought of the FLN—for Jeffrey James Byrne (2016), for at least some of its leaders, the FLN was a left-wing revolutionary movement, inspired by Russian revolutionary Vladimir Lenin, Chinese revolutionary Mao Zedong and Vietnamese revolutionary Hồ Chí Minh with the goal of becoming a Third Worldist (see Glossary) pilot state. This interpretation might be viewed sceptically by those who consider most FLN leaders much more attached to Islam than Marxism.

What is more interesting than the question 'what was the FLN?'—to which perhaps the only response is that it was heterogeneous, but not devoid of ideology—is 'why are debates about what it was so politically charged?' With its arguments about who was the 'father' of Algerian nationalism and clashes surrounding the relative 'contribution' of different political movements and cultural associations to the FLN's political DNA, the search for the origins of Algerian nationalism has often resembled the construction of a family tree. In Algeria today, those who are officially recognised as having participated in the Revolution are referred to as belonging to 'the revolutionary family'. As Omar Carlier (1997, 137) underlines: 'These questions are not just mere matters of technical or archival scholarship.' Arguing about who was the first, or the most 'truly' nationalist Algerian nationalist is inextricable from disputes over what the Algerian state and nation should look like in the present, and who is legitimate to lead it. For 20 years after independence, the post-1962 party of the FLN dominated Algerian public history with an official version of events which gave them a starring role. From the 1980s onwards, arguments about the present state of politics in Algeria have often taken place through proxy debates about the past. Branches of Algerian nationalism which were snapped off during the War of Independence, such as Messali Hadj's brand of popular nationalism or Ferhat Abbas's commitment to secular democracy, are presented as alternative pasts which could have provided alternative (i.e. 'better') futures. Long occulted in Algerian official history, we must be mindful of the air of nostalgia which often hangs around popular discussion of figures such as Messali Hadj and Abbas today, and that a revisionist foregrounding of their roles and visions is often developed with the aim of criticising the post-independence political system. More recent scholarship has focused less on the relative 'contribution' of different parties and associations in the emergence of an armed anti-colonial movement in 1954. Instead, it has examined how these groups participated in the creation of a wider political culture and language for making claims and articulating criticisms within a repressive political system—practices which extended into post-independence Algeria (Rahal 2018).

Thematic pathway 3 textboxes: *Manoeuvring for change within the limits of the possible* (Chap. 2, p. 24), *New interpretations of the Elus and Ferhat Abbas* (Chap. 2, p. 26), *New possibilities as seen by Messali Hadj* (Chap. 2, p. 29), *The ENA—Bringing together working-class and anticolonial struggles* (Chap. 2, p. 31), *The religious as reference* (Chap. 2, p. 32). *The 'ulama—more important in writing history than making it?* (Chap. 2, p. 34), *The PCA is not the PCF* (Chap. 2, p. 40), *The so-called Berber crisis* (Chap. 2, p. 54), *Who were 'the people'?* (Chap. 3, p. 67), *Gradually building the Front* (Chap. 3, p. 81), *Lacoste Promotion* (Chap. 3, p. 84), *The DAF* (Chap. 3, p. 88), *Melouza* (Chap. 3, p. 104), *Oujda* (Chap. 3, p. 109), *The term* mujahidin (Chap. 3, p. 127), *Women in the ALN* (Chap. 3, p. 128), *Why we need to know about the implosion of the FLN in summer 1962* (Chap. 3, p. 143), *'True' and 'false'* mujahidin (Chap. 4, p. 168), *Alternative versions of the past as a way to criticise the politico-military system* (Chap. 4, p. 178) and *Weaponising the language of the national past in the 2019 protests in Algeria* (Chap. 4, p. 186).

Thematic Pathway 4: The Terms of Future Debates: Questioning the Utility of 'Unhealed Wounds' as a Way of Understanding the Political, Social and Cultural Legacies of the War. Thinking Instead About How the War Provides a Set of Codes and Political Tools to Talk About Issues in the Present

One of the most hotly debated topics, in academic work, amongst politicians and in the media, are the legacies of the war. To what extent have Algeria and France failed to 'come to terms' with the conflict, and to what extent can this be used to explain contemporary issues such as crises of political legitimacy, a lack of social cohesion and racism? In 1991, Benjamin Stora published his highly influential *La Gangrène et l'oubli* [Gangrene and Forgetting], in which he argued that the unhealed wounds of the Algerian War were continuing to exert a divisive impact on French society, Algerian society and Franco-Algerian relations. The idea of bringing about greater social cohesion through confronting the multiple facets of France's past has been influential in French policy-making circles in recent years. The mission statement of France's National Museum for the History of Immigration, of which Stora is president of the steering committee, declares that it seeks to be 'a major element in the Republican and social cohesion of France'. A key theme for critics of the post-independence Algerian state is that the 'unfinished business' and 'hidden histories' of the War of Liberation are in part to blame for political problems in the present. Both the French and Algerian press make regular references to 'Franco-Algerian memory wars', a term which implies a conflict between the French state and the Algerian state, or between the Algerian people and the French people over how to interpret the past.

Scholars have expressed growing scepticism about both the idea that France and Algeria are collectively haunted by the past, and the capacity that 'coming to terms with the past' has to 'fix' the present. Instead of studying how the past shapes the present, this book flips the question round and focuses on how present political needs and socio-economic demands in Algeria and France can prompt politicians, associations and individuals to selectively revisit the past, plucking out people and events to make their point more forcefully. This approach also involves critiquing the overused term 'Franco-Algerian memory wars' by analysing how debates about the past have unfolded differently in France and Algeria since 1962, developing their own sets of codes and references.

> Chapter 4 'Legacies, 1962–2020' is centred around this thematic pathway, which will begin to be explored in earlier chapters through the following textboxes: *The so-called Berber crisis* (Chap. 2, p. 54), *Lacoste promotion* (Chap. 3, p. 84), *The DAF* (Chap. 3, p. 88), *The French army's use of torture* (Chap. 3, p. 94), *What happened to the 'disappeared'?* (Chap. 3, p. 95), *Oujda* (Chap. 3, p. 109), *17 October 1961* (Chap. 3, p. 135), *Charonne and the PCF* (Chap. 3, p. 138), *Rue d'Isly, 26 March 1962* (Chap. 3, p. 141) and *Why we need to know about the implosion of the FLN in summer 1962* (Chap. 3, p. 143).

References

Abbink, Jon, Klaas van Walraven, and Mirjam de Bruijn. 2002. *Rethinking Resistance: Revolt and Violence in African History.* Leiden: Brill.

Adel, Khedidja. 2019. La prison des femmes de Tifelfel. Enfermement et corps en souffrance [The Women's Prison of Tifelfel. Imprisonment and Suffering Bodies]. *L'Année du Maghreb* 20 (1): 123–158. https://doi.org/10.4000/anneemaghreb.4674.

Benkhaled, Walid, and Natalya Vince. 2017. Performing Algerianness: The National and Transnational Construction of Algeria's 'Culture Wars'. In *Algeria: Nation, Culture and Transnationalism, 1988–2015,* ed. Patrick Crowley, 243–269. Liverpool: Liverpool University Press.

Benrabah, Mohamed. 2013. *Language Conflict in Algeria: From Colonialism to Post-independence.* Bristol: Multilingual Matters.

Byrne, Jeffrey James. 2016. *Mecca of Revolution: Algeria, Decolonization and the Third World Order.* Oxford: Oxford University Press.

Carlier, Omar. 1997. Scholars and Politicians: An Examination of the Algerian View of Algerian Nationalism. In *The Maghrib in Question: Essays in History and Historiography,* ed. Michel Le Gall and Kenneth Perkins, 136–169. Austin: University of Texas Press.

Chaalal, Omar Mokhtar, and Djelloul Haya. 2013. *Aux sources de novembre* [The Sources of November]. Algiers: APIC éditions.

Conklin, Alice L. 1997. *A Mission to Civilize: The Republican Idea of Empire in France and West Africa, 1895–1930*. Stanford, CA: Stanford University Press.

Connelly, Matthew. 2002. *A Diplomatic Revolution: Algeria's Fight for Independence and the Origins of the Post-Cold War Era*. Oxford and New York: Oxford University Press.

Eldridge, Claire. 2009. 'We've never had a voice': Memory Construction and the Children of the Harkis (1962–1991). *French History* 23 (1): 88–107. https://doi.org/10.1093/fh/crn062.

Horne, Alistair. 1977. *A Savage War of Peace: Algeria, 1954–62*. London: Macmillan.

Kateb, Kamel. 2005. *Ecole, population et société en Algérie* [School, Population and Society in Algeria]. Paris: L'Harmattan.

Lorcin, Patricia. 1995. *Imperial Identities: Stereotyping, Prejudice and Race in Colonial Algeria*. New York, NY: I.B. Tauris.

McDougall, James. 2005. Savage Wars? Codes of Violence in Algeria, 1830s–1990s. *Third World Quarterly* 26 (1): 117–131. https://doi.org/10.1080/0143659042000322946.

———. 2006. *History and the Culture of Nationalism in Algeria*. Cambridge: Cambridge University Press.

———. 2017. *A History of Algeria*. Cambridge: Cambridge University Press.

Meynier, Gilbert. 2002. *Histoire intérieure du FLN 1954–1962* [The Internal History of the FLN]. Paris: Fayard.

———. 2007. *L'Algérie des origines. De la préhistoire à l'avènement de l'islam* [Algeria from Its Origins. From Prehistory to the Coming of Islam]. Paris: La Découverte.

Perville, Guy. 2008. A la mémoire: Charles-Robert Ageron (1923–2008) [In Memory of Charles-Robert Ageron (1923–2008)]. *Outre-mers* 360–361: 373–388. https://www.persee.fr/doc/outre_1631-0438_2008_num_95_360_4804. Accessed 1 June 2020.

Rahal, Malika. 2018. *L'UDMA et les UDMISTES: Contribution à l'histoire du nationalisme algérien* [UDMA and Its Members: Contribution to the History of Algerian Nationalism]. Algiers: Barzakh.

Sessions, Jennifer. 2011. *By Sword and By Plow: France and the Conquest of Algeria*. Ithaca, NY: Cornell University Press.

Shepard, Todd. 2006. *The Invention of Decolonization. The Algerian War and the Remaking of France*. Ithaca and London: Cornell University Press.

———. 2015. 'Of sovereignty': Disputed Archives, 'wholly modern' Archives, and the Post-Decolonization French and Algerian Republics, 1962–2012. *The American Historical Review* 120 (3): 869–883. https://doi.org/10.1093/ahr/120.3.869.

Siari Tengour, Ouanassa. 2014 [2012]. La révolte de 1916 dans les Aurès. [The 1916 Revolt in the Aures]. In *Histoire de l'Algérie à la période coloniale* [History of Algeria During the Colonial Period], eds. Abderrahmane Bouchène, Jean-Pierre Peyroulou, Ouanassa Siari Tengour, and Sylvie Thénault, 255–260. Paris: La Découverte.

Soufi, Fouad. 2000. Oran, 28 février 1962, 5 juillet 1962. Deux événements pour l'histoire, deux événements pour la mémoire. [28 February 1962, 5 July 1962. Two Events for History, Two Events for Memory]. In *La Guerre d'Algérie au miroir des décolonisations françaises: en honneur de Charles-Robert Ageron* [The Algerian War in the Mirror of French Decolonisations: In Honour of Charles-Robert Ageron],

635–676. Paris: SFHOM. A version of this text is available online: https://histoire-coloniale.net/Oran-1962-par-Fouad-Soufi-1-l.html. Accessed 1 June 2020.

Stora, Benjamin. 1989. L'effet "89" dans les milieux immigrés algériens en France (1920–1960). *Revue des mondes musulmans et de la Méditerranée*: 52–53: 229–240. https://www.persee.fr/doc/remmm_0997-1327_1989_num_52_1_2303. Accessed 1 June 2020.

———. 1991. *La Gangrène et l'oubli: la mémoire de la guerre d'Algérie*. [Gangrene et Forgetting: The Memory of the Algerian War]. Paris: La Découverte.

———. 2005. *Les mots de la guerre d'Algérie* [The Words of the Algerian War]. Toulouse: Presse universitaires du Mirail.

Temlali, Yassine. 2015. *La Genèse de la Kabylie: aux origines de l'affirmation berbère en Algérie (1830–1962)* [The Genesis of Kabylia: The Origins of the Berber Affirmation in Algeria (1830–1962)]. Algiers: Barzakh.

Thénault, Sylvie. 2012 [2005]. *Histoire de la guerre d'indépendance algérienne* [History of the Algerian War of Independence]. Paris: Flammarion.

Vince, Natalya. 2015. *Our Fighting Sisters: Nation, Memory and Gender in Algeria, 1954–2012*. Manchester: Manchester University Press.

Weil, Patrick. 2008. *How to Be French: Nationality in the Making Since 1789*. Trans. Catherine Porter. Durham, NC: Duke University Press.

Zekkour, Afaf. 2011. Muslim Reformist Networks in the City of Algiers. *Le Mouvement Social* 236: 23–34. https://doi.org/10.3917/lms.236.0023.

CHAPTER 2

Origins, 1914–54

Seeking to go beyond the 'missed opportunities' and 'inevitable violence' interpretations of the Algerian War of Independence, this chapter examines a period of 40 years in which Algerian anti-colonial activists sought to acquire political rights, improve Algerians' socio-economic situation and campaign for cultural recognition. The years 1914–54 were some of the most tumultuous in world history, including two world wars, the rise of fascism, Nazism and communism, and the beginnings of the Cold War. Algerian anti-colonial activism in its different manifestations, French government decision-making, and settler attitudes and behaviour were shaped by the interaction between this broader context and the particular dynamics of the French empire and colonial Algeria.

The Impact of the First World War: Connecting Conscription and Citizenship, the Experience of Mainland France and Settler Anxiety

The First World War was central to the emergence of Algerian political nationalism in a number of ways. Firstly, this was because of the connection which was made between Algerians' conscription in the French army and access to political rights. This set the stage for much of the political debate in the 1920s, 'centred on the notion of a "mutual obligation" between the inhabitants of Algeria and the colonial system that governed them' (Hassett 2019, 75).

The need for troops in the French army to combat the Central Powers of Germany, Austria-Hungary and the Ottoman empire meant that conscription was applied to France's colonial subjects for the first time. 172,019 Algerian soldiers were brought into the French army, with around 120–125,000 men seeing frontline action. Nearly 26,000 Algerians were killed or disappeared, and 72,000 injured (Meynier 2015, 398). Throughout the nineteenth and early twentieth centuries, the French state had recruited—sometimes voluntarily, sometimes through coercion—men from its African colonies into army

© The Author(s) 2020
N. Vince, *The Algerian War, The Algerian Revolution*,
https://doi.org/10.1007/978-3-030-54264-1_2

units in order to conquer, or repress revolt in, other parts of its empire. This allowed colonial wars to be fought on the cheap, reducing the financial, demographic and political cost of sending white men to fight wars thousands of miles away. Although obligatory military service for all 'indigenous' Algerians (<<Chap. 1, p. 7) was introduced in 1912, both the civilian and military authorities were reluctant to generalise compulsory enlistment. Instead, they preferred to rely on existing methods of recruitment, such as providing financial incentives or using local Algerian elites to rally or coerce quotas of men. Civilian and military authorities had two main concerns about the impact of conscription. They were anxious that taking troops out of Algeria to fight in France left the colony vulnerable in case of internal unrest—unrest which would be more likely if conscription was introduced and proved unpopular. They were also worried about conscription fuelling demands for full citizenship. Since the emergence of the modern nation-state in Europe in the nineteenth century, accepting the risk of dying for the nation has been inextricably linked with being entitled to rights: in short, if you were a soldier, you were a citizen (see Glossary, blood tax/ blood debt).

The Young Algerians (Jeunes algériens) were a small group of French-educated Algerian intellectuals and professionals who since the early twentieth century had been lobbying for improvements in the rights and access to education of Algerians. In 1912, they petitioned the French government, demanding that military service be linked to an increase in the number of 'indigenous' elected representatives and the size of the 'indigenous' electorate. They also called for the end to discriminatory taxation and legal codes (the *indigénat*). The leader of the Young Algerians was the Emir Khaled (1875–1936), the grandson of the Emir Abdelkader, who had led armed resistance against the French invasion in the 1830s and 1840s. In 1913, the Emir Khaled—a captain in the French army—made a speech in Paris in which he declared that France could 'quite reasonably confer rights upon those who have accepted all of the duties, including the blood tax' (Mann 2017, 48). The Young Algerians were not the only colonised subjects making such an argument. In French West Africa, which provided around 166,000 soldiers to the French army during the First World War (Fogarty 2008, 27), politician Blaise Diagne (1872–1934) actively promoted recruitment amongst his fellow black Africans in the Senegalese 'Four Communes' of Gorée, Dakar, Rufisque and Saint-Louis as part of his campaign for their right to French citizenship to be recognised. In late September 1916, Diagne was successful and the National Assembly in Paris voted a law conferring full citizenship on the inhabitants of the Four Communes. Just a few weeks earlier, systematic conscription had been introduced across the empire, as the army's need for troops took precedence over the anxieties of colonial administrations.

The impact of the First World War went well beyond political claim-making. In addition to those soldiers who were transported to fight in Europe, conscription amongst French men in mainland France meant that Algerians went to work in France in unprecedented numbers. Before 1914, there were little more than 10,000 Algerian workers across France and Belgium. During the First World War, it is estimated that between 120,000 and 130,000 Algerians came to France to work in war industry factories and on the farms of conscripted French soldiers, around two thirds of whom were officially recruited, the rest travelling freely to the metropole (Meynier 2015, 404–405). In total then, during the First World War, up to 300,000 Algerians went to France.

The effects of this were profound. Algerians in the army experienced significant discrimination in terms of leave entitlements, access to promotion, pensions and the kind of food which they were served compared to French soldiers—discrimination which they, and some of their French officers, actively and often successfully challenged during the course of the war. At the same time, military paternalism and the welcome accorded to colonial troops by large sections of the French population in metropolitan France were in many ways preferable to the repression, humiliation and hostility of colonial Algeria. To a certain extent, this fuelled the myth of a 'true France' (<<Chap. 1, p. 6), adhering to its proclaimed slogan of liberty, equality and fraternity, and which could be rediscovered in Algeria if only the layers of colonial perversion could be peeled away.

The experiences of Algerian workers were more negative, but no less important in the development of Algerian nationalism. Frequently viewed with suspicion by fellow French workers as rivals bringing wages down or strike-breakers, they nevertheless gained experience of trade unionism through the organisation of their own strikes. The structures of unions and left-wing political parties in metropolitan France would form the initial basis for the organisational structures of the nationalist movement (Meynier 2015) (>>Chap. 2, pp. 28–9).

Back in Algeria, there was resistance to conscription, there were desertions, and the propaganda produced by both Germany and its Ottoman Empire ally called upon Algerians to unite as Muslims to fight against the Christian invader. 'Hadj Guillaume'—aka the Kaiser Wilhelm II—was depicted as the benevolent facilitator of the Central Powers' 'jihad' (holy war). Overall, however, not only did Algerians fight in France, but they fought hard and they fought well. In Algeria, there were only a few localised revolts, notably the Beni Chougran revolt near Mascara in 1914 and a revolt in the Aures region in 1916 (Siari Tengour 2014). This was simplistically interpreted by the government in Paris and the colonial authorities as evidence of 'loyalty' to the 'motherland'. A more likely explanation is that Algerian soldiers in the French army fought hard and well as the result of the process by which armies create group solidarity and institutional loyalty (i.e. soldiers fight for their fellow soldiers, not for the political causes of governments), or, as in the case of the majority of civilians in Algeria, they adopted a wait-and-see attitude. Meynier (2015) argues that this view of Algerian soldiers as 'loyal' marginalised the voices of advocates of colonial reform during the interwar period. If Algerians would fight for France despite not being citizens, despite being subject to the repressive *indigénat*, change was seen as unnecessary. Paradoxically, this sense of false security was accompanied by a growing sense of anxiety that any attempt to reform the colonial system would bring about its collapse. This siege mentality would block reform right up until the War of Independence was well underway (for an English-language summary of Meynier's work, see Meynier 2016).

Connecting the local, national, transnational and global, and debating the nature of Algerian nationalism: manoeuvring for change within the limits of the possible

From the First World War onwards, Algerian political actors were aware that their demands for rights, and later, outright independence, did not just depend on Algerians' relationship with France, but also on the international pressure which could be directed towards their colonial ruler. In 1918, American President Woodrow Wilson championed the right of all peoples to self-determination—that is the right to choose ('determine') their own state and form of government (see Glossary). This seized the attention of the Young Algerians. In reality, and despite his universal language, Wilson was really only referring European peoples' right to self-determination, but that did not stop the idea resonating with anti-colonial elites in Asia and Africa (Manela 2007). As the victors of the First World War, including Britain, France and the United States, sat down to draw up the Treaty of Versailles in 1919, the Emir Khaled secretly passed on to the American peace commissioner, George B. Noble, a petition addressed to Wilson. In this petition, Khaled denounced the inequalities, exploitation and disrespect for Algerian culture under colonial domination, which, he argued, meant that France no longer had the legitimacy to rule in Algeria. The American government appears to have passed the letter on to the French government, who kept its existence secret (Belmessous 2013, 162–163). It was only six decades later that the letter was rediscovered in the archives. Published in 1980, it went some way to resolving what had been heated debates about whether the Emir Khaled was the 'first Algerian nationalist' or 'just' a reformer seeking to improve, rather than bring down, colonialism (Ageron 1966).

Such debates remain popular, because of the ways in which they are entangled with questions about present-day political legitimacy. However, arguing over whether individuals were 'revolutionaries' or 'reformists' implies that individuals' words and acts were formulated in vacuum. The Emir Khaled had no choice but to function within national and international contexts whose parameters he did not control. The real significance of the Emir Khaled's letter was that it reveals that when he was presented with a strategic opportunity—the redrawing of the world's borders at Versailles and the emergence of an apparently anti-imperial American president—he made explicitly *nationalist* demands. All his claims addressed to the French state before and after 1919 focused on Algerians gaining more rights *without* breaking away from France. Within the confines of the French colonial context, this was judged a more effective strategy to bring about change.

POST-FIRST WORLD WAR REFORM: TIMID LEGISLATION,
SETTLER RESISTANCE AND THE SHIFTING MEANINGS
OF 'ASSIMILATION' AMONGST THE ALGERIAN
FRENCH-EDUCATED ELITE

Whereas men from the four communes in Senegal were granted full French citizenship in the course of the First World War, Algerians got the 1919 Jonnart law, taking its name from the Governor General of Algeria, Charles Jonnart (1857–1927). In the face of the impassioned opposition of the colonial administration and settler political representatives in Algeria, the law, when it was finally passed, was much watered down from its original version. Naturalisation was made easier for some categories of Algerians, such as war veterans, but they still had to give up their Muslim personal status (see Glossary). Algerians were still not allowed to elect deputies to the French parliament (National Assembly) in Paris. Voting rights were given to around 425,000 Algerian men in local and regional elections, which represented approximately 43 per cent of the male population over the age of 25 (McDougall 2017, 152).

This was timid legislation. Nevertheless, one consequence of increasing the number of 'indigenous' local councillors was that it allowed new voices to be heard within local councils. The so called 'old turbans' ('Vieux Turbans'), conservative notables who were likely to side with the colonial authorities as long as the latter did not interfere too much in the organisation of their day-to-day lives, were gradually sidelined. The Young Algerians brought new ideas to local election campaigns, for example, denouncing the *indigénat*. Some assimilationist Young Algerians favoured individually renouncing their Muslim personal status to become French citizens through naturalisation and adopting French culture. Other Young Algerians, inspired by *islah*—Islamic reformist movements originating in the Middle East—defended maintaining the Muslim personal status, and underlined the centrality of the Arabic language and Islam to Algerians. The Emir Khaled's approach brought these two tendencies together (Fromage 2014a; in English see Aissaoui 2017). For the Emir Khaled, assimilation meant political equality, without becoming culturally French, and by the end of the First World War this French army captain was campaigning for the recognition of the distinctiveness of Algerians as defined by their religion and language. The Young Algerians also began to increase their influence beyond a narrow social elite into the populations of smaller towns where they had family connections. Sensing the growing threat which the Emir Khaled's message represented, in 1923 he was exiled to Egypt.

Four years after his departure, the small number of Algerians with positions on elected bodies within the colonial system sought to coordinate their efforts more effectively, rebuilding the Young Algerian movement on a more solid basis. The result was the Fédération des élus (Federation of elected representatives). The Fédération des élus was created in 1927 and divided into three departmental federations in 1930. The most active federation (Fromage

2014b) was that in the Constantine region, run by Mohamed Salah Bendjelloul (1893–1985). His right-hand man was the pharmacist Ferhat Abbas. The programme of the Elus was a Young Algerian one—equality, justice, respect.

Debating the nature of Algerian nationalism: new interpretations of the Elus and Ferhat Abbas

In Algerian official history, and much scholarship, the Elus and Ferhat Abbas's post-Second World War party, the Democratic Union of the Algerian Manifesto (Union démocratique du manifeste algérien, UDMA), were for a long time dismissed as a timorous, elitist and assimilationist. A new generation of scholars, such as Malika Rahal (2018) and Julian Fromage (2014b), have critiqued this interpretation by deepening our understanding of the message of the Fédération des élus and their contribution to creating a political culture beyond the elite, and by underlining the regional differences within each movement in their ways of doing politics. For Fromage (2015), members of the Fédération were not nationalists, but they contributed to the shift from anti-colonialism to nationalism, whether they intended to or not, through the campaigns they led and the language they used. Fromage argues that they sought to integrate Algerians into a redefined French citizenship, which included obligatory, universal education, the application of the 1905 law in Algeria separating Church and state (*laïcité*, which meant freeing Algerian mosques from French state control), freedom of the press and some redistribution of land to dispossessed Algerian farmers (<<Chap. 1, p. 4). At its height in 1937, the Constantine branch had 4400 members. Although the leaders were French-educated notables, most of the membership came from rural local assemblies (*djemaas*) and was composed of men who had benefitted from the Jonnart extension of the franchise. The Fédération des élus was attracting around 200,000 votes (Fromage 2015), and sought to remain legal within the narrow framework of the colonial system by using arguments which were 'rational' to Paris and Algiers, for example, by appealing for an extension of the benefits of 'French civilisation' to all Algerians through better educational provision.

SOCIALISM, COMMUNISM AND NATIONALISM: INTERNATIONAL POLITICAL EARTHQUAKES, TRANSNATIONAL ALLIANCES AND ON-THE-GROUND REALITIES

Up until the end of the First World War, colonialism was an accepted fact for all French political parties. For those the right, imperialism embodied French greatness on the world stage. On the centre and left, that is to say for the Radical Party (Parti radical) and the French Section of the Workers' International (Section française de l'Internationale ouvrière, SFIO, the future Socialist

Party), colonialism was justified by the 'civilising mission'. Abuses of autochthonous peoples in the colonies were condemned as the result of the failure to live up to this mission, rather the inevitable consequence of imperial rule. Moreover, late-nineteenth-century and early-twentieth-century socialism, which sought to unite the working-class across borders, was ideologically suspicious of nationalism, which sought to unite people across social classes within the boundaries of the nation—although this did not stop the vast majority of socialist parties supporting 'their' nation during the First World War.

The Russian Revolution in 1917 would introduce an element of disruption into this consensus. Lenin, leading figure of the revolution and the first head of the Soviet Union, argued that bringing about the collapse of capitalism and the liberation of the working class required not only the working class to rise up against factory owners and politicians in the metropole, but also needed colonised peoples to rebel against their colonial rulers. In 1920, the Second World Congress of the Communist International (Comintern, 1919–43), held in Petrograd (St Petersburg) and Moscow, set out the twenty-one conditions which socialist and communist parties around the world had to meet in order to join the organisation. Condition number eight stated that adherents had to denounce their 'own' imperialists (i.e. colonialism and support for it in their own country) and support the liberation movements of colonised peoples (Suny 2003).

In France, the conflict over whether or not to adhere to the Comintern split the SFIO. The majority voted to join and became the French Communist Party (Parti communiste français, PCF). This included the majority of members of the Algerian SFIO. The SFIO continued as a socialist party which was not a member of the Comintern. The eighth condition was one of the points of contention in debates over whether or not to adhere to the Comintern. That said, even the majority who voted to adhere to the Comintern were rather vague in their commitment to the eighth condition and it is questionable how much they thought through its full implications (Marangé 2016a; in English see Sivan 1973).

Apart from a few notable figures—such as the historian and journalist Charles André Julien (1891–1991) who regularly wrote about the socio-economic exploitation of Algerians and European racism (Drew 2014, 29 and 31)—interwar communism in Algeria mainly concerned urban, working-class Europeans who took little interest in the misery of Algerians. The eighth condition was rejected outright by a group of communists of European origin in Sidi Bel Abbes, in the west of Algeria. They were expelled from the PCF in 1922 and condemned by Russian revolutionary Leon Trotsky, who accused them of employing 'pseudo-Marxist phraseology in order to cover up a purely slave-holder's point of view, essentially in support of the imperialist rule of French capitalism over its colonial slaves' (Drew 2014, 34). As for the SFIO, which gradually rebuilt its presence in Algeria from the 1920s onwards, it insisted on the need for the social and economic situation of 'Muslims' to be improved before they could be politically assimilated (i.e. given more political rights). Many members of the SFIO were teachers, some of the most passionate believers in the 'civilising mission' (Marynower 2011).

Socialists and communists of European origin living in Algeria in the interwar period could not imagine their presence there as anything other than legitimate (<<Chap. 1, p. 4, 8). It is therefore hardly surprising that, in the 1920s, it was in metropolitan France that the PCF was most active in developing anticolonial activities (Derrick 2002). This was significant because it was a French political party engaging in anti-colonialism for the first time, but this should be contextualised in terms of the size and influence of the PCF: in 1924, they attracted about 10 per cent of the vote (although this was 20 per cent some regions). By 1936 (>>Chap. 2, pp. 36–7), this had increased to 15 per cent, but it was not until after the Second World War that the PCF could attract 25 per cent of voters. Nevertheless, not being settlers, or the descendants of settlers, white metropolitan French communists could be much more critical of the idea that Algeria was French and were more sympathetic to the struggles of colonised peoples.

There were increasing numbers of Algerians living in metropolitan France. At the end of the First World War, the majority of colonial troops and workers had been forcibly repatriated to Algeria, but their numbers began to steadily grow in the course of the 1920s. There were between 70,000 and 90,000 Algerians in the Paris region alone by 1930, alongside approximately 5000–13,000 people from the Caribbean and West Africa and 2500 each from Vietnam and China (Goebel 2016, 1448). Apart from a small number of university students, the vast majority of these people were young men in hard, manual labour jobs who had left behind rural poverty in the colony to live in overcrowded, insalubrious conditions in the metropole.

This was a fertile recruiting ground for French trade unions and left-wing parties. By 1924, as a result of the concerted efforts of the PCF, its trade union and the Intercolonial Union (Union intercoloniale, UIC, 1921–26/27), the PCF had approximately 8000 North African members or supporters (Aissaoui 2009, 15). This recruitment was buoyed by both the PCF's general appeal to the working class and its critique of colonialism. In the 1920s, the PCF supported the campaign of guerrilla warfare led by Abd el-Krim (Mohamed Ben Abdelkrim el-Khattabi, 1882–1963) against the Spanish, and then against the French, in Morocco (the Rif War). The UIC was founded in 1921 by Nguyễn Ái Quốc of Vietnam, the future Hồ Chí Minh, and a group of lawyers from the Caribbean. The organisation rapidly came under the control of the PCF. The UIC brought together migrants in mainland France from French colonies in Indochina, Guadeloupe, Martinique, Madagascar and North and sub-Saharan Africa. Although it only had a few hundred members and it only existed for five or six years, it provided an important forum for the circulation of critiques of empire across the world. The North African section of the UIC was led by Abdelkader Hadj Ali (1883–1957), an Algerian worker and First World War veteran who lived in France. Five years after its foundation, the UIC was broken up into a series of more regionally-and nationally-focused organisations. In 1926, the PCF and the UIC played a key role in the founding of the North African Star (Etoile nord africaine, ENA). The PCF provided much of the ENA's infrastructure support through funding, meeting spaces and access to printing presses. Abdelkader Hadj Ali and fellow Algerian communist Abdelkader Menouar were its first leaders (Amiri 2014, 577).

THE NORTH AFRICAN STAR: DEMANDING AN 'IMPOSSIBLE' INDEPENDENCE AND EVERYDAY ACTIVISM

The ENA was created—as the name suggests—on a platform of independence for all North Africans: Moroccans, Tunisians and Algerians, as well as on a wider agenda of solidarity between colonised people and workers against imperialism and oppression. Born from the French communist and trade union movement, the ENA sought to recruit members primarily amongst North African workers in France, although it also sought to appeal to small businessmen (shopkeepers and restaurant owners). By January 1927, it had an estimated 3000 members—this would grow to around 4000 in early 1928 (Stora 1986, 64 and 79). The ENA would rapidly become synonymous with its general secretary, Ahmed Messali Hadj (1898–1974). The relationship between the ENA and the PCF would also become increasingly strained.

Debating the nature of Algerian Nationalism: new possibilities as seen by Messali Hadj

Messali Hadj was born in the western Algerian town of Tlemcen, into a locally well known, but not wealthy, family. He completed his primary education at a French school in Tlemcen, and also received a religious education with a local Sufi-influenced brotherhood. He served in the French army in the First World War. In 1923, he went to Paris and worked various jobs in factories and as a travelling salesman. According to his first biographer (Stora 1986), at this point Messali Hadj was marked by three key political events. Firstly, the use of colonial troops in the French and Belgian occupation of the Ruhr in 1923, in response to Germany defaulting on reparation payments set out in the Treaty of Versailles. For Messali Hadj, this demonstrated the limits of using the 'blood debt' argument as the basis for demands for greater political rights: colonial troops were still serving in the French army, and still being denied citizenship. Secondly, in 1924, Abdelkader Hadj Ali nearly won a seat in legislative elections as a PCF candidate in the Parisian region. Hadj Ali had been able to stand for office because he had been naturalised as a French citizen in 1911. Thirdly, Messali Hadj noted the PCF's opposition to the Rif War. These

---

(*continued*)

(continued)
events indicated that the ballot box could be a path to bring about change and the left in Europe could be an ally in challenging colonial domination. The Rif War also highlighted that, although France and Spain were rivals in their occupation of Morocco, the imperial powers would join together to brutally crush those who contested colonial rule—but not before they sustained defeats. For Messali, these events represented both the limits of citizenship in a colonial context, and offered glimpses of possibilities for bringing about change. Given settler hostility and police repression in the colonies, it is hardly surprising that the first movement which explicitly called for Algerian independence should have emerged in the relatively freer space of metropolitan France.

In February 1927, Messali Hadj and other senior members of the ENA attended the first International Congress against Colonial Oppression and Imperialism in Brussels, Belgium, alongside many other groups formerly connected to the UCI. The Brussels meeting marked the official creation of the League Against Imperialism and for National Independence (LAI, 1927–37), supported by the Comintern in Moscow. This first meeting sought to bring together workers in imperialist countries and colonised peoples. Its 175 delegates included representatives from China, Egypt, Syria, India (including future Indian prime minister Jawaharlal Nehru of the Indian National Congress), Dutch East India (including future Indonesian vice-president Mohamed Hatta of Perhimpoenan Indonesia), Senegalese activist Lamine Senghor of the Committee for the Defence of the Black Race as well as representatives from movements fighting racism and discrimination in South Africa and the United States. Presenting the ENA's declaration to the congress, Messali Hadj, described Algerians as 'prisoners in our own country'. There was no freedom of association or of the press. Algerians did not benefit from the same workers' rights as their French counterparts and could not travel freely. Algerian children had very limited access to education and the teaching of Arabic was being eliminated. The expropriation of land meant that famine was a systematic occurrence. The 'civilising mission', Messali Hadj declared, was a lie, as were claims that Algerians were not 'ready' for independence. The ENA's resolutions to the congress demanded the independence of Algeria, the withdrawal of French troops, the creation of a national Algerian army and the redistribution of land from large colonial landowners to those peasants who had been expropriated. In the meantime, the ENA would also campaign for greater political, legal, socio-economic and educational rights within the colonial system.

Debating the nature of Algerian nationalism: the ENA—bringing together working-class and anti-colonial struggles

For many historians, Messali Hadj's explicit demand for independence was a key change in tone, and to quote the subtitle of Stora's biography of Messali Hadj, it made him the 'pioneer of Algerian nationalism'. Striking a somewhat discordant note in this general consensus, Michael Goebel (2016, 1464) argues that Messali Hadj was encouraged by the LAI congress organisers to put more emphasis on demanding independence, whereas his own focus was—at that point—primarily on combatting everyday discrimination and the lack of civil rights, attacking low wages, brokering medical care and access to legal advice, and getting state benefits paid to the children living in Algeria of Algerian workers in France. This is not to make a false distinction between socio-economic demands and political demands: as Goebel (2016, 1455) states, 'mutual aid, local community work, and anticolonialism were inseparably interwoven'. For the ENA, as for other parties in the LAI, the struggle of Algerians as workers oppressed by capitalism was intertwined with the political struggle of Algerians oppressed by an imperial power—the Algerian, Vietnamese and West African working classes were paid less and struggled to access benefits even more than their white French counterparts precisely because they were colonised.

Messali Hadj's desire for an autonomous organisation, the religious undertones he brought into the movement and his explicit call for independence were growing sources of tension between the ENA and the PCF. In France, the PCF was more attached to the idea of colonised people's 'lack of readiness' than the Comintern was in Moscow. Seeing what was meant to be a satellite organisation slip from its control, the PCF reduced its financial support for the ENA. The ENA was also increasingly harassed by the police and its newspaper banned. In 1929, the ENA itself was banned for 'threatening the unity of national territory'. The ENA entered a difficult period, compounded by the economic crisis in France which resulted in tens of thousands of now-unemployed Algerian workers—its militant base—returning to Algeria.

The charismatic Messali Hadj nevertheless continued giving speeches at meetings, writing newspaper articles and petitioning international organisations—including the League of Nations (1920–46), the post-First World War organisation established to resolve disputes between nations peacefully. In 1933, the ENA was relaunched with Messali Hadj as president. Its organisational structure was based on that of the PCF, but it was now pointedly independent of the communists.

Debating the nature of Algerian nationalism: the religious as reference
Religious references became increasingly important, as Messali Hadj insisted that preserving spiritual identity was a powerful weapon (<<Chap. 1, p. 7). The ENA's newspaper was called *El Ouma* [*umma*], the Arabic term usually used to refer to the international community of Muslim believers, but which in this context can be understood as a religious *and* national community (Courrèye 2014). The November 1933 issue of *El Ouma* declared that the motto of all 'good nationalists' should be 'I love my country and for it I want to die. I love my country and I want to see it free' (Aissaoui 2009, 21) (>>Chap. 3, p. 127).

It was around this time that the ENA designed the first models of their flag—a red star and crescent on a white and green background, similar to what would become the Algerian flag—the likely artist behind this was Messali Hadj's French wife, Emilie Busquant (1901–53). A few clandestine ENA cells began to form in Algeria. By 1933–4, *El Ouma* had a circulation of around 44,000 (Stora 1986, 120) and Messali Hadj's public meetings were attracting audiences of hundreds, and sometimes, thousands. The ENA message was also being relayed in bars, restaurants and music concerts. Arrest and imprisonment were quick to follow.

Beyond communities of colonised peoples living in the metropole, anti-colonialism attracted little interest from the wider metropolitan public. In 1930, the centenary of the French invasion of Algiers was commemorated with much pomp and ceremony. This glorification of empire was repeated on an even grander scale in Paris in May 1931. The Colonial Exhibition, which celebrated the vastness, exoticism and wealth of the French empire, attracted eight to nine million visitors and 29 to 33 million separate entries. The PCF called for a boycott of the exhibition and staged a counter exhibition on 'The truth about the colonies'. It only attracted about 5000 visitors (Evans 2000).

CULTURAL RESISTANCE TO COLONIAL DOMINATION: FROM HISTORY, LANGUAGE, RELIGION AND THE MUSLIM PERSONAL STATUS TO FOOTBALL AND SCOUTING

For many Algerians, these celebrations of empire were experienced as yet another humiliation. For Abdelhamid Ben Badis (1890–1940): 'Today men without hearts seek to revive hate and resentment. These military parades and all these vain displays which satisfy their pride as conquerors are the ultimate insult to our dignity and an attack on the memory of our glorious fathers' (Hodier and Pierre 1991, 32). In 1931, Ben Badis founded the Association of Algerian Muslim 'Ulama (Association des 'ulama [sometimes transliterated oulémas] musulmans algériens/jam'iyyat al-'ulamā' al-muslimīn al-jazā'iriyyīn,

AUMA/AOMA). The *'ulama* were Islamic teachers and writers. The AUMA was the formalisation of a growing religious, cultural and social movement which sought to 'purify' Islam from within and revive a Muslim, Arabic-language culture within Algeria.

The Algerian *'ulama* were driven by, and were part of, the transnational networks of the Islamic reformist movement (*islah*) which swept across North Africa and the Middle East from the late nineteenth century onwards. Ben Badis had been educated at al-Zaytuna university in Tunisia, a centre of Islamic learning. In the 1920s and 1930s, members of the AUMA were in contact with the editors of a number of Egyptian newspapers which promoted *islah* and, like Messali Hadj, the *'ulama* were in regular contact with the Lebanese politician and author Shakib Arslan (1869–1946) who promoted the unity of the Muslim world against imperialism. In the 1950s, the AUMA would play a key role in representing Algeria on the international, pan-Arab, pan-Islamic scene (Courrèye 2016, 172–174).

The *'ulama*'s oft-cited declaration, attributed to Ben Badis, linked language, religion and nationality: 'Islam is our religion, Arabic is our language, Algeria is our homeland'—although this was not formulated as a demand for independence. The slogan on the *'ulama* newspaper *al-Muntaqid* was 'For the welfare of the Algerian nation with the aid of democratic France' (McDougall 2006, 64). By insisting on the centrality of Islam and Arabic, the *'ulama* constructed a collective identity distinct from that France, and they were fervently against Algerians choosing to become full French citizens through naturalisation. Nevertheless, they did not so much reject external 'Western influence' as seek to purify cultural practices from within. The *'ulama* sought to rid Algerian Muslims of what they considered to be archaic and ignorant local customs such as worshipping saints, superstitious practices and Sufi mysticism, which, in their view, deviated from a 'pure' and 'authentic' Islam.

AUMA groups developed across Algeria, promoting *islah* through religious instruction and Arabic teaching for adults and children. Members of the AUMA wrote tracts and newspaper articles and staged plays. In some larger towns and cities, the *'ulama* opened up their own schools, providing a modern education for boys and girls in all aspects of the curriculum (i.e. not just the Qur'anic recitation classes traditionally delivered by mosques) (Courrèye 2014). The education of girls was seen as particularly important, to provide educated Muslim wives for educated Muslim men—the *'ulama* were critical of mixed marriages. Both Abbas and Messali Hadj were married to French women, and this was a common practice for Algerian men living in France. The *'ulama* viewed this as damaging to the family and the transmission of religious values to the next generation (Macmaster 2011).

Leading AUMA figure Ahmad Tawfiq al-Madani (1899–1983), also educated at al-Zaytuna university, produced extensive historical writings in Arabic celebrating the glorious Muslim and Arab ancestors of Algeria (McDougall 2006). This reappropriation of Algerian history counterbalanced the colonial narrative of Algeria's past, which claimed that before 1830 the territory was populated by different ethnolinguistic groups with no sense of shared identity and no central state, and thus insisted that it was only through colonialism that 'Algeria' came into existence (<<Chap. 1, p. 4, 8). Although the primary aim of the *ulama* was not to overthrow the colonial power, but rather to transform their fellow Muslims, they were seen as a danger by the colonial authorities. The colonial authorities were swift to clamp down on unauthorised preachers in mosques and close AUMA schools.

Debating the nature of Algerian nationalism: The *ulama*—more important in writing history than making it?

The *ulama* were long presented as having played a crucial role in revealing to Algerians what it meant to *be* Algerian. This interpretation of the *ulama* as having made a major contribution to a national awakening was often the work of historians who had close personal ties to the AUMA. Yet as James McDougall (2006) has argued, the *ulama* did not, as they claimed, 'recover' Algerian history and culture, rather, they reinvented it for the context of the 1930s. Moreover, McDougall underlines, we should be wary of thinking about their role in Algerian history (simply) in terms of their 'contribution' to the War of Independence. A direct connection cannot be made between the AUMA and its leaders and the turn to armed conflict in 1954. The attacks of 1 November 1954 took them by surprise—at that point they neither approved of, nor had they envisaged, that independence would be achieved through armed struggle. They were slowly incorporated, individually, into the FLN in the course of 1956 (>>Chap. 3, p. 78, 81). The *ulama*'s political significance and influence came into its own *after* independence in 1962 when their mastery of the language of cultural authenticity—the 'Arab-Muslim Algerian identity', their ready-made history of Algeria and their homogenising, unitary vision of Algerian culture found its place as of the official identity of the newly independent state (>>Chap. 4, p. 168, 175, 177, 186).

The *ulama* motto 'Islam is our religion, Arabic is our language, Algeria is our homeland' is often pitched as a rejection of the idea that Algerians could *ever* become French, in direct opposition to the demands of the Fédération des élus for legal and political rights which would bring about greater equality by making Algerians *more* French. Yet this dichotomy is flawed. Ferhat Abbas, whose political career began as a locally-elected representative with the Fédération des élus, and ended in 1963 when he resigned as president of the post-independence Constituent Assembly, was long discredited in Algerian official history as a reformist, middle-class Francophile assimilationist. An article which Abbas wrote in

(continued)

(continued)
1936, titled 'La France, c'est moi' [France is me], in which he declared
that the Algerian nation did not exist either in the past or in the present,
prompted a sharp rebuttal from the *'ulama* at the time of its publication
and was often used against Abbas subsequently (McDougall 2006,
84–85). Far less often cited is another statement made by Abbas, a decade
earlier in 1926, in which he declared that: 'Islam remains our unwavering
faith, the belief which gives meaning to our life, our spiritual motherland,
the Muslim personal status is our true country [*pays réel*]' (Rahal 2014,
443–445). Abbas never sought to be naturalised as a full French citizen—
that is, he refused to give up his Muslim personal status. Abbas, the Emir
Khaled, Messali Hadj and the *'ulama* were *all* attached to the ethno-
religious legal category which stopped them from becoming full French
citizens (<<Chap. 1, p. 7), which they understood as the embodiment of
the Algerian collective identity (or 'personality' to use a term commonly
employed at the time). Even when demands for naturalisation were made,
these were demands for the 'indigenous' to be made full French citizens
en masse, like the Jews of Algeria (<<Chap. 1, p. 8), without the require-
ment for individuals to renounce their personal status. The Young
Algerians, the Elus, the ENA and the *'ulama* were all promoters of the
Arabic language, even those senior figures who were more comfortable
expressing themselves in French in their writing and speeches.

The *'ulama* were part of a broader expansion of associational life amongst
Algerians in the interwar period. For Omar Carlier (1995, 53), youth began to
emerge as a distinct force, with their own set of political and cultural models
and sporting, educational and musical activities. Political parties and associations of all political persuasions were keen to both channel and harness this
potential (Krais 2017). Two examples will be presented here: football and
scouting.

After the First World War, football became widely popular in Algeria and
France—it was a game played by soldiers when they were on breaks from front
line combat. Sport as a tool of inter-community integration only functioned in
pockets in Algeria, as a result of settler hostility to 'indigenous' inclusion,
although some Algerian players had very successful careers in football clubs in
metropolitan France, and indeed in the French national team. As clubs and
leagues formed in Algeria, it became clear that in many towns there was a
divide between 'European' clubs and 'Muslim' clubs. 'Muslim' clubs often
distinctly displayed their Muslim identity. For example, the Mouloudia football
club, founded in 1921 in the Algiers's Casbah (see Glossary), took its name

from the festival which marks the birth of the prophet Mohamed (Mouloud) and wore a green and red kit—the colours which would later become those of the Algerian flag.

Sports which required relatively little investment in expensive equipment such as football levelled the playing field between Europeans and Algerians in a very literal way, providing an opportunity to challenge colonial hierarchies when Algerian teams inflicted defeats on their European counterparts. Levels of violence between rival fans was high, sometimes resulting in full blown riots (Dine 2002, 498). As a result, in 1928, the Governor General of Algeria ordered that all 'Muslim' teams contain at least three 'European' players, a quota increased to five in 1934—although this was largely ignored (Evans 2012, 64). Within and across Algeria, football, and sport more generally, was increasingly the opportunity for new forms of socialisation and organisation amongst Algerians (for a local study of Constantine, see Boulebier 2007), and in some cases was a springboard for political activity. Twenty years later, during the War of Independence, the FLN's touring football team would be part of the nationalist campaign to win over international support (Evans 2010; Amara 2005).

In Algiers in 1935, Mohamed Bouras (1908–41), an attendee of both an *'ulama* cultural circle and a fan of Mouloudia, created the first section of the Algerian Muslim Scouts (Scouts musulmans algériens, al-kashāfa al-islamiyya al-jazā'iriyya, SMA). Bouras entered into contact with various other scout groups which had emerged in Algeria since the start of the decade and per-suaded them to become federated into a national organisation (Kaddache 2003a). The *'ulama* played a central role in founding scout groups. Alongside the usual scout activities—camping, exercise and drills aimed at building physi-cal and moral character—there was a clear political dimension to the SMA. They wore red and green badges which closely resembled the future Algerian flag and they promised to follow the principals of Islam and be 'faithful to the motherland'. Deliberately ambiguous to the ears of the colonial authorities, it was clear to scouts and their leaders that this 'motherland' was Algeria, not France (Kaddache 2003a). Many of the men who would go on to join the FLN's rural and urban guerrilla networks had been members of the scout movement as children.

The 1936 Popular Front: From Hope to Disillusion? Or Just One More Example of the Fundamental Contradictions of Liberal Colonialism?

France in the mid-1930s was in crisis. The economic impact of the 1929 Wall Street Crash continued to reverberate. There was growing apprehension about the prospect of another war in Europe, with the rise of Adolf Hitler in Germany and Benito Mussolini in Italy. In France, fascist leagues were growing in strength. In the face of this threat, in 1936, the centre and left political parties (Radicals, Socialists and Communists), trade unions and the anti-colonial Tunisian Neo Destour, Moroccan Action Committee (Comité d'action marocaine) and the Algerian ENA joined together to create the Popular Front. In the middle of one of the biggest strike movements in the history of France, in which Algerian workers participated, a Popular Front government was voted into power on a programme of 'bread, peace and liberty'. For the first time, France had a socialist prime minister, Léon Blum (1872–1950), and the PCF were part of the parliamentary majority.

The Popular Front promised to dissolve the fascist leagues and reform the press; work for peace through the League of Nations, collective security and progressive disarmament; and improve the lot of the worker through public works and a reduction in the working week without a reduction in pay. Alongside this radical programme for reform in France was a more limited proposal for a parliamentary fact-finding mission to investigate the political, economic and cultural situation in North Africa and Indochina in a bid to 'humanise' colonialism (Chafer and Sackur 1999).

For the French left and for anti-colonial movements in the colonies, this was a time of hope. For the right, and for settlers in Algeria, this was a time of fear, with the Popular Front seen as the harbinger of communist revolution and/or the end of French Algeria. This fear swelled support for and radicalised the Algerian extreme right (Kalman 2013). Also galvanised by the Popular Front, delegates from the Fédération des élus, the AUMA, the SFIO and the Algeria section of the PCF (in October, this would become the Algerian Communist Party, PCA) formed the first Algerian Muslim Congress (Congrès musulman algérien). 6000 representatives met in Algiers on 7 June 1936 and put together a charter of demands (Marynower 2014). These included Algeria being directly attached to France (i.e. not ruled by a Governor General in Algeria—this demand was a way to undercut settler dominance of Algerian politics), universal suffrage and the possibility for Algerians to be elected to the National Assembly in Paris. The Congress also demanded the application of the 1905 law separating Church and State (i.e. the end of French interference in mosques) and the adoption of Arabic as an official language alongside French (Benkada 2004). Messali Hadj's ENA did not support the charter, rejecting the idea that Algeria should be attached to France.

A delegation was sent to present the charter to the Popular Front government. They made little headway—in Paris, reform in the colonies was not a priority. On 2 August 1936, the delegation returned to Algiers, empty handed, but greeted by rally of 10,000 people in the Algiers municipal stadium. Messali Hadj, back in Algeria for the first time for more than a decade, made a fiery speech. He recognised the work of the Congress, but argued that Algeria could never be integrated into France, because the French presence in Algeria was the result of a brutal conquest. Brandishing a handful of soil, to enthusiastic applause, he declared 'this land is not for sale!' (Evans 2012, 69) (<<Chap. 1, p. 4).

For the members of the Algerian Muslim Congress, the ENA and colonised peoples across the French empire, the Popular Front was a disappointment. As the Popular Front government struggled to hold a diverse alliance together, the Spanish Civil War began in 1936 and the Nazi threat grew ever more menacing. Colonial injustices and inequalities were further pushed into the background. The missions of inquiry barely had time to report back before the government fell in 1938, although some of their propositions would find their way into post-Second World War colonial reforms. The main proposal put forward in Algeria was the Blum-Viollette reform. Maurice Viollette (1870–1960) was the former liberal-leaning Governor of Algeria (1925–27), unaffectionately known amongst the settler population as 'Viollette L'Arbi' (Viollette the Arab) for his supposedly excessive sympathy for the colonised population. The Blum-Viollette bill proposed full citizenship for 25,000 Algerians (war veterans, students, elected officials and trade union leaders) without losing their Muslim personal status. Presented to parliament in December 1936, it was passionately opposed by pro-colonial deputies in the National Assembly. Blum hesitated to confront the opponents of the bill, and it disappeared with the fall of the Popular Front government in 1938.

A missed opportunity? One interpretation of the Popular Front—a disappointment with far-ranging impact

For a long time, particularly in histories produced in France, the death of the Blum-Viollette proposal was presented as key moment in which post-First World War hopes of colonial reform were buried. Its failure was seen as evidence of the intractable resistance to any kind of reform, notably amongst the Europeans of Algeria, even when moderate changes were presented by French-educated Algerians and pushed by the government in Paris.

But rather than a 'missed opportunity' thwarted by intransigent settlers, the failure of the reform is best understood as the result of the inherent and long-standing contradictions of the French empire, and the tension between 'liberal humanist rhetoric that promised change and a continuity of authoritarian practices' (Chafer and Sackur 1999, 10). Nor was the failure of the Blum-Viollette proposal necessarily a definitive turning point for Algerian anti-colonial activists. Without underestimating the impact of the disappointment of the Popular Front on politicians such as Abbas, they did not give up on reform in 1938. They continued to see reform as one of the means for bringing about change in the colonial system right up beyond 1954. Neither were Messali Hadj's hopes dashed, because well before 1936 he already had little hope in the ability of the colonial system to reform itself. Messali Hadj had vigorously opposed the Blum-Viollette bill, which he saw as a means to separate the elite from the masses.

A missed opportunity? Newer interpretations of the Popular Front— marking the shift of mass politics to Algerian soil

More recent scholarship has been less interested in the question of whether the Popular Front was a moment of disappointed hopes or not. Instead, historians have argued that the real significance of the Popular Front moment was the way in which it enabled Algerian political partici- pation in Algeria to expand beyond a narrow elite of the Elus or the AUMA. The ENA, which had a more working-class base than the Elus or the AUMA, had been established in metropolitan France in 1926 because of the particularly repressive context in Algeria. The public meetings, strikes and marches in Algeria which accompanied the Popular Front in 1936 on both sides of the Mediterranean enabled Algerians to participate in activities which were usually very difficult for them to organise, because of the *indigénat*. A political space thus opened up, however briefly, for demands for political and social rights and cultural recognition to be made publicly to large audiences in Algeria (Marynower 2014). When the Popular Front government dissolved the ENA in January 1937, Messali Hadj reformed the organisation as the Algerian People's Party (Parti du peuple algérien, hizb al-shāab al-jazā'iri, PPA) and rebuilt the membership *on Algerian soil*. By 1939, PPA rallies were attracting up to 25,000 people in Algeria. This in turn reinforced the extreme-right view in Algeria that the metropole was incapable of addressing the 'indige- nous' problem (Kalman 2013, 132). The fear of being 'submerged' was exacerbated further by the growing 'Muslim' birth rate, far outstripping that of 'Europeans' and the increasing numbers of 'Muslims' living in towns and cities, although the majority were still rural inhabitants.

The Popular Front also marked a break in the connection between French communism and anti-colonialism. After 15 years of taking—on the Comintern's orders—an anti-colonial line (<<Chap. 2, p. 27), in 1934 Moscow decided that combatting Nazism and Fascism took precedence over combatting impe- rialism. The PCF was instructed to make a temporary alliance with the centrist and centre-left parties in France—which it did in 1936—and continued colo- nial rule was accepted for the time being. In 1937, the PCF General Secretary, Maurice Thorez (1900–64), argued that 'the right to divorce does not mean an obligation to divorce' (Derrick 2002, 64). In 1939, Thorez declared that the Algerian nation did not yet exist, describing Algeria as a melting pot of races, a 'nation in the process of formation' (Drew 2014, 111).

Debating the nature of Algerian nationalism: the PCA is not the PCF

This retreat from the PCF's former anti-colonial positions was not the whole story, because in Algeria on the ground something different was happening. In contrast to the PCF's growing electoral success in mainland France, the Algerian section of the PCF had become moribund since the late 1920s. In addition to internal purges, state repression and a sense that the PCF was not giving a clear political direction, the party was failing to engage with the social and economic misery endured by the majority of Algerians and the daily oppression brought about by the *indigénat*. It also had very few Algerians amongst its leadership and membership. In the mid-1930s, French-born professional revolutionary and committed Leninist André Ferrat (1902–88) and Algerian communists Amar Ouzegane (1910–81) and Benali Boukkort (who had links to the PCF, the ENA and the LAI) were amongst those who set about addressing this problem, with the result being the creation of a separate Algerian Communist Party (Parti communiste algérien, al-hizb al-shuyūʿī al-jazāʾiri, PCA) in October 1936. In internal communications with the Comintern, the expressed goal of the PCA was to create an 'anti-imperialist front' (Marangé 2016b). In public pronouncements, the PCA was more cautious: it endorsed the Blum-Viollette reforms. By the end of 1937, membership had grown to 5000 members, 2000 of whom were 'Muslim'. Unlike many of the members of European origin, who were atheists, most Algerian communists did not see religion as a form of reactionary superstition in contradiction with Marxism. In 1935, Boukkort published *Peuple d'Algérie, quels sont tes amis?* [People of Algeria, who are your friends?] in which he argued Islam and communism were compatible: 'If the prophet Mohammed lived today, in this period where Muslims are subjugated and chained in the majority of countries, he would call them to the liberation struggle' (Drew 2014, 90). The PCA nevertheless faced competition from the PPA, and as the popularity of Messali Hadj's party grew, that of the PCA waned.

THE SECOND WORLD WAR: THE COLONIES TAKE CENTRE STAGE AS A LOCATION OF EUROPEAN POLITICS, BUT THERE IS LITTLE INTEREST IN LISTENING TO COLONISED PEOPLES

In August 1939, the USSR and Nazi Germany signed an ideologically improbable, but in both countries' view, strategically necessary, non-aggression pact. The pact removed Hitler's fears of a war on two fronts in the East and the West, and opened up the way for the German invasion of Poland. The PCF and PCA were promptly banned after the signing of the pact, as was the PPA, accused of being defeatist.

When war broke out in September 1939, Algerian troops were once again recruited and conscripted into the French army (<<Chap. 2, p. 21). In 1940, about ten per cent of the French army were colonial subjects. A total of 640,000 men were mobilised, of whom 176,000 were Algerian (Frémeaux 2004, 217). In the build-up to the Second World War, French politicians and the press had constantly reassured the metropolitan public that the empire provided the men, raw materials and strategic positions to protect France from attack. In reality, the empire was very poorly integrated into French military planning and strategy. After France fell to the Germans after only six weeks of fighting in May-June 1940, very few leaders in positions of influence could imagine continuing the struggle from or within the empire (Ageron 1982; in English see Thomas 2013a). The attempt of a group of French parliamentarians to relocate the government from Paris to North Africa was scuppered by the manoeuvrings of Prime Minister Philippe Pétain (1856–1951). Instead, Pétain, the First World War hero who had transposed the artillery and aerial bombing of European warfare 1914–18 to crush the Rif uprising in Morocco in 1925 (<<Chap. 2, p. 28), concluded an armistice with Germany on 22 June 1940. As a result of this agreement, France was divided into two, with the north and west (including Paris) forming part of an occupied zone under German control. The French army was demobilised and its navy and air force put out of action. The 'unoccupied zone' in the south, as well as all of France's colonies, were placed under the control of Pétain and his government in tourist spa town of Vichy—the French state at this time is often referred to as the Vichy regime (>>Chap. 4, p. 165, 179).

Pétain's desire to remake France in order to promote the values of 'work, family and motherland', abandoning what he saw as the 'decadent' Republican values of 'liberty, equality and fraternity', would lead to enthusiastic collaboration with the Nazis. In June 1941, the Nazi-Soviet pact ended and the USSR joined the Second World War on the side of the allies, a further impetus to communists swelling the ranks of the anti-Nazi, anti-Vichy resistance. There were many French resistances, but it was Charles de Gaulle who emerged as the—not undisputed—leader of the unified resistance. In June 1940, de Gaulle was an officer in the French army who refused to accept the armistice. Fleeing to London, he formed a government-in-exile and sought to organise the internal and external resistance to the Nazi occupation and the Vichy regime under his authority: this was the Free French.

As mainland France had been defeated and occupied, the colonies took centre stage like never before. For both collaborationist Pétain and resister de Gaulle, the colonies were what made France (still) great, despite defeat and division. Some the earliest resistance to the Vichy regime came from the colonies. The French-Guianese Governor of Chad, Félix Eboué (1884–1944), the first black man to be appointed to a post of such seniority in the colonial administration, rallied to the Free French in summer 1940, bringing with him much of French Equatorial Africa. Later, colonial troops played a central role in the liberation of France and Italy. In summer 1944, of 633,000 men in the

French army, 60 per cent were 'indigenous' soldiers, many North African, many Algerian (Frémeaux 2004, 218). Yet whilst empire was the location for much Franco-French fighting about what the future of France should be, the starting point for the liberation of Europe, and the homeland of many of the troops who led this liberation, barely any thought was given to the political situation or daily lives of colonised peoples (Thomas 2015, 582).

CITIZENSHIP IS NOT A PROTECTION, ANTI-COLONIAL ACTIVISTS REJECT COLLABORATION

In Algeria, authoritarian, traditionalist, anti-communist, xenophobic and anti-Semitic Vichy France closely matched the political sympathies of many settlers (Cole 2019; Kalman 2013; Abitbol 1989). In October 1940, Jews were stripped of the French citizenship which they had held since the Crémieux decree in 1870 (<<Chap. 1, p. 8), and reverted back to being 'French nationals' alongside the 'Muslim' population. Both the Nazis and the Vichy regime sought to make alliances with Arab nationalists in the Middle East and North Africa, working on the principal that 'the enemy of my enemy is my friend'— that is, they claimed that had a shared enemy in British imperialism and Zionism in Palestine (at this point under British mandate). These overtures met with little success. In France, a very few members of the PPA flirted with Nazism. In 1941, Mohamed Bouras of the SMA was shot, accused of spying for the Germans: although the Vichy regime was collaborating with the Nazis, it did not want to be bypassed by its 'Muslim' subjects directly making contact with them. Mahfoud Kaddache (2003b, 587) insists that Bouras's only motivation was to obtain weapons.

Supporters of the Vichy regime perhaps anticipated that 'Muslims' with second-class citizenship might be satisfied by the Jewish population's return to the ranks of the 'indigenous', possibly looking back to sporadic incidents of Muslim anti-Jewish violence, notably in Constantine in 1934 (Cole 2019). They were to be disappointed. Both Ferhat Abbas and Messali Hadj asserted that they were not looking for equality through a race to the bottom (Le Foll Luciani 2015). Messali Hadj rejected repeated invitations to work with the Vichy regime and collaborate with the Nazis and he expelled those members of the PPA who did. In March 1941, a sentence of 16 years' hard labour was handed down to Messali Hadj. He was banned from mainland French territory for 20 years and had all his property confiscated (Katz 2015, 145).

For Abbas, who had held out some hope for the liberation of Algerians through obtaining full French citizenship, the lesson from the revocation of the Crémieux decree was that citizenship was not an inalienable right. It could be taken away. In the Manifesto which he composed in 1943 (>>Chap. 2, pp. 45–6), he made explicit reference to the abrogation of the Crémieux decree: 'From now on, an Algerian Muslim will demand nothing else than to be an

Algerian Muslim'—that is to say, henceforth Algerian citizenship and nationality offered better protection than French citizenship and nationality (Le Foll Luciani 2015; in English see Lane 2007).

THE IMPACT OF THE SECOND WORLD WAR: INTERNATIONAL REORDERING WITHOUT COLONIAL REORDERING, EVERYDAY MISERY

Algeria would remain under the control of the Vichy regime until the US–British landings of 100,000 Allied soldiers in Morocco and Algeria on 8 November 1942, which began Operation Torch. With an eye on staying on the winning side, Pétain's second-in-command Admiral François Darlan, who by chance was in Algiers as the Americans landed, went over to the side of the Allies, forming an alternative North African administration. Following Darlan's assassination two months later, he was replaced by de Gaulle's rival for the leadership of the Free French, Henri Giraud. In June 1943, De Gaulle and Giraud formed the French Committee of National Liberation (Comité français de libération nationale, CFLN), making Algiers the capital of the fight to regain control of metropolitan France from the Germans and the collaborationist Vichy regime. De Gaulle then began the process of wresting the CFLN from the control of Giraud, and in June 1944 became president of the Provisional Government of the French Republic (Gouvernement provisoire de la République française, GPRF). The similarity of these names and acronyms to those which the FLN would adopt just over a decade later are worth noting—in 1958, the FLN would establish its Provisional Government of the Algerian Republic (Gouvernement provisoire de la République algérienne, GPRA). In doing so, like de Gaulle in 1944, they brought into existence a government which had not yet secured a territory to rule over (>>Chap. 3, p. 98, 146).

For most Algerians, the switch from being ruled over by enthusiastic Vichy collaborationists to Algiers becoming the capital of the Free French did not change much. Beyond a few men at the top, there was a continuity of personnel. Amongst those few men at the top, as the struggles between Darlan, Giraud and de Gaulle revealed, there was much infighting (Thomas 2013a). Messali Hadj, like many other political prisoners, not only remained in prison, but was also deported to Brazzaville in French Equatorial Africa in April 1945. Much Vichy legislation remained in force. The Crémieux decree was only tardily reinstated in October 1943, nearly a year after the Free French had taken control of Algeria. The new political order did not seem to be functioning any differently than the now much decried Vichy regime.

At the same time, the Second World War had a profound impact on Algeria and Algerians. France had been humiliatingly defeated by the Germans in 1940 and Algeria was liberated by the British and the Americans in 1942. Many would consider that the war was decisively won not by the Western Allies, but by the USSR in Stalingrad in 1943. In August 1941, just before the US entry into the war, American President Franklin D. Roosevelt and British Prime

Minister Winston Churchill signed the Atlantic Charter. This declared that the Second World War was not being fought for territorial gain, but for the right of all peoples to self-determination (<<Chap. 2, p. 24; >>Chap. 3, p. 73). The American Secretary of State, Cordell Hull, even proposed putting colonial empires under international trusteeship at the end of the war (Chafer 2002, 55). In September 1941, de Gaulle declared his adhesion to the principles of the Charter in the name of the Free French.

De Gaulle had no intention of giving up France's colonies—for him, the Atlantic Charter meant self-determination for people living in Nazi-occupied Europe. This international agreement nevertheless gave hope to nationalists across Africa and Asia (Klose 2013, 11–17). During the November 1942 landings, the US air force had dropped thousands of leaflets across North Africa, which bore the American flag, a portrait of Roosevelt and the message that the Allies had come to free the people 'from the grip of conquerors who seek to deprive you of your sovereign rights, your religious freedom and the right to lead your way of life in peace' (Evans 2012, 77). The leaflet was meant to refer to the Vichy regime. It is easy to see how this might be interpreted as referring to French colonial rule more generally.

> **Connecting the local, national, transnational and global: African American soldiers on the streets of Algeria**
> On the streets of Algeria after the Allied landings, a new global power was in town. The dollar was a more sought-after currency than the franc. Hunger-stricken local populations saw American soldiers arrive with chewing gum, cigarettes, chocolate bars and big loaves of bread in their pockets. In Larb'a, near Algiers, where US soldiers were stationed to provide logistical support to military convoys, African American soldiers supported Algerians against their competitors of European origin in boxing matches, and Algerians cheered on African-American GIs in their frequent street fights with white American soldiers (Hadjerès 2014, 119–120). Both Algerians and African Americans were living in a situation of legal, political, economic, social and cultural inequality as they were being called upon by their respective governments to fight for 'freedom'.

In addition to the damage done to the image of the invincible coloniser through France's reduced international status and very visible infighting, Martin Thomas (2011) underlines the long-term damage to economic stability in the colonies. The Vichy authorities drained the colonies of basic foodstuffs both to meet vociferous German demands and for their own use in the unoccupied zone. Allied blockades led to a dramatic decrease in imports of essential supplies such as sugar, groundnut oil, petroleum and cement into Algeria.

After the British-American landings in Morocco and Algeria in November 1942, railway lines and trains were requisitioned to enable Allied troops and equipment to be transported to Tunisia to fight German and Italian forces. One impact of this was that the harvest of 1943 could not be internally distributed within North Africa or exported to foreign markets and there were fuel shortages in major cities. Nor, under the Allies, was there any significant increase in ships to transport foodstuffs to the colonies despite a few US food shipments of products such as milk powder. In the 1930s, the economic situation was already bad for Algerians. Under Vichy, the Allies and the Free French, the economic needs of the colony were unashamedly subservient to the needs of the metropole and the war effort even if this left colonised populations struggling to survive on below-subsistence levels of food.

The results of major food shortages and the decline in medical facilities and sanitation were mass starvation and the rapid spread of diseases such as typhus, cholera and tuberculosis. Crucially, as Martin Thomas underlines, although the deprivations of war affected everyone in the colonies, the impact on colonised populations was far more devastating. In Algeria, settler deaths rose from 11,482 in 1939 to 17,143 in 1942. Deaths amongst Algerians more than doubled over the same period, with 233,388 deaths in 1942 alone. More Algerians starved and more Algerians died of illnesses as a result of 'a racially ordered economic system that privileged the requirements not just of the colonial state but of its European elites' (Thomas 2011, 247–248).

ALGERIAN ACTIVISTS DEMAND TO BE ALGERIAN CITIZENS, THE FRENCH GOVERNMENT WANTS TO KEEP ITS EMPIRE MORE THAN EVER

By 1943, claims of French superiority and its promises of bringing prosperity and civilisation had been starkly undermined by the international context and the day-to-day reality of many Algerians. The French empire was vulnerable like never before. France's leaders—both in Vichy and in Algiers—knew it. So did Algerian political actors, as did their counterparts in France's other colonies.

In January 1943, leaders of the clandestine PPA, including Mohamed Lamine Debaghine (1917–2003) in the absence of Messali Hadj, who was still in prison, the AUMA and those close to Ferhat Abbas met and agreed that Abbas should put together a text to be collectively discussed. Although the follow-up meeting was banned, on 10 February 1943, a first version of Abbas's text was ready. It was titled 'Algeria Before the Global Conflict: the Algerian People's Manifesto'. At the end of the following month, the manifesto was presented to the French and Allied authorities.

The Manifesto reveals a clear change in position on the part of Abbas and many of the signatories, who were drawn from middle-class Algerian elected representatives. It not only denounced the social, economic and cultural ruin wreaked by colonialism, the political exclusion and legal discrimination to which 'Muslims' were subject and decried failed reform projects, but also attacked the false hope of assimilation, described as a 'dangerous machine in the service of colonisation'. Campaigns for the right to full French citizenship now belonged to a bygone age (<<Chap. 2, pp. 25–6). 'Europeans' and 'Muslims' were now definitively separate 'blocs' and the Manifesto signatories demanded the right to be Algerian citizens and have an Algerian government and constitution. This constitution would guarantee equality without distinction of race or religion, land reform, Arabic as an official language alongside French, a free press, free compulsory education for boys and girls and end state interference in religious practice—all within the framework of an association with France (Rahal 2015). These demands were not rejected outright, but when 'Muslim' elected representatives in the Financial Delegations (Délégations financières, the central assembly in Algiers) refused to vote the budget in the absence of reforms, the supposedly liberal Governor General Georges Catroux (1877–1969) arrested Abbas and Abdelkader Sayah, the president of the 'Muslim section' of the Financial Delegations.

A missed opportunity? Assessing the Brazzaville Conference
In early 1944, a representative of the Algerian Governor General was sent, as an observer, to the Brazzaville conference in French Equatorial Africa. Held from 30 January to 8 February, the conference brought together senior colonial officials from across the empire, now under the control of the Free French. With the spectre of the 1941 Atlantic Charter looming, they discussed how to consolidate the French presence in sub-Saharan Africa and Madagascar. The Brazzaville conference has often been presented as a turning point in French imperial policy, at which French politicians and civil servants recognised the need for a new relationship with the colonies, according more rights and autonomy to colonised peoples and investing in the colonies in order to secure the longevity of France's empire. The significance of Brazzaville has perhaps been overstated—what was agreed was more mundane and vague: France had to maintain its empire, and to do this some reforms were needed (Chafer 2002, 56). Back in Algeria, an order issued on 7 March 1944 scrapped the *indigénat*, gave French citizenship to about 60,000 men without them having to renounce their Muslim personal status and accorded the right to elect representatives to the Financial Delegations as part of a 'second electoral college' (>>Chap. 3, p. 72, 82, 112) to all Algerian men over 21. This was a version of the failed Blum-Viollette reform (<<Chap. 2, p. 38), for which Algerian politicians had long since lost their enthusiasm.

In the eastern Algerian town of Setif, on 14 March 1944, Ferhat Abbas established the Friends of the Manifesto and of Liberty (Amis du manifeste et de la liberté, AML). The AML sought to build a wide membership drawn from different groups such as the PPA, the AUMA, the Elus and the membership of the PCA (the party itself refused to adhere) as well as the wider population. Abbas was also in contact with Robert Murphy, Roosevelt's Atlantic Charter envoy in Algeria (Klose 2013, 24), in a bid to develop external allies. The AML was spectacularly successful. The number of AML sections in Algeria multiplied, membership grew to 100,000, pamphlets and the AML newspaper were widely distributed, and meetings attracted hundreds of thousands of people. The PPA was particularly influential in building the AML's grassroots membership (Evans 2012, 79–80). The AML was, for the moment, tolerated by the colonial authorities, but also feared. The wider settler population was particularly fearful of what it saw as growing 'Muslim militancy'.

8 May 1945

In May 1945, Messali Hadj was in prison in Brazzaville. In the many street demonstrations which took place to celebrate the end of the Second World War, 'Free Messali!' became a common slogan when Algerians participated. During the Mayday celebrations of 1 May 1945, whilst the French trade unions' slogans applauded the anti-Nazi resistance, Algerian participants, notably those in or close to the PPA, shouted 'Free Messali!' In Oran and Algiers, clashes broke out between marchers and the police. The police shot at the crowds and a number of PPA leaders were arrested. More demonstrations were planned for 8 May 1945, Victory in Europe (VE) day, which formally marked the surrender of Nazi Germany. The AML sought to use these demonstrations to remind both the French and the Allies of Algerian nationalist demands, through a pacifist show of strength. The demonstrations—and their aftermaths—which would acquire notoriety were those in the Constantine region in eastern Algerian, in and around the towns of Setif and Guelma (Fig. 2.1).

In Setif on 8 May 1945, around 8000 Algerian men, women and children marched through the town centre. Like Europeans participating in other VE day celebrations happening at the same time, they placed a wreath on the local war memorial and bore the flags of the Allied countries. However, they were also carrying a model of an Algerian flag, a red star and crescent on a green and white background. Algerian scouts (<<Chap. 2, p. 36) sang *Min Djibalina* [From our mountains]: 'From our mountains the voices of free men shout out/call out, calling/summoning us to independence'. Placards and banners appeared, declaring 'Free Messali' and 'Long live free and independent Algeria'. When police demanded that the flags and banners be taken down, scuffles broke out. Shots were fired by the police and a riot started. Angry demonstrators attacked European businesses, homes and Europeans. The news relayed to neighbouring rural areas, and Algerians in some of these places also attacked

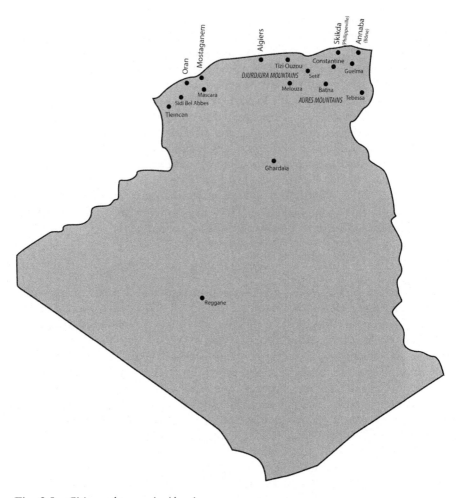

Fig. 2.1   Cities and towns in Algeria

Europeans and their property. In total, 102 Europeans were killed, including farm owners, low ranking local officials, women and children.

These deaths were dwarfed by the several thousand Algerians killed in the massacre which followed in the weeks and months after 8 May 1945, across towns and the countryside in the Constantine region. This repression was carried out by both regular French army forces and civilian militias composed of Europeans of all political tendencies. The formation of militias had been allowed, and indeed encouraged, by local and regional administrators and elected representatives and they were assisted by the police force and gendarmerie. The French army response included troops on the ground, many of whom were colonial troops from Morocco and France's West African colonies ('tirailleurs sénégalais') (>>Chap. 3, pp. 124–6), in addition to aerial bombardment of villages and navy shelling onto coastal regions. The French army soldiers were fighting a war—except this was a war waged against a civilian population (in English see Peyroulou 2008; Evans 2012; McDougall 2017). In some areas, the violence was indiscriminate, wiping out whole families. In other areas, militias deliberately targeted and killed young nationalist men, seeking to wipe out a whole generation of political activists. Rape and pillage accompanied the murders, with bodies burnt in mass graves.

On 15 May 1945, the AML was banned and Abbas arrested and charged with 'attacking French sovereignty', despite the fact he was not in Setif on 8 May. The *'ulama* leader Cheikh Mohamed Bachir El-Ibrahimi (1889–1965) was also arrested—he had only been released a few months earlier, having been under house arrest since 1940. Messali Hadj continued to remain in prison in Brazzaville. An investigation into the atrocities was rapidly hushed up. The PCA initially joined the majority settler reaction to Setif, blaming the AML and Algerians for the violence. It denounced 'fascists' on both sides, although a few months later the PCA changed position and campaigned for an amnesty for all those imprisoned Algerians accused of participating in riots (Drew 2014, 149–153). The AML collapsed under the weight of colonial repression and mutual recriminations between Abbas and the PPA about their respective responsibility in the events surrounding the massacre. Abbas felt that the PPA had tricked him into falling into a trap of confrontation through the Setif demonstration. The PPA denounced Abbas as a 'traitor' when he did not support their demands for immediate independence (Stora and Daoud 1995, 148 and 156).

The French official figure for the number of Algerians killed in the aftermath of the 8 May 1945 demonstrations was 1340. The BBC and Radio Madrid put the figure at 10,000. In June 1945, the PPA presented the figure of 35,000, which later was increased in the nationalist press to 45,000 (Rey Goldzeiguer 2002, 11–12). The exact figure has provoked much highly politicised debate amongst historians—it probably lies between the BBC and the PPA figure—as have conflicts over terminology—that is, whether to refer to what happened in Setif as 'events', a 'massacre' or 'genocide'. Only the most diehard settler would today contest the fact the repression was totally disproportionate.

From summer 1945 onwards, Setif was a persistent theme in the nationalist press. Later interviews with participants and eyewitnesses (for example, Ainad Tabet 2002; Chaalal and Haya 2013) and the memoirs of leaders of the FLN would all insist on 8 May 1945 and its aftermath as the decisive turning point. It is presented as the point of no return, after which the only solution was independence, and the only means to achieve this was armed struggle. For Mohamed Harbi (2005), senior figure in the wartime FLN turned historian: 'The Algerian War did indeed begin in Setif on 8 May 1945' (>>Chap. 4, p. 184).

The relationship between politics and violence: an inevitable turn to violence after Setif?
In recent years, a new generation of historians has questioned this straight line drawn from Setif in 1945 to the first attacks of the FLN in 1954. Rather seeing the period 1946 to 1956 as simply the prelude to 1 November 1954, Malika Rahal (2013a, 2013b, 2018) describes this period as 'the decade of political parties'. In these ten years, there were concerted efforts to challenge the colonial system through the ballot box, or, at the very least, keep Algerian nationalist demands publicly visible, which in turn created a dynamic space for discussion and political activity. Members of these parties did not all immediately rally to the FLN in 1954, and when they did—for many this was in 1956 (>>Chap. 3, p. 81)—they brought with them the experiences and practices of political organisation which they had developed in the previous decade.

THE DECADE OF POLITICAL PARTIES, 1946–56: CHANGE THROUGH THE BALLOT BOX, THE PERSISTENCE OF UNEQUAL CITIZENSHIP AND PERVASIVE FRENCH ELECTORAL FRAUD

In 1946, two new political parties were created. Released from prison in March 1946, Abbas founded the Democratic Union of the Algerian Manifesto (UDMA), whilst Messali Hadj established the Movement for the Triumph of Democratic Liberties (Mouvement pour le triomphe des libertés démocratiques, MTLD). The UDMA project was to create an Algerian Republic, in which there was a place for European settlers and the Jewish population, linked to France through a federal structure. One of Abbas's motivations for forming the UDMA was to stand in the June 1946 elections to the Constituent Assembly which would determine the constitution of the new French Republic (the Fourth Republic, 1946–58). After 1945, for the first time, African deputies could be elected to go to Paris, via a 'second electoral college' composed of non-citizens. Léopold Sedar Senghor (1906–2001, the future president of Senegal, 1960–80) and Félix Houphouët-Boigny (1905–93, the future president of Côte d'Ivoire, 1960–93) were already part of the first Constituent Assembly and lobbying intensely for greater political rights and civil liberties in the colonies. Abbas would be one of eleven UDMA deputies to join them from June to November 1946. The UDMA secured eleven out of thirteen 'second college' seats for Algeria, with 71 per cent of the vote—although the abstention rate was 50 per cent as the PPA had called for a boycott (Meynier 2002, 76).

Keen to maintain a visible presence in the legal political sphere to stop this territory being captured by other, more reformist, political parties (i.e. the UDMA), Messali Hadj founded the MTLD shortly after his release from prison in October 1946. The MTLD did not replace the PPA, which had been banned in 1939, rather it was its legal wing for the purposes of electoral politics. The MTLD campaigned in Algeria on a platform of sovereignty and independence. It secured five seats in elections to the National Assembly in the November 1946 elections, including the seat of Mohamed Khider (1912–67). The PCA, having reversed its previous critique of the Algerian demonstrators at Setif as Hitler sympathisers and pseudo-nationalists, reengaged with anti-colonialism, attacking racist prejudices and the socio-economic vested interests of settlers (Sivan 1976, 160).

In the 1946 constitution of the new Fourth Republic, the French empire was rebranded 'French Union'. Whilst French sovereignty was reaffirmed, limited political and social reforms for the benefit of colonised populations were introduced, largely as a result of the intense work of black deputies from sub-Saharan Africa (Chafer 2002, 61–67). Algeria got its own specific legislation and a new legal framework in 1947. The Statute of Algeria abolished the Financial Delegations and replaced them with an Algerian Assembly (1948–56), which held some budgetary powers and was given the task of applying legislation. This Assembly was elected through two electoral colleges, with each college containing sixty deputies. Both electoral colleges also sent 15 deputies to the National Assembly in Paris. The demography meant that a 'European' (see Glossary) vote was worth much more than a 'Muslim' (see Glossary) one (McDougall 2017, 184). The first college represented the 'Europeans' and naturalised 'Muslims' of Algeria. This was the equivalent to approximately 532,000 voters, about 10 per cent of whom were naturalised 'Muslim' men, whilst the rest were 'European' men and women. French women in metropolitan France and 'European' women in Algeria had obtained the right to vote in 1946. The second college represented the numerically much bigger group of 1.3 million 'Muslim' men who maintained their Muslim personal status. 'Muslim' women were not given the right vote, supposedly out of respect for 'tradition', even though a number of majority-Muslim countries had already, or would very soon, accord women the right to vote (>>Chap. 3, p. 112). Both 'Muslim' and 'European' deputies from Algeria in the National Assembly boycotted the vote on the new Statute of Algeria—for Algerian deputies it did not go far enough, for Europeans it went too far, and both groups could agree that they disagreed with the principle of a government in Paris passing legislation on Algeria.

Beyond the legally enshrined inequalities contained in the Statute of Algeria, the voting system in Algeria was plagued with perfectly illegal, but widely tolerated and practised, electoral fraud (Evans 2012, 104–106). The purpose of this fraud was to keep out of political power anyone who challenged the colonial status quo and the unequal relationship between 'Europeans' and 'Muslims'. After the MTLD's success in municipal elections in October 1947, the April 1948 elections to the Algerian Assembly were marked by the MTLD offices being raided, its newspaper being banned, a refusal to issue voting cards to those who might vote MTLD or UDMA, voters being physically threatened and outright cheating. In such a context, the nine deputies which the MLTD secured in the Algerian Assembly (although only five could take their seats as the other four were arrested), and the eight which the UDMA managed to get elected, was a victory. It still gave them little voice. The elections were a stark reminder to Algerian anti-colonialists that the political process was rigged against them.

Whilst the colonial authorities cheated in elections in Algeria, the creation of two new international organisations hinted that the Algeria problem might be resolved elsewhere. In October 1945, the United Nations (UN) was founded (>>Chap. 3, p. 74, 77, 133). Its Charter enshrined the language of self-determination evoked in the 1941 Atlantic Charter (<<Chap. 2, p. 44), declaring that it would bring about peace and friendly relations between nations based on 'respect for the principle of equal rights and self-determination of peoples'. France was one of the fifty signatories of the UN Charter, but did not consider that it applied to Algeria (or indeed its empire more generally). Its colonial subjects had other ideas.

Algerians were not just looking to the UN. In March 1945, the Arab League was established in Cairo. Seen as a symbol of Arab unity and identity against colonialism, the Arab League was galvanised by the independence of Syria and Lebanon in 1946 and the expulsion of Palestinians after the creation of the state of Israel in 1948. The Arab League and its members' support of the demands of Algerian nationalists was not always consistent, or unconditional, but in the late 1940s and 1950s, Cairo was a hub for North African nationalists. PPA member Chadli El-Mekki went to Cairo in 1945. He would be joined in 1951 by fellow PPA members Hocine Aït Ahmed (1926–2015), Mohamed Khider (1912–67) and, in 1952, Ahmed Ben Bella (1916–2012) (El-Mechat 2014). Members of the PPA-MTLD also had close contacts with nationalists in the Moroccan Istiqlal and the Tunisian Neo-Destour parties. Egyptian support for Algerian nationalism would be boosted by the Egyptian revolution and the coming to power of Gamal Abdel Nasser (1918–70) in 1952 (>>Chap. 3, pp. 88–9).

THE FIRST STIRRINGS OF ARMED ACTION: THE SPECIAL ORGANISATION (OS), A BANK ROBBERY AND CONNECTING ALGERIAN ARMED ACTION TO BROADER INTERNATIONAL CONFLICTS AND INTERESTS

Aït Ahmed, Khider and Ben Bella's arrival in Cairo was precipitated by their participation in a not entirely successful armed robbery. Whilst the MTLD contested elections, a paramilitary branch of the PPA was created in February 1947 to prepare for an eventual armed uprising. This was called the Special Organisation (Organisation spéciale, OS). A clandestine network composed of relatively few people stretched across the Algerian territory, the OS leaders sought to collect funds and arms and build underground cells of reliable activists. The most visible of the OS's activities was an armed robbery planned by Aït Ahmed, with the support of Ben Bella, at the main post office in Oran in April 1949. The robbery team were well informed by an insider and tried to pass themselves off as professional gangsters from mainland France. However, they had no prior experience in bank robberies and, after various false starts, the raid yielded a smaller haul than anticipated, as they could not get the safe open. The money that they did manage to steal was transported to Algiers in the official vehicle of MTLD National Assembly deputy Mohamed Khider (de Rochebrune and Stora 2011). A year later, in 1950, Ben Bella would be arrested and sentenced to eight years in prison. That same year, the colonial authorities also dismantled the OS, with those not arrested pushed deeper underground. In 1952, Ben Bella escaped from prison and went to Cairo, joining Aït Ahmed and Khider, who now represented the PPA-MTLD abroad. In 1952, Messali Hadj was once again arrested, expelled from Algeria and placed under house arrest in France.

The relationship between politics and violence, and connecting the local, national, transnational and global: Aït Ahmed's 1948 report
Although at the head of the OS, Aït Ahmed did not believe that independence could be won solely through armed struggle. In 1948, he wrote a highly perceptive report, commissioned by the MTLD, on the relationship between political and armed action. Drawing lessons from a series of military theorists as well as conflicts in Ireland, Yugoslavia and Indochina, Aït Ahmed's concluded that the large settler minority, the proximity to France and the legal status of Algeria as three departments of France all pointed to the fact that force of arms alone was not enough to win. For Aït Ahmed, there also needed to be a political strategy, which included firmly locating the Algerian anti-colonial struggle within broader international conflicts and interests, adopting a flexible attitude towards different international actors—notably the Western and Communist blocs—and leveraging them against each other (Connelly 2001, 222–223) (>>Chap. 3, p. 65, 76). His report was approved by the MTLD Central Committee with almost unanimity. In the early 1950s, a Committee for the Freedom of North Africa was established in New York to lobby on behalf of the PPA, Istiqlal and Néo-Destour (Thomas 2002, 232). This would metamorphose into separate Moroccan (Istiqlal), Tunisian (Néo-Destour) and, in due course, FLN lobbies and propaganda offices based in the United States.

THE SHIFT TO THE NATIONAL LIBERATION FRONT (FLN): PPA-MTLD INFIGHTING AND A FRUSTRATED YOUNGER GENERATION

Mohamed Harbi argues that the chain of events leading to the formation of the FLN and the attacks of 1 November 1954 is, above all, the story of the internal history of the PPA-MTLD (Harbi 1975, 34). Infighting and rivalry propelled a faction within the PPA-MTLD to create a new nationalist organisation and accelerate the shift to armed action with the proclaimed aim of forging unity and ending a sense of stagnation. The FLN was thus, as Omar Carlier (1995, 306) argues, 'both the successor and the destroyer of the PPA'.

There were a number of overlapping sources of tension within the PPA-MTLD. In terms of leadership, some members of the senior leadership increasingly resented Messali's Hadj's dominance of the organisation, accusing him of developing a cult of personality around himself. Others were fiercely loyal, including for a long time most of the party base in rural areas in Algeria and Algerian emigrants in France. From a strategic point of view, a number of mainly younger PPA-MTLD figures were impatient at what they considered to be Messali Hadj's lack of direction. Elections were rigged against the MTLD from the outset. The OS had been relatively easily dismantled by the French. Against accusations of pointless legalism, Messali Hadj and his supporters argued that the shift to armed action, or the threat of a shift to armed action, should only be used as leverage to bring about a political solution (Stora 1986, 205). Violence was not an aim in itself and its precipitous use would only result in exposing the party, its supporters and the wider population to repression.

Debating the nature of Algerian nationalism and the terms of future debates: the so-called Berber crisis

The majority of members and leaders of the PPA-MTLD saw Islam as a constituent part of Algerian identity, bringing Algerians together across linguistic groups and different regions. They also made common cause with Arab countries for political reasons—they were waging similar anti-colonial struggles—above and beyond cultural or religious affinities. Yet some members of the PPA-MTLD were attached to a narrower vision of an 'Arabo-Islamic' Algerian identity, and a sense of cultural belonging to an 'Arab nation', as essential components of Algerianness. Others were more inclined to envisage a secular and multicultural Algeria (Temlali 2015). These debates would come to a head in 1949, during the misleadingly-labelled 'Berber crisis'.

Both at the time and subsequently, this has been presented as cultural confrontation between those from the Berber-speaking regions of Algeria (notably Kabylia), who supposedly favoured a vision of a plural Algeria, and Arabic speakers from other regions who are depicted as supporting a narrower 'Arabo-Islamic' version. In reality, the two sides in this conflict did not neatly divide into linguistic, cultural or regional groups—there were Berber speakers and activists from Kabylia on both sides. The conflict was as much, if not more, about the incapacity of the leadership of PPA-MTLD to enable internal debate to take place without feeling that its very existence was threatened. It was so preoccupied with the need to maintain a united front against French colonial rule that it had no

(*continued*)

(continued)

mechanisms for enabling discussion amongst its membership (Hadjerès 2014). The 'Berber crisis' was thus a political struggle in which 'culture' was weaponised. Accusing someone of being a 'Berberist'—as Messali Hadj and his supporters did—was a way to close down debate. It alluded to colonial attempts to divide-and-rule by creating a false 'racial' distinction between Berber (Tamazight) speakers and Arabic speakers and privileging 'Berbers' over 'Arabs' in discourse and some policy (e.g. access to schooling) (<<Chap. 1, pp. 8–9). What the term 'Berberist' implied was someone that was anti-national—a regionalist possibly working for the colonial power, or at the very least reproducing its categories. References to the 'Berber crisis' or the 'anti-Berber crisis' of 1949 would become important in political debates from the late 1970s onwards in Algeria (>>Chap. 4, pp. 175–7, 186).

In the 1940s and early 1950s, disagreements about leadership, tactics and political and cultural identity were often exacerbated by intense personal rivalries. Struggles amongst members of the leadership for control of the direction of the PPA-MTLD played out in ferocious arguments amongst leaders and physical fights and refusals to pay party dues at the grassroots. By 1953, the senior leadership of the party was increasingly struggling to find a way work together and two rival camps had emerged—the 'Messalists' (i.e. Messali Hadj and his supporters) and the 'Centralists' (i.e. members of the Central Committee of the PPA-MTLD). On 23 March 1954, the Revolutionary Committee for Unity and Action (Comité revolutionnaire d'unité et d'action, CRUA) was created by a group of centralists and former members of the OS, with the aim of—as their name suggests—going beyond divisions by launching the armed struggle. From this was born the meeting of 'the 22' in June 1954 in Algiers. All 22 men present at this meeting were former members of the OS and they agreed to launch the armed struggle without delay. Organisational responsibility for this was delegated to five men drawn from the 22: Mostefa Ben Boulaïd (1917–56), Larbi Ben M'Hidi (1923–57), Rabah Bitat (1927–2000), Mohamed Boudiaf (1919–92) and Mourad Didouche (1922–55, often presented in Algeria with his surname first, as Didouche Mourad). They were joined in August by Belkacem Krim (1922–70, nearly always referred to by both his surname and his first name in Algeria, as Krim Belkacem). They would come to be known as the 'six historic leaders'. Supporting them from Cairo by developing international contacts, sources of weapons and propagating propaganda were Aït Ahmed, Khider and Ben Bella.

These nine men were all young. Apart from the 42-year-old Khider, they were aged between 27 and 37. With the exception of Didouche, who was from Algiers, they all came from rural backgrounds across Algeria, albeit somewhat more privileged rural backgrounds compared to the grinding poverty and illiteracy of the Algerian rural majority. Ben Bella, Krim Belkacem, Boudiaf and Ben Boulaïd were veterans of the Second World War, although only Boudiaf had spent a significant period of time in France, so they had not had the same socialisation as the first Algerian workers to join the ENA. They had all received at least a primary education in a French school (in 1954, this was the case for only 14 per cent of Algerian children, in 1930, when these men would have been of school age, this figure was eight per cent). They were less urban, and less highly educated than, say, the *'ulama* leaders or Abbas (Meynier 2002). This made them connected to, but also gave them a certain authority to lead, the masses. The first men to join the rural guerrilla often had a similar kind of profile (Branche 2019).

Recent scholarship (Sidi Moussa 2019) has underlined that we should not see the CRUA as simply surpassing and confining to oblivion the PPA-MTLD in the course of 1954. Whilst members of the CRUA were planning the armed uprising, neither the 'Messalists' nor the 'Centralists' had lost hope of reuniting the movement—the Messalists hoped to do so under the leadership of Messali Hadj, whereas the Centralists wanted to do this with Messali Hadj brought under the control of the party. It is retrospectively that the actions of the CRUA acquired their historical significance. In late autumn 1954, the six historic leaders would meet a number of times and decide to call their movement the National Liberation Front. The first series of armed attacks committed in its name would take place shortly afterwards.

CONCLUSION: 1914–54: THE IMPORTANCE OF CHANGING TACTICS AND CHANGING YOUR MIND AS THE CONTEXT SHIFTS

Until recently, Algerian political and cultural movements from the First World War until the outbreak of the Algerian War/ Algerian Revolution in 1954 have been neatly schematised into different 'types'. The middle-class Young Algerians, Fédération des élus and UDMA were presented as working within the system to bring about greater equality for the colonised population through political and cultural assimilation. The *'ulama* were described as the religious reformists who were promoting cultural revival, and the celebration of an Algerian cultural difference based on Arabic and Islam, but were not demanding independence. The European settlers' domination of the PCA and Marxist atheism were seen as making it very difficult for the party to engage with the question of independence, or indeed the Muslim majority population, even if the party criticised social and racial injustices. Messali Hadj's ENA, and then PPA and MTLD, were pitched as the radical nationalists with a popular base and the straightforward goal of independence.

Although each of these stereotypical descriptions has some factual basis, they have been challenged and nuanced by historians in recent years. More importantly though, new historical work has demonstrated that this kind of classification is not very useful. Such a classification suggests that each of these groups neatly encapsulates a different set of unchanging ideas: that is, you either bring down the colonial system *or* improve it, you engage in either cultural revival *or* political activism. Yet this was not an either/or situation: there was significant crossover in goals, tactics and practices across parties and associations. In varying degrees, all of these groups were campaigning for the recognition of an Algerian cultural identity, for political and legal rights, for access to education and social security benefits—in short, for the right to exist and not be crushed by colonial rule. Many Algerians belonged to more than one of these groups—it was entirely possible to be a member of the UDMA and the *'ulama* or the *'ulama* and the MTLD at the same time. Rivalries could be fierce, but they were often just as fierce amongst members of the same party as they were between parties—for example between Ben Badis and Cheikh Tayeb El Okbi (1890–1960) within the *'ulama*, between Abbas and Bendjelloul within the UDMA or between the Messalists and the Centralists in the MTLD.

Moreover, the demands and tactics of these parties and movements were not decided in a vacuum. All of these groups were also attentive to what was going on internationally. From the cultural renaissance (*nahda*) and reform (*islah*) movements spreading across the Arabic-speaking and Muslim worlds to the Comintern's demand that communist parties denounce their own imperialists, from the Rif War in Morocco and Mustafa Kemal Atatürk's creation of the Turkish Republic to France's Second World War defeat and the emergence of two new world powers, the United States and the USSR, Algerian anti-colonial parties and movements were inspired by ideas and tactics developed elsewhere, and glimpses of how they might leverage changes in the international political system.

At home in Algeria, anti-colonial leaders and their supporters were obliged to function within the considerable constraints of the colonial system. The *indigénat*, which radically curtailed the ability of Algerians to organise public meetings or indeed move about freely, was only abolished in 1944, and on the ground many of its practices remained. Moreover, after the violent repression at Setif on 8 May 1945, there was a further shift away from an intelligence-based state (i.e. based on the targeted gathering of intelligence to pre-empt specific challenges to colonial rule) towards a police state—that is to say, widespread repression of the Algerian population as a whole through greater police powers, the growing use of detention centres to house suspect elements not convicted of committing specific crimes and even greater restrictions on Algerian political activities (Thomas 2013b).

For those who opposed the colonial system, focusing on cultural or sporting activities—producing theatre plays, singing at weddings or creating football teams—rather than making outright political demands was not (just) a choice to focus on cultural revival, it was also necessary in order to exist. It is no accident that the ENA was created in mainland France, where there was less repression of political activity than in Algeria. When considering the political language used to articulate demands, it has to be remembered that not only was the press censored, but also that newspapers could be fined if they published an article which displeased the colonial authorities. Too many fines could put a newspaper out of existence. This is why parties and associations had to carefully choose their language. An emphasis on the Republic, citizenship, rights and culture were not as obviously threatening to the colonial authorities as the words sovereignty, self-determination and independence (although in terms of culture, the French authorities were made very nervous by the words Arabic and Islam). Demonstrating one's service to France, for example by foreground- ing one's status as a war veteran, and attachment to Republican values was not an act of servile adhesion to empire if this was used as the basis to make demands for change. Instead, such 'assaults of loyalism' (Fromage 2014b, 399) could be a pragmatic, legal strategy to challenge the colonial status quo by declaring one's attachment to an idealised vision of the core values of 'Frenchness' (in short: 'we really want to be French, but you are not letting us').

There was, necessarily, an ebb and flow between legalism and clandestine activity, public displays of compliance and open defiance of the system, elite political lobbying and mass rallies, songs and sport and the secret gathering of arms. This developed in relation to what the French government and colonial authorities were doing at different points in time—and they oscillated between some enthusiasm for reform (for example, during the Popular Front) and the conviction that survival depended on brutal repression (for example, in Setif and Guelma). Clearly, 'the French' were not a homogenous group either. The reformist plans of Viollette 'the Arab' during the Popular Front were not the same strategies as the electoral fraud to prevent MTLD and UDMA candidates being elected practiced by Marcel-Edmond Naegelen (1892–1973) as Governor General of Algeria between 1948 and 1951. In turn, Naegelen's Republicanism would not have been shared by far-right settler militias who went out 'Arab bashing'.

After the Second World War, however, as the agenda for colonial reform took shape on the international stage through the language of self- determination, the French state and the colonial authorities sought to resist change and reinforced their repressive apparatus in order to do so. In turn, Algerians changed their minds about what was going to work to bring about change. They changed their minds based on their experiences (of the Second World War, of Setif, of participation in elections) and based on what they saw happening in the world around them (the rise of Egyptian and Turkish nation- alism, the Anglo-American landings in North Africa, the Battle of Stalingrad, the uprising against French rule in Indochina). By 1954, the founders of the FLN had decided that colonial abuses could only be stopped by bringing down the whole system.

REFERENCES

Abitbol, Michel. 1989. *The Jews of North Africa during the Second World War*. Trans. Catherine Tihanyi Zentelis. Detroit: Wayne State University Press.

Ageron, Charles-Robert. 1966. Enquête sur les origines du nationalisme algérien. L'emir Khaled, petit-fils d'Abdelkader, fut-il le premier nationaliste algérien? [Investigation into the Origins of Algerian nationalism. Was the Emir Khaled, the Son of Abdelkader, the First Algerian Nationalist?]. *Revue des mondes musulmans et de la Méditerranée* 2: 9–49. https://doi.org/10.3406/remmm.1966.929.

———. 1982. La perception de la puissance française en 1938–9: le mythe imperial [The Perception of French Power in 1938–9: The Imperial Myth]. *Revue française d'Histoire Outre-Mer* 69 (254): 7–22. https://doi.org/10.3406/outre.1982.2331.

Ainad Tabet, Redouane. 2002 [1985]. *8 Mai 1945, le génocide* [8 May 1945, the Genocide]. Algiers: ANEP.

Aissaoui, Rabah. 2009. *Immigration and National Identity: North African Political Movements in Colonial and Postcolonial France*. London and New York: Tauris Academic Studies.

———. 2017. 'Between two worlds': Emir Khaled and the Young Algerians at the Beginning of the Twentieth Century in Algeria. In *Algeria Revisited: History, Culture and Identity*, ed. Rabah Aissaoui and Claire Eldridge, 56–78. London and New York: Bloomsbury.

Amara, Mahfoud. 2005. Global Sport and Local Identity in Algeria: The Changing Role of Football as a Cultural, Political and Economic Vehicle. In *Transition and Development in Algeria: Economic, Social and Structural Challenges*, ed. Margaret Majumdar and Mohammed Saad, 145–158. Bristol: Intellect.

Amiri, Linda. 2014 [2012]. La Fédération de France du FLN, acteur majeur de la guerre d'indépendance [The Federation of France of the FLN, Major Actor in the War of Independence]. In *Histoire de l'Algérie à la période coloniale* [History of Algeria During the Colonial Period], eds. Abderrahmane Bouchène, Jean-Pierre Peyroulou, Ouanassa Siari Tengour, and Sylvie Thénault, 576–582. Paris: La Découverte.

Belmessous, Saliha. 2013. *Assimilation and Empire: Uniformity in the French and British Colonies, 1541–1954*. Oxford: Oxford University Press.

Benkada, Saddek. 2004. La revendication des libertés publiques dans le discours politique du nationalisme algérien et de l'anticolonialisme français (1919–1954). [The Demand for Public Freedoms in the Political Discourse of Algerian Nationalism and French Anti-colonialism (1919–1954)]. *Insaniyat* 25–26: 179–199. https://doi.org/10.4000/insaniyat.6387.

Boulebier, Djamel. 2007. Constantine, fait colonial et pionniers musulmans du sport. [Constantine, Colonialism and the Muslim Sporting Pioneers]. *Insaniyat* 35–36: 21–61. https://doi.org/10.4000/insaniyat.3702.

Branche, Raphaëlle. 2019. Combattants indépendantistes et société rurale dans l'Algérie colonisée [Combatants for Independence and Rural Society in Colonial Algeria]. *Revue d'histoire* 141: 113–127. https://doi.org/10.3917/vin.141.0113.

Carlier, Omar. 1995. *Entre nation et jihad: histoire sociale des radicalismes algériens*. [Between Nation and Jihad: A Social History of Algerian Radicalisms] Paris: Presses de Sciences Po.

Chaalal, Omar Mokhtar, and Djelloul Haya. 2013. *Aux sources de novembre* [The Sources of November]. Algiers: APIC éditions.

Chafer, Tony. 2002. *The End of Empire in French West Africa: France's Successful Decolonisation?* Oxford and New York: Berg.

Chafer, Tony, and Amanda Sackur, eds. 1999. *French Colonial Empire and the Popular Front: Hope and Disillusion.* Basingstoke: Palgrave Macmillan.

Cole, Joshua. 2019. *Lethal Provocation: The Constantine Murders and the Politics of French Algeria.* Ithaca, NY: Cornell University Press.

Connelly, Matthew. 2001. Rethinking the Cold War and Decolonization: The Grand Strategy for the Algerian War for Independence. *International Journal of Middle East Studies* 33 (2): 221–245. https://doi.org/10.1017/S0020743801002033.

Courrèye, Charlotte. 2014. L'école musulmane algérienne de Ibn Bâdîs dans les années 1930, de l'alphabétisation de tous comme enjeu politique [The Algerian Muslim School of Ibn Bâdis [Ben Badis] in the 1930s, Literacy for all as a Political Tool]. *Revue des mondes musulmans de la Méditerranée* 136. https://doi.org/10.4000/remmm.8500.

———. 2016. L'association des Oulémas Musulmans Algériens et la construction de l'Etat algérien indépendant: foundation, héritages, appropriations et antagonisms. [The Association of the Algerian Muslim 'Ulama and the Construction of the Independent Algerian State]. PhD Thesis, INALCO, Paris.

Derrick, Jonathan. 2002. The Dissenters: Anti-Colonialism in France. In *Promoting the Colonial Idea: Propaganda and Visions of Empire in France,* ed. Tony Chafer and Amanda Sackur, 53–68. Basingstoke: Palgrave Macmillan.

Dine, Philip. 2002. France, Algeria and Sport: From Colonisation to Globalisation. *Modern and Contemporary France* 10 (4): 495–505. https://doi.org/10.1080/0963948022000029574.

Drew, Alison. 2014. *We Are No Longer in France. Communists in Colonial Algeria.* Manchester: Manchester University Press.

El-Mechat, Samya. 2014 [2012]. Les pays arabes et l'indépendance algérienne, 1945–1962. [The Arab Countries and Algerian Independence, 1945–1962]. In *Histoire de l'Algérie à la période coloniale* [History of Algeria During the Colonial Period], ed. Abderrahmane Bouchène, Jean-Pierre Peyroulou, Ouanassa Siari Tengour, and Sylvie Thénault, 644–651. Paris: La Découverte.

Evans, Martin. 2000. Projecting a Greater France. *History Today* 50 (2): 18–32.

———. 2010. Patriot Games: Algeria's Football Revolutionaries. *History Today* 60 (7): 42–44.

———. 2012. *Algeria: France's Undeclared War.* Oxford: Oxford University Press.

Fogarty, Richard S. 2008. *Race and War in France: Colonial Subjects in the French Army, 1914–1918.* Baltimore: Johns Hopkins University Press.

Frémeaux, Jacques. 2004. Les contingents impérieux au cœur de la guerre [Imperial Contingents in the Heart of the War]. *Histoire, économie et société* 23 (2): 215–233. https://doi.org/10.3917/hes.042.0215.

Fromage, Julien. 2014a [2012]. L'expérience des "Jeunes algériens" et l'émergence du militantisme moderne en Algérie (1880–1919). [The Experience of the 'Young Algerians' and the Emergence of Modern Activism in Algeria (1880–1919)]. In *Histoire de l'Algérie à la période coloniale* [History of Algeria During the Colonial Period], ed. Abderrahmane Bouchène, Jean-Pierre Peyroulou, Ouanassa Siari Tengour, and Sylvie Thénault, 238–244. Paris: La Découverte.

———. 2014b [2012]. Le docteur Bendjelloul et la Fédération des élus musulmans. [Dr Benjelloul and the Federation of Muslim Representatives]. In *Histoire de l'Algérie à la période coloniale* [History of Algeria During the Colonial Period], ed.

Abderrahmane Bouchène, Jean-Pierre Peyroulou, Ouanassa Siari Tengour, and Sylvie Thénault, 398–401. Paris: La Découverte.

———. 2015. La moblisation des élus musulmans fédérés au cours des années 1930: chaînon manquant entre anticolonialisme et nationalisme? [The Mobilisation of the Federated Muslim Representatives in the 1930s: The Missing Link Between Anticolonialism and Nationalism?]. In *La guerre d'Algérie revisitée: nouvelles générations, nouveaux regards* [The Algerian War Revisited: New Generations, New Perspectives], ed. Aissa Kadri, Moula Bouaziz, and Tramor Quemeneur, 89–99. Paris: Karthala.

Goebel, Michael. 2016. 'The capital of men without a country': Migrants and Anticolonialism in Interwar Paris. *The American Historical Review* 121 (5): 1444–1467. https://doi.org/10.1093/ahr/121.5.1444.

Hadjerès, Sadek. 2014. *Quand une nation s'éveille. Mémoires – tome 1 – 1928–1949* [When a Nation Awakes. Memoirs – Volume 1 – 1928–1949]. Annotated and Postfaced by Malika Rahal. Algiers: Inas Editions.

Harbi, Mohamed. 1975. *Aux origines du FLN: le populisme revolutionnaire en Algérie* [The Origins of the FLN: Revolutionary Populism in Algeria]. Paris: Bourgois.

———. 2005. La guerre d'Algérie a commencé à Sétif [The Algerian War Started in Sétif]. *Monde diplomatique*, March 1. http://www.monde-diplomatique.fr/2005/05/HARBI/12191#nb4. Accessed 1 June 2020.

Hassett, Dónal. 2019. *Mobilising Memory: The Great War and the Language of Politics in Colonial Algeria, 1918–1939.* Oxford: Oxford University Press.

Hodier, Catherine, and Michel Pierre. 1991. *1931: l'Exposition coloniale [1931: the Colonial Exhibition].* Brussels: Complexe.

Kaddache, Mahfoud. 2003a. 'Les soldats de l'avenir': les Scouts musulmans algériens (1930–1962) ['The soldiers of the future': Algerian Muslim Scouts (1930-1962)]. In *De l'Indochine à l'Algérie. La jeunesse en mouvements des deux côtés du miroir colonial, 1940–1962* [From Indochina to Algeria. Youth in Movement on Both Sides of the Colonial Mirror, 1940–1962], ed. Nicolas Bancel, Daniel Denis, and Youssef Fates, 68–77. Paris: La Decouverte.

———. 2003b. *Histoire du nationalism algérien. Tome 2, 1939–1951* [History of Algerian Nationalism; Volume 2, 1939–1951]. Paris and Algiers: Paris-Méditerranée, EDIF.

Kalman, Samuel. 2013. *French Colonial Fascism: The Extreme Right in Algeria, 1919–1939.* Basingstoke: Palgrave Macmillan.

Katz, Ethan. 2015. *The Burdens of Brotherhood: Jews and Muslims from North Africa to France.* Cambridge, MA: Harvard University Press.

Klose, Fabian. 2013. *Human Rights in the Shadow of Colonial Violence. The Wars of Independence in Kenya and Algeria.* Trans. Dona Geyer. Philadelphia, PA: University of Pennsylvania Press.

Krais, Jakob. 2017. The Sportive Origin of Revolution: Youth Movements and Generational Conflicts in Late Colonial Algeria. *Middle East – Topics & Arguments* 9: 132–141. https://doi.org/10.17192/meta.2017.9.6965.

Lane, Jeremy F. 2007. Ferhat Abbas, Vichy's National Revolution, and the Memory of the 'Royaume arabe'. *L'Esprit Créateur* 47 (1): 19–31.

Le Foll Luciani, Pierre-Jean. 2015. Les juifs d'Algérie face aux nationalités française et algérienne (1940–1963) [The Jews of Algeria Faced with French and Algerian Nationalities]. *Revue des mondes musulmans et de la Méditerranée* 137: 115–132. https://doi.org/10.4000/remmm.9057.

Macmaster, Neil. 2011. The Role of European Women and the Question of Mixed Couples in the Algerian Nationalist Movement in France, Circa 1918–1962. *French Historical Studies* 34 (2): 357–386. https://doi.org/10.1215/00161071-1157376.

Manela, Erez. 2007. *The Wilsonian Moment: Self-Determination and the International Origins of Anticolonial Nationalism*. New York, NY: Oxford University Press.

Mann, Michelle. 2017. The Young Algerians and the Question of the Muslim Draft, 1900–1914. In *Algeria Revisited: History, Culture and Identity*, ed. Rabah Aissaoui and Claire Eldridge, 39–55. London and New York: Bloomsbury.

Marangé, Céline. 2016a. De l'influence politique des acteurs coloniaux [The Political Influence of Colonial Actors]. *Vingtième siècle. Revue d'histoire* 131: 3–16. https://doi.org/10.3917/ving.131.0003.

———. 2016b. André Ferrat et la création du Parti communiste algérien (1931–1936) [André Ferrat and the creation of the Algerian Communist Party]. *Histoire@Politique* 29: 190–219. https://doi.org/10.3917/hp.029.0190.

Marynower, Claire. 2011. Réformer l'Algérie? Des militants socialistes en "situation coloniale" dans l'entre-les-deux-guerres [Reform Algeria? Socialist Activists in a 'colonial situation' in the Interwar Period]. *Histoire@politique* 13: 112–124. https://doi.org/10.3917/hp.013.0010.

———. 2014 [2012]. 1936. Le Front Populaire en Algérie et le Congrès musulman algérien. [1936. The Popular Front in Algeria and the Algerian Muslim Congress]. In *Histoire de l'Algérie à la période coloniale* [History of Algeria During the Colonial Period], ed. Abderrahmane Bouchène, Jean-Pierre Peyroulou, Ouanassa Siari Tengour, and Sylvie Thénault, 401–404. Paris: La Découverte.

McDougall, James. 2006. *History and the Culture of Nationalism in Algeria*. Cambridge: Cambridge University Press.

———. 2017. *A History of Algeria*. Cambridge: Cambridge University Press.

Meynier, Gilbert. 2002. *Histoire intérieure du FLN 1954–1962 [The Internal History of the FLN]*. Paris: Fayard.

———. 2015 [1981]. *L'Algérie révélée: la guerre de 1914–1918 et le premier quart du XXe siècle* [Algeria Revealed: The 1914–18 War and the First Quarter of the Twentieth Century]. Saint Denis: Editions Bouchène.

———. 2016. Algerians and the First World War. *Orient XXI*. https://orientxxi. info/l-orient-dans-la-guerre-1914-1918/algerians-and-the-first-world-war,0645,0645. Accessed 1 June 2020.

Peyroulou, Jean-Pierre. 2008. Setif and Guelma (May 1945). Mass Violence and Resistance – Research Network. https://www.sciencespo.fr/mass-violence-war-massacre-resistance/en/document/setif-and-guelma-may-1945. Accessed 1 June 2020.

Rahal, Malika. 2013a. A Local Approach to the UDMA: Local-Level Politics During the Decade of Political Parties, 1946–56. *Journal of North African Studies* 18 (5): 703–724. https://doi.org/10.1080/13629387.2013.849897.

———. 2013b. Algeria: Nonviolent Resistance Against French Colonialism, 1830s–1950s. In *Recovering Nonviolent History: Civil Resistance in Liberation Struggles*, ed. Maciej J. Bartkowski, 107–123. Boulder, CO: Rienner.

———. 2014 [2012]. Ferhat Abbas, de l'assimilation au nationalism. [Ferhat Abbas, from Assimilation to Nationalism]. In *Histoire de l'Algérie à la période coloniale* [History of Algeria During the Colonial Period], ed. Abderrahmane Bouchène, Jean-Pierre Peyroulou, Ouanassa Siari Tengour, and Sylvie Thénault, 443–446. Paris: La Découverte.

———. 2015. 10 février 1943 – Le Manifeste du peuple algérie [10 February 1943 – The Manifesto of the Algerian People]. *Textures du temps*. https://texturesdutemps. hypotheses.org/1458. Accessed 1 June 2020.

———. 2018. *L'UDMA et les UDMISTES: Contribution à l'histoire du nationalisme algérien* [UDMA and Its Members: Contribution to the History of Algerian Nationalism]. Algiers: Barzakh.

Rey Goldzeiguer, Annie. 2002. *Aux Origines de la Guerre d'Algérie 1940–1945. De Mers-el-Kébir aux massacres du Nord Constantinois* [The Origins of the Algerian War 1940–1945. From Mers-el-Kébir to the Massacres in the North Constantine Region]. Paris: La Découverte.

de Rochebrune, Renaud, and Benjamin Stora. 2011. *La Guerre d'Algérie vue par les Algériens. Des origines à la Bataille d'Alger* [The Algerian War Seen by Algerians. From Its Origins to the Battle of Algiers]. Paris: Denoël.

Siari Tengour, Ouanassa. 2014 [2012]. La révolte de 1916 dans les Aurès [The 1916 Revolt in the Aurès]. In *Histoire de l'Algérie à la période coloniale* [History of Algeria During the Colonial Period], ed. Abderrahmane Bouchène, Jean-Pierre Peyroulou, Ouanassa Siari Tengour, and Sylvie Thénault, 255–260. Paris: La Découverte.

Sidi Moussa, Nedjib. 2019. *Algérie. Une autre histoire de l'indépendance.* [Algeria. Another History of Independence]. Paris: PUF.

Sivan, Emmanuel. 1973. 'Slave owner mentality' and Bolshevism: Algerian Communism, 1920–1927. *Asian and African Studies* 9 (2): 154–195.

———. 1976. *Communisme et nationalisme en Algérie 1920–1962* [Communism and Nationalism in Algeria 1920–1962]. Paris: Presses de Sciences Po.

Stora, Benjamin. 1986. *Messali Hadj (1898–1974): pionnier du nationalisme algérien* [Messali Hadj (1898–1974), Pioneer of Algerian Nationalism]. Paris: L'Harmattan.

Stora, Benjamin, and Zakya Daoud. 1995. *Ferhat Abbas, une utopie algérienne* [Ferhat Abbas: An Algerian Utopia]. Paris: Denoël.

Suny, Ronald Grigor. 2003. 'Don't paint nationalism red!' National Revolution and Socialist Anti-imperialism. In *Decolonization: Perspectives from Now and Then*, ed. Prasenjit Duara, 176–198. London and New York: Routledge.

Temlali, Yassine. 2015. *La Genèse de la Kabylie: aux origines de l'affirmation berbère en Algérie (1830–1962)* [The Genesis of Kabylia: The Origins of the Berber Affirmation in Algeria (1830–1962)]. Algiers: Barzakh.

Thomas, Martin. 2002. Defending a Lost Cause? France and the United States Vision of Imperial Rule in French North Africa, 1945–1956. *Diplomatic History* 26 (2): 215–130. https://doi.org/10.1111/1467-7709.00308.

———. 2011. Resource War, Civil War, Rights War: Factoring Empire into French North Africa's Second World War. *War in History* 18 (2): 225–248. https://doi. org/10.1177/0968344510394265.

———. 2013a. *Fight Or Flight: Britain, France, and Their Roads from Empire.* Oxford: Oxford University Press.

———. 2013b. Intelligence and the Transition to the Algerian Police State: Reassessing French Colonial Security After the Sétif Uprising, 1945. *Intelligence and National Security* 28 (3): 377–396. https://doi.org/10.1080/02684527.2013.789637.

———. 2015. France and Its Colonial Civil Wars, 1940–1945. In *The Cambridge History of the Second World War: Volume 2, Politics and Ideology*, ed. Richard Bosworth and Joseph Maiolo, 518–604. Cambridge: Cambridge University Press.

CHAPTER 3

The Course of the War, 1954–62

NOVEMBER 1954, 12 NOVEMBER 1954: TWO DECLARATIONS

On 1 November 1954, a series of assassinations, bomb explosions and acts of sabotage and arson took place across Algeria. The attacks were accompanied by a proclamation issued by the newly formed National Liberation Front. The FLN declared that its goal was 'national independence', defined as 'The restoration of the sovereign, democratic, and social Algerian state, within the framework of Islamic Principles', at the same time ensuring 'The respect of all fundamental liberties without distinction of race or religion' (see Shepard 2015, 96–100, for an English translation of the full text). The proclamation called upon all nationalist activists, across rival parties and their internal factions, and all Algerians of all social classes, to unify their efforts to achieve independence, under the sole leadership of the FLN. The struggle was envisaged on a number of fronts. The FLN's National Liberation Army (Armée de libération nationale, jaysh al-taḥrīr al-watani, ALN) would wage armed action, whilst the FLN kept the door to political negotiation open, on the condition that France accept the principle of self-determination.

Simultaneously, the FLN would hasten a favourable resolution of the conflict by making it an international issue, drawing in the USSR, the United States and newly independent Asian, Middle Eastern and African states, to apply pressure on France (<<Chap. 2, p. 53). The 1 November attacks were deliberately planned to take place across the Algerian territory to demonstrate that this was not a local revolt. The founders of the FLN (<<Chap. 2, pp. 55–6) had thus divided Algeria into different military zones (later *wilayat*, see Glossary and >>Chap. 3, p. 86). Zone 1 (the region of the Aures mountains) was the responsibility of Mostefa Ben Boulaïd. Mourad Didouche was head of Zone 2 (North Constantine region), zone 3 (Kabylia) was under the authority of Krim Belkacem and Amar Ouamrane, zone 4 (the Algiers region) went to Rabah Bitat and Larbi Ben M'Hidi led zone 5 (the Oran region) (Fig. 3.1).

© The Author(s) 2020
N. Vince, *The Algerian War, The Algerian Revolution*,
https://doi.org/10.1007/978-3-030-54264-1_3

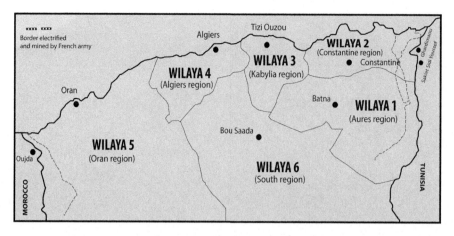

Fig. 3.1 The *wilayat* of the ALN in Algeria and its military bases in Oujda (Morocco) and Ghardimaou (Tunisia). The French army's Pédron, Morice and Challe electrified/mined defensive borders are also indicated

To begin with, the ALN had few arms and no more than 1000 men. Despite the 'national' character of the 1 November attacks, the political and military organisation was mostly present in the mountainous regions of Kabylia and the Aures, where the rocky terrain and thick vegetation provided the best protection against capture by the French army and police. The vast majority of Algerians did not read the 1 November declaration. The FLN was a largely unknown organisation, and its networks in Algeria in the first months of the war were based on family ties and political contacts from the PPA-MTLD. For Algerian workers and small business owners in France in particular, anti-colonial politics was inseparable from the figure of Messali Hadj, who had played such a central role in building the nationalist movement from the metropole (<<Chap. 2, pp. 29–32). Many erroneously but reasonably assumed that Messali Hadj had approved the attacks or had played a role in their organisation.

The FLN's first—and indeed ongoing—challenge was to establish itself as the sole representative of Algerian nationalism and make the organisation synonymous with 'the people'. On 5 November 1954, the French authorities dissolved the MTLD. On 8 November, Messali Hadj, under house arrest in France, issued a statement which was vague enough to allow MTLD supporters to believe that he had been consulted about the 1 November attacks: 'those explosions in Algeria are precisely the disastrous result of the colonial policy which continues obstinately to ignore Algerian realities', he declared (Aissaoui 2012, 228). This ambiguous show of unity was short-lived: on 3 December, Messali Hadj created the Algerian National Movement (Mouvement national algérien, al-haraka al-wataniyya al-jazā'iriyya, MNA), led by himself. Messali Hadj had not abandoned the idea of unity—but on his own terms, with the nationalist movement united behind him. This position was firmly rejected by the FLN. The distinction between the MNA and FLN was not necessarily obvious to many Algerians for a number of months. Messalists continued to fund Krim Belkacem, for example, not realising until spring 1955 he had rallied to the FLN (Aissaoui 2012, 229).

Debating the nature of Algerian nationalism: who were 'the people'?
Addressing 'the Algerian people', the 1 November 1954 declaration insisted: 'The National Liberation Front is your front. Its victory is yours.' The same idea would later become part of the masthead of the FLN newspaper *El Moudjahid*—'The revolution by the people and for the people'. Such neat slogans conceal the fact that the FLN had to not only rally 'the people', but also define who was included in 'the people', and on what basis they belonged to the national community. Was 'Algerianness' culturally defined, based on being Muslim as the phrase 'within the framework of Islamic principals' suggested? Or was Algerianness defined by adhering to a set of values such as sovereignty, democracy, equality and non-discrimination, as the 1 November declaration also stated, in which case there was a place in the liberation struggle and in an Algerian Algeria for those of European and Jewish origin? Defining 'the people' was a complex and hotly debated task which had begun well before 1954 (<<Chap. 2, pp. 34–5, 54–5) and continued long into the post-independence period (>>Chap. 4, pp. 158–9, 168–9, 175–8, 185–6). The FLN/ALN began, however, in the first months of the war by assassinating those whom they considered indisputable traitors to 'the people' and thus unequivocally outside the boundaries of the emerging national community—that is to say, Algerians who worked for the local colonial administration.

On 12 November 1954, in response to the 1 November attacks, the Minister for the Interior in the centre-left coalition government, François Mitterrand (1916–96, president of France 1981–95), insisted in a speech to the National Assembly in Paris that 'Algeria is France [...] Algeria's departments are departments of the French republic' and announced the imminent arrival of additional troops to defend the local population (Shepard 2015, 101–103). For politicians such as Mitterrand, and Prime Minister Pierre Mendès-France (1907–82), it was inconceivable that the situation in Algeria could be compared to that in Indochina. French military defeat at the hands of the communist-nationalist Viet Minh at Dien Bien Phu in May 1954 had led to the collapse of the previous government and the election of Mendès-France's coalition on a programme of withdrawal from its east Asian colony. Nor, for these politicians, was Algeria in any way comparable to Tunisia and Morocco. The French government had already begun to embark on a process of moving towards 'internal autonomy' for these North African protectorates (see

Glossary), a process which would culminate in Tunisian and Moroccan independence in 1956. The view that Algeria was France, part of the Republic and under the same laws as the metropole, was the position of the overwhelming majority of the French political class in 1954, despite this flying in the face of the lived reality of the vast majority of Algerians (<<Chap. 1, pp. 4–10).

The responses of successive French governments and civil servants to the FLN was remarkably consistent right up until late 1959. This is despite what the numerous changes of government—and indeed the collapse of the Fourth Republic and the creation of the Fifth Republic in 1958—might suggest. Firstly, politicians insisted that Algeria was France. There was no question of independence, and no question of foreign countries or international organisations interfering in France's 'internal affairs'. The French government would repeatedly argue that the FLN 'outlaws' were just an unrepresentative minority of religious fanatics and criminal bandits, in thrall to Egyptian President Nasser, and that they would be dealt with by the police and army (Evans 2012, 123). There was a widely shared fear that the loss of Algeria would lead to the loss of France's status in the world. Secondly, political, social and economic reforms and initiatives were developed, which sought to simultaneously tighten French control and surveillance of the Algerian population and convince Algerians that they would be materially and politically better off under French rule than in an independent state. From 1955 onwards, this became 'an extension of political rights and economic assistance unparalleled in the history of Western overseas imperialism' (Shepard 2006, 45).

The 1 November proclamation and the initial French response thus clearly set out the three interconnected arenas in which the War of Independence would be fought between 1954 and 1962. Firstly, this was a military confrontation, in Algeria and in mainland France. Secondly, this was a war between two competing claims: 'Algeria is France' versus 'Algeria is the FLN'. Which of these claims was most true, or rather could be the most convincingly made to win 'the hearts and minds' of the population of Algeria, as well as international audiences? Thirdly, this war was never just a Franco-Algerian confrontation, it was also fought on the world stage and shaped by a shifting global context.

Importing Ideas About Revolutionary Warfare into Algerian Local Networks, the French Military Response and the April 1955 State of Emergency

The founders of the FLN knew that they were not going to achieve independence by defeating the French army, one of the largest and best equipped in the world. Instead, the tactics it adopted were those which would come to be known in military-speak as revolutionary warfare or asymmetric warfare (Alexander and Keiger 2002; Vaïsse and Jauffret 2001). In asymmetric warfare, smaller powers (in this case, the FLN and its military branch, the ALN) use tactics which larger powers (in this case, France) are not expected to use, such as guerrilla warfare and urban terrorism. The goal is to wear down the political will of larger powers to remain, either through growing 'war weariness' of the human and material costs as the conflict drags on or through discrediting the moral authority of the larger power by exposing the tactics it uses to crush the weaker power (Mack 1975).

The FLN leadership drew upon the methods of Chinese communist revolutionary Mao Zedong and Viet Minh leader Hồ Chí Minh, and was in direct contact with both by 1959 (Byrne 2009, 430). It was inspired by the way in which Viet Minh General Vo Nguyen Giap had brought about French defeat at Dien Bien Phu, by unexpectedly transporting heavy weapons through very difficult terrain and digging tunnels to besiege the French position. It took to heart Mao's much-quoted dictum for the conduct of revolutionary warfare: the guerrilla's relationship to the rural population is that of the fish to water. To enable guerrillas to swim, breathe and multiply and (i.e. move about, be fed, escape capture and increase their numbers), they first have to ideologically win over the population to their cause.

Winning over local populations was a gradual task, which took place over a number of months. Growing numbers of men, and some women, joined the rural, and later urban, guerrilla. Women in civilian support networks prepared food for men in the rural guerrilla when they arrived in villages after trekking through the mountains. Women washed their clothes and healed their wounds with medicinal plants. Children kept watch for French soldiers and sometimes took food out to the *mujahidin* (see Glossary). Those men who did not fight were expected to pay a 'revolutionary tax' to support the struggle. In response, the French army developed a strategy of counter-revolutionary warfare to cut off the supply lines which enabled rural guerrillas to function. The French army sought to turn local populations against guerrillas through psychological warfare aimed at 'winning hearts and minds' (>>Chap. 3, pp. 99–101). It forcibly displaced entire regions of rural inhabitants away from areas where the ALN was particularly active (>>Chap. 3, p. 102). Throughout the war, the French state and army used the euphemistic term 'pacification' to refer to this counter-revolutionary programme, which also included collective punishment and extra-judicial killings as well as regular warfare.

Initially, the first rural populations to be 'won over' to the FLN, or more precisely, the ALN, were those brought into the struggle by members of their family who were already in the organisation. In a highly secret operation, the bonds of family were initially seen as surer method of recruitment than seeking to cultivate shared political beliefs—meetings to raise political consciousness would come later. Algeria on the eve of the War of Liberation was a primarily rural society. Only a quarter of the population lived in towns (Aït-el-Djoudi 2007, 54). Gilbert Meynier (2002, 177) underlines that for 'the masses, before discovering the *jabha* [front, i.e. the FLN], they would discover the *jaych* [army, i.e. the ALN]'. In the village of Agraradj in Kabylia, Fatima Benmohand Berci remembers her first contact with the soldiers of the ALN in the following terms:

Krim Belkacem came and he gave an outfit to everyone. They all had a *burnus* [a long, hooded cloak made out of coarse fabric]. Nobody knew. They forbade tobacco and chewing tobacco [tobacco was an emblematic colonial crop and buying cigarettes was a source of tax revenue for the colonial state]. Only people they trusted knew. Very few women knew, apart from those who were in on the secret, the ones who they really trusted. During the night, they came in the houses, they took all the shotguns of civilians (Vince 2015, 30).

The ALN merged modern guerrilla warfare strategies with much older, more familiar methods used in traditional 'peasants' revolts'. These included targeting those seen as having become rich through unfair means (e.g. landowning settlers), pitilessly punishing traitors, and becoming larger-than-life characters by encouraging tales to be told about their feats and French army defeats (Branche 2019). Rural populations were also won over through evoking collective memories of past violence committed against them by the French. These included the 'enfumades' (acts of 'smoking out') in the Dahra in the west of Algeria in 1845, when families hiding in caves were suffocated to death by fires deliberately lit by the French army, the dispossession of land in the east after the failed 1871 Mokrani uprising and the massacres following the 8 May 1945 demonstrations (<<Chap. 2, pp. 47–9).

In addition to commandeering arms from villagers, the FLN/ALN's weapons came from two main sources. Firstly, weapons from the Eastern bloc (East Germany, Czechoslovakia, Yugoslavia and the USSR) were smuggled into Algeria via Egypt and Tunisia. Secondly, arms were captured from French army troops during ambushes. In addition to these ambushes, rural guerrilla units also carried out attacks such as sabotaging roads and railway lines and burning down crops on European-owned farms. In November 1954, there were 178 such attacks recorded. In December 1954, this figure rose to 201. After a winter lull, attacks took place on an increasing scale in 1955 with 196 attacks recorded in April, 455 in May, 501 in June and 441 in July (Evans 2012, 125).

In response, the French government sent more and more troops. At the end of 1954, there were around 50,000 soldiers in Algeria. In late 20 January 1955, the French army, by now numbering over 80,000 troops, conducted its first operations in the Aures mountains to track down the rural guerrillas and impose collective punishments, such as burning down politically suspect villages, killing livestock and destroying food stores. By June 1955, there were 100,000 French troops in Algeria (Alexander and Keiger 2002, x). Despite this, the fact that the FLN/ALN was increasingly taking root in local populations is reflected in the gradual extension of a state of emergency by Edgar Faure's government. Faure's government had replaced that of Mendès-France in February 1955. On 3 April 1955, a state of emergency was declared in the regions of Batna, Tebessa and Tizi Ouzou. It was extended to the whole of Algeria in August 1955. The state of emergency gave supplementary powers to the General Government in Algiers and its regional representatives. These included internment (>>Chap. 3, p. 94), curfews, banning people from moving from a designated area, confiscating weapons, night time house searches, house arrest, enhanced surveillance and the ability to close 'suspect' cafes and cinemas as well as censorship of the press. The process of identifying, arresting or killing the enemy led to many other Algerians, not yet engaged in the FLN, to be stopped at road blocks and have their papers checked, in addition to enduring the collateral damage of operations to arrest and kill rural guerrillas. This contributed to antagonising the whole Algerian population.

THE FRENCH POLITICAL RESPONSE: THE 'THIRD WAY'

The 1 November 1954 attacks were the impetus for the French state to—finally—make good on the claim that 'Algeria is France'. In the 1920s and 1930s, reforming citizenship law, and notably extending full citizenship to all Algerians without individuals being obliged to renounce their personal status (see Glossary), had been central to the political demands of the Emir Khaled and the Jeunes Algériens, the Fédération des Elus and the UDMA (<<Chap. 2, p. 25, 35). The response of the French state had been timid—minor reforms in 1919 (<<Chap. 2, p. 25), 1944 (<<Chap. 2, p. 46) and 1947 (<<Chap. 2, p. 51) had only given full citizenship to a very small number of men, maintaining settler political dominance despite their numerical inferiority. Large swathes of rural Algeria had little or no contact with the French state at all: there were no schools, no doctors, no infrastructure such as gas or electricity and few representatives of the state in the form of local administrators. This lack of direct contact with local populations was rapidly pinpointed by the French government as an explanation for why the FLN appeared to be implanting itself into rural communities with such ease.

In January 1955, Mitterrand announced major plans to open up educational and employment opportunities for the 'Muslim' majority. These included a series of public works to improve roads, bringing post offices and town halls to remoter parts of Algeria, removing some of the barriers which excluded 'Muslims' from participating in political life and integrating the Algerian police force into the metropolitan French one. These were not particularly innovative measures—similar kinds of reforms had been mooted in previous decades—but the rebellion made implementing change a political imperative. The 'third way' promoted by Mendès-France and Mitterrand rejected both settler intransigence and FLN nationalism, in order to build a more equal society in Algeria, under the control of France. Reforming in order to better remain would enable France to sustain its rank as a global power, despite challenges to this status from the USSR, the United States and pan-Arab nationalism (Evans 2012, 130).

The belief that tackling poverty and political inequality would diminish support for independence was shared by many French politicians and civil servants. For some, this vision of change was very instrumental: it was a means to an end, a way to subdue the rebellion. Others were more idealistic, envisioning the creation of a new French Algeria. On the more idealistic end of the spectrum was Jacques Soustelle (1912–90), who was Governor General of Algeria between February 1955 and February 1956. A member of the French resistance during the Second World War and a left-wing supporter of de Gaulle, Soustelle was an ethnographer by training who had conducted extensive fieldwork in Mexico, specialising in the cultures and societies of its indigenous peoples. From this experience emerged Soustelle's ideas about 'integration'. This meant promoting political equality (including removing unfair 'second colleges' (<<Chap. 2, p. 51) and reforming local government) and providing greater social and economic opportunities for autochthonous peoples, whilst respecting the distinctiveness of their languages and cultures (i.e. without cultural assimilation). For Soustelle, being Muslim was not a barrier to being French, and French reformers needed to recognise and respect that Algerians could be Muslim and French. In doing so, he believed, the ground would be laid for the creation of a modern, inclusive Franco-Algerian nation (Tyre 2006; Shepard 2006, 47–48, 2011). Soustelle was initially viewed with suspicion by much of the settler community as a reformer who would seek to undermine their dominant position in Algeria. Settler hostility towards his appointment, and a general fear on the French right that reform meant accommodating terrorism, was one of the factors in the collapse Mendès-France government in February 1955. Soustelle was, however, popular with settlers by the time he left office (>>Chap. 3, p. 80, 110, 134).

18–24 April 1955, Bandung, Indonesia: Imperialism Under International Attack

The flirtation of Gaullists such as Soustelle with a more inclusive, Franco-Algerian vision of the nation ended around mid-1955, when a bloc of previously colonised countries began to assertively make their own demands on the world stage. After the Second World War, the centre of power had shifted away from Europe towards two new rival superpowers, the United States and the USSR. As the process of decolonisation gathered pace, the United States, the Soviet Union and the old European colonial masters sought to sustain or establish their influence over newly independent nation-states. Between 18 and 24 April 1955, the first Afro-Asian conference was held in Bandung, Indonesia. Indonesia had achieved independence from Dutch colonial rule the previous decade. Six hundred leaders and delegates attended from 29 states from across Africa, Asia and the Middle East. Many of these countries were former colonies. Participants included the Egyptian President Nasser, the Indian Prime Minister Jawaharlal Nehru as well as Chinese Prime Minister Zhou Enlai and the Yugoslavian President Josip Broz Tito. Around 30 nationalist movements from countries still under colonial rule were also represented as observers. These included Tunisia's Neo Destour, Morocco's Istiqlal—and the Algerian FLN. Amongst the Algerian delegation were Hocine Aït Ahmed and M'hamed Yazid (1923–2003).

Participants at Bandung represented around two-thirds of the world's population. Ideologically, some were closer to the United States, others were closer to the USSR, but they all took the position of being anti-imperial and 'non-aligned'—that is to say, they sought to be neutral in the Cold War. They did not want to be forever locked in political, economic and cultural thrall to their former colonial masters. Nor did they want to be new markets for the United States to sell Coca Cola and access cheap raw materials. Nor did they want to become communist puppets (see Glossary, Third Worldism). Bandung was a political alternative, a successor to the 1927 League Against Imperialism and Colonialism conference in Brussels (<<Chap. 2, p. 30). Indeed, Indonesian President Sukarno referred to the 1927 conference in his opening speech. The Bandung conference's closing statement included a declaration of support for the 'rights of the people of Algeria, Morocco and Tunisia to self-determination and independence', urging 'the French government to bring about a peaceful settlement of the issue without delay'.

Connecting the local, national, transnational and global: why was Bandung significant?
Self-determination was the language of the 1941 Atlantic Charter (<<Chap. 2, pp. 43–4) and the 1945 United Nations Charter (<<Chap. 2, p. 52). France had been a signatory to both, although French politicians and civil servants had not envisaged that the 'provinces' of Algeria, an integral part of French territory, would be included in the UN's remit, nor that Algeria's 'Muslims' would be considered a distinct people with the right to self-determination. The Bandung conference explicitly made the language of self-rule, sovereignty and independence that of colonised peoples, too: 'Bandung surely helped the newly independent states become parts of the UN system […] it [also] brought into the imagination of that system a shared anti-imperial rhetoric' (Chakrabarty 2010, 51). The presence of FLN representatives at Bandung began the process of legitimising the idea that Algeria was a distinct nation on the world stage, and that the FLN was the organisation which was best placed to represent this nation. This was to the detriment of Messali Hadj, who had spoken so passionately nearly 30 years previously at the 1927 League Against Imperialism and Colonialism conference, and who now was increasingly sidelined.

Bandung frightened the imperial powers. In May 1955, future French Prime Minister (1959–62) Michel Debré (1912–96) penned an article titled 'The lessons of Bandung'. Just a few years previously, in 1951, Debré had expressed concerns about European integration (i.e. the development of what would become the European Union) on the basis that France was a 'Muslim power' and therefore should not be geographically confined to Europe (>>Chap. 3, p. 130). In 'The lessons of Bandung', Debré saw the countries of the Global South, including Muslim-majority countries, in a much more fearful light. He argued that Bandung marked the beginnings of a new Islamic onslaught against France, which would kill off any Franco-Algerian projects. He called for France to resist, and made a parallel with the eighth-century defeat of the Moors at Poitiers in western France (Tyre 2006, 290–291). The American reaction to Bandung was different—they moved to improve relations with the non-aligned states, fearing they might lose them to communism if the United States seemed too hostile. French diplomat Maurice Couve de Murville (1907–99, prime minister 1968–9) told politicians in Paris to prepare themselves for the re-emergence of a form of American anti-colonialism which risked undermining France's place in the world (Thomas 2002, 241) (>>Chap. 3, p. 75, 77, 89, 106–7).

It should be underlined that just because another country was a former colony it was not automatically sympathetic to the FLN or Algerian independence. This can be seen in Tunisian, Moroccan and Egyptian political and material support for the FLN. On the one hand, these countries were the FLN's most committed international supporters. On the other hand, this support could wax and wane depending on how keen they were to sustain or develop good relations with France at any given time (>>Chap. 3, pp. 88–90, 106–7). A growing number of former colonies becoming independent and joining the UN, and therefore participating in UN votes on international issues, was not necessarily of automatic benefit to the FLN, or other anti-colonial nationalist movements. Whilst the Afro-Asian group in the UN (composed of many of the countries represented at Bandung) supported self-determination in Algeria, the Brazzaville group tended to vote with France to keep Algeria off the UN agenda. The Brazzaville group was composed of the majority of France's former sub-Saharan African colonies, which became independent in 1960 and thereafter members of the UN: Cameroon, Central African Republic, Côte d'Ivoire, Dahomey (Benin), Gabon, Mauritania, Haute Volta (Burkina Faso), Madagascar, Niger, Senegal and Chad. The group did not include Mali and Guinea, who were firmly pro-Algerian independence.

The FLN and France: Neither Autonomous Actors Nor Pawns of the Superpowers in the Cold War Context

Seeking to form alliances with the non-aligned movement and use these connections to lobby the UN was just one part of the FLN's efforts to make the Algerian struggle for independence an international issue. In theory, both the superpowers which emerged after 1945 were anti-colonial and thus potential sources of support for nationalist movements seeking patronage. At the same time, in both Washington and Moscow, ideological sympathy for anti-colonialism was always in proportion to other strategic priorities and perceived opportunities and threats.

The United States had been at the origin of the 'Wilsonian moment' of 1919 (<<Chap. 2, p. 24) and the 1941 Atlantic Charter, both of which had championed ideas of self-determination. The United States had an interest in colonial reform, despite its own stark failings in relation to the civil rights of African Americans. It also had an economic interest in decolonisation—the economic protectionism of colonial rule in Africa was obstructing American access to new markets. John F. Kennedy would become a popular figure for many Algerians in 1957 when, as Senator and Chairman of the Senate Foreign Relations sub-committee on UN Affairs, he vigorously attacked French policy and actions, declaring the Algerian struggle for independence a matter which the United States could not ignore (Barkaoui 1999, 32–33). Kennedy still has a major square in Algiers named after him, although once he became president in 1961 he followed much the same policy towards Algeria as his predecessor, Dwight D. Eisenhower (president 1953–61). Both sought to apply pressure, but not too much pressure, on France to find a negotiated solution.

The United States would always see communism as a bigger global threat than European imperialism. Fear of the 'domino effect' of communist contagion explains why, following the establishment of the People's Republic of China in 1949 and the outbreak of the Korean War in June 1950, the Americans stepped in where the French had left off in Vietnam in 1954, having already heavily subsidised their European ally's failed military campaign there. In North Africa, French diplomatic efforts to win the support of the United States presented French rule as the guarantee of stability. They claimed that they were the last bulwark keeping out those they labelled communists and illiberal anti-western religious fanatics. US politicians and policy makers were not necessarily convinced, however, that North Africa was a credible frontline in the Cold War—unless a badly managed French withdrawal from the region inadvertently made it so (Thomas 2002, 218).

For much of the War of Independence, from the FLN's perspective, US scepticism about the sustainability and desirability of 'French Algeria' was of more political use than the USSR's ideologically strong, but inconsistently applied, opposition to imperialism. In the 1920s, Moscow had actively supported anti-colonial movements (<<Chap. 2, p. 27), before putting its anti-colonialism on the back burner from the 1930s onwards as the fight against fascism and Nazism took precedence (<<Chap. 2, p. 39). Joseph Stalin (leader of the USSR mid-1920s–53) was not that interested in North Africa and did not hold anti-colonial leaders in high regard. The huge electoral success of the PCF in France in the aftermath of the Second World War—a party which was not in favour of Algerian independence in the 1940s and 1950s—gave the USSR hope that one day soon a communist party under their control might take power in Paris. The USSR was also keen to encourage French reticence about the US political and military presence in Europe, as well as being suspicious of American ambitions in Africa and Asia, if these countries were no longer under colonial rule. All of these factors encouraged the USSR to avoid

criticism of France (Zoubir 1995, 441; Thomas 2002, 223). Nevertheless, after Stalin's death in 1953, Nikita Khrushchev (leader of the USSR 1953–64) gave a new impetus to Soviet policy in the decolonising world. The USSR began to actively support anti-colonial movements even when these were not communist in nature. This support was both diplomatic, in UN debates, and military, through supplying weapons and training students. In the Algerian case, the USSR supplied weapons and took Algerian students into its universities. For the USSR, this was a low-cost, high-value means to destabilise the West and create future allies.

Connecting the local, national, transnational and global: leveraging Cold War rivalries

The decolonising world was much more than just a theatre for Cold War proxy wars. Since 2000, a significant amount of academic research has focused on how anti-colonial movements actively manipulated Cold War rivalries (including rivalries between the USSR and communist China) in order to advance their causes internationally and gain legitimacy. The FLN played Cold War rivals off against each other to push countries to recognise the FLN, and later its provisional government (>>Chap. 3, p. 115), as the legitimate representative of the Algerian people. If countries were not willing to formally recognise the FLN, FLN representatives encouraged them to at least distance themselves from supporting the French position that Algeria was France and that the 'rebellion' was a French internal affair. This in turn was used as a means to put pressure on France to come to the negotiating table on the FLN's terms. For Matthew Connelly (2001, 221), 'rather than being mere pawns of the great powers, the Algerians rewrote the rules of the game' (see also Byrne 2016; Westad 2006) (>>Chap. 3, p. 98).

This required careful diplomacy. With regard to the United States, the challenge was to suggest that a future post-independence Algeria might look unfavourably on the United States and more favourably towards the USSR, or even that more 'red' (i.e. communist) guerrillas might seize the initiative, if the United States did not apply pressure on France to negotiate in a timely way on terms favourable to the FLN. The message that Aït Ahmed sought to communicate to the US government was that 'the attitudes of an independent North Africa towards the West would depend on the circumstances in which she won her independence' (Connelly 2001, 225). At the same time, the FLN had to be careful not to create fear amongst the Americans that Algeria was the next Cold War battlefield—in which case the United States would be obliged to support France under their commitment to NATO (created in 1949).

President Eisenhower and his political and military advisors were in turn faced with a delicate balancing act between contradictory interests (Thomas 2002). Some American politicians and policy makers argued that long-term American strategic and economic interests might be best served by accommodating North African nationalism. They believed that this would ensure it remained 'moderate', and avoid damaging the United States's reputation with recently independent nation-states, including in the (oil-rich) Arab world, or even worse, pushing nationalists into the arms of the USSR and communism. For others, there was a more immediate desire to maintain a good relationship with France in the interests of European stability and military access to the Mediterranean. French politicians, in turn, grew increasingly frustrated with American ambivalence-verging-on-hostility towards the French presence in North Africa and remained suspicious that what the Americans really wanted to do was muscle in on their regions of influence. At the same time, France could not be too anti-American—it was economically dependent on the US as a result of the huge economic assistance which the United States was providing to Western Europe for post-war reconstruction (Marshall Aid) (>>Chap. 3, p. 106).

Shortly after the Bandung conference in April 1955, M'hamed Yazid (1923–2003)—whose wife was American—set up an FLN representation in New York to lobby UN member states, including the United States and the Afro-Asian group (those countries linked to the Bandung conference who were members of the UN), to get the 'Algerian question' on the UN agenda. In October 1955, through the efforts of the FLN's New York office and the Afro-Asian group, UN members narrowly voted to formally discuss the conflict in Algeria. The French government was furious at what it saw as meddling in its internal affairs. France's delegation to the UN was recalled and France threatened leave the UN. In the end, the UN did not pass any motion on Algeria, but for the FLN, getting Algeria on the agenda as an international issue was already a symbolic victory (>>Chap. 3, 133).

20 August 1955 and Its Aftermath: Defining 'Us' and 'Them'

Algeria had been brought to the attention of many UN member states by events which had taken place that summer. In August 1955, a series of attacks coordinated by the FLN against the European population in the North Constantine region was followed by large-scale repression by the French state and European settlers against the Algerian population. According to Charles-Robert Ageron (1997, 27), 'For both France and the Algerian nationalist militants, the Revolution that had been announced on 1 November became the Algerian War.'

By summer 1955, the FLN was under pressure politically and militarily. ALN groups in mountainous regions were being tracked down by the French army with increasing efficiency, and the organisation had not yet firmly established its hegemony over the nationalist movement or the Algerian population. The FLN's claim to embody the Algerian people and present independence as the only solution to end the violence was at risk of being undermined. Notably, it was threatened by political discussions to resolve the crisis through political, economic and social reforms which Governor General Soustelle and his advisors had been having, or were trying to set up, with the UDMA, the *ulama* and members of the MTLD who had not joined either the FLN or Messali Hadj's MNA.

In the North Constantine region in the weeks before August 1955—which had been the location of the Setif massacres ten years previously (<<Chap. 2, pp. 47–9)—tensions were rising between the European and Algerian populations. ALN guerrillas were carrying out an increasing number of attacks on European targets. The French army response had included imposing collective punishments on the Algerian populations of villages suspected of supporting the ALN. Following the death of Didouche in battle in January 1955, Youcef Zighoud (1921–56, often presented in Algeria with his surname first, as Zighoud Youcef) had been made head of the ALN in the Constantine region (the zone/*wilaya* 2). A founding member of the FLN (one of the '22'), Zighoud considered that it was a military and political necessity to directly implicate the wider population in the struggle by getting them to participate in armed action. For Zighoud, this would fulfil a number of aims. Firstly, it would relieve the beleaguered ALN soldiers in the mountains by forcing French soldiers to leave rural areas in order to deal with violence in cities, towns and other more populated areas. Secondly, it would underline the ability of the FLN to organise the Algerian population. Thirdly, it would make a definitive distinction between 'us' (Algerians) and 'them' (Europeans) as being on different sides of a conflict which could only be resolved through armed struggle and the end of French rule in Algeria—not reformist negotiation.

The date chosen for action was 20 August, two years to the day since the Sultan of Morocco had been deposed by France in 1953. Opposition demonstrations were planned in Morocco to mark this event, and Zighoud thus sought to give a wider, North African resonance to his plan. This plan consisted of a series of attacks in the north-east of the Constantine region, across an area between Philippeville (today known as Skikda), Constantine, Guelma and Collo (a 245 km round trip; covering approximately 3000 km²) (Fig. 2.1). Thousands of civilians, mostly peasants, and a few hundred ALN soldiers were divided into a mixture of smaller groups and larger crowds. Some were armed with knives, a few with shotguns, whilst other men, women and children were unarmed. The action consisted of peaceful demonstrations but also armed attacks on local town halls, roads, European farms and people—soldiers, gendarmes, civilians, adults and children. Civilian targets included both Europeans (such as families living around the mineral mines of El Halia) and those considered 'moderate' Algerians, such as the nephew of Ferhat Abbas, who was a local UDMA leader and pharmacist like his uncle. In total, this group of ALN soldiers and civilians killed 123 people, 52 of whom were Algerians.

The European reaction was ferocious: 'The number of [European] deaths was similar to that of 8 May 1945 and the repression just as disproportionate' (Thénault 2012a, 55). Between 20 and 25 August 1955, around 10,000 Algerians were killed. Little attention was paid to whether or not punishments were being meted out to culprits or suspects—this was collective punishment on a huge scale for being Algerian. Algerians were rounded up and summarily executed by the French army. European civilians organised 'self-defence' groups (militias) and carried out revenge 'Arab hunts' ('ratonnades', from the racist term 'raton', rat, used to refer to Algerians). Algerian homes, villages, businesses and livelihoods were also destroyed (Mauss-Copeaux 2011).

The relationship between politics and violence: one interpretation of 20 August 1955—a point of no return?
Not all of the FLN leaders were convinced that the 20 August 1955 operation had been a success. For Ramdane Abane (1920–57, more often presented in Algeria with his surname first, as Abane Ramdane) and Larbi Ben M'Hidi, attacking European settlers fuelled accusations that the FLN was composed of fanatical extremists and the price paid by the Algerian civilian population in reprisal attacks was both predictable and far too high. Yet Zighoud achieved his political aim. The attacks attracted international media attention. The indiscriminate and disproportionate French repression which followed forced those Algerians still hesitating or reluctant to support the FLN to pick their side: they were either with 'us' (the FLN, and its goal of independence through violence) or 'them' (the French colonial authorities and their blind repression) (Ageron 1997, 44–45). In the aftermath, Dr Mohamed Salah Bendjelloul, founder of the Fédération des élus, and socialist deputy Mostepha Benbahmed— neither of whom were pro-FLN—explained to French parliamentarians that 'The repression was carried out in such a way that our Muslim populations are no longer able to recognise themselves as French' (Ageron 1997, 46). In late September, 61 elected representatives considered to be 'moderates', including a number of members of the Algerian Assembly (<<Chap. 2, p. 51), signed a declaration in which they denounced the blind repression of Philippeville, described Soustelle's 'integration' as a failure and declared that the majority of Algerians now supported 'the Algerian national idea' (Evans 2012, 142). By April 1956, the Algerian Assembly was no longer functioning and was dissolved.

The sense of belonging to a European 'side' under existential threat was also heightened. The French and colonial press presented 20 August as the product of collective Muslim criminal madness, rather than a political act. Examples of violence committed against Europeans were recounted in gory detail, published alongside explicit photographs. These images were subsequently used to motivate French conscripts in the war. Later still, digitised, these now circulate on numerous *pied-noir* (see Glossary) websites as proof of the barbarianism of the FLN and the abandonment of the European population by the French state (>>Chap. 4, p. 160–1). Arriving in the Constantine region, Governor General Soustelle was horrified. He came to the conclusion that the FLN had succeeded in making local populations so scared about accepting French educational and medical intervention that the organisation would have to be militarily crushed before his ambitious reform programme could have any chance of success (Tyre 2006, 286). The violent repression to which Algerians were subject received little press attention. One exception was the French newspaper *L'Express*. In December 1955, *L'Express* published photographs showing an unarmed Algerian civilian being shot by a French gendarme. These images were also printed in the leading American magazine *Life*. This met the indignation of the French government who tried to claim that the gendarme had been bribed by Americans to commit the murder (Kuby 2012).

SPRING 1956, TWO FRONTS: GROWING FLN HEGEMONY, A FRENCH REPUBLICAN FRONT GOVERNMENT

The relationship between politics and violence: another interpretation of 20 August 1955—not so significant?
In historiography on both sides of the Mediterranean and of a variety of political tendencies, there is agreement that 20 August 1955 was a key moment in the conflict. Yet we should not be too hasty to label it a point of no return, as it was described in both settler and FLN propaganda at the time. Events remained localised. Not all Algerian 'moderates', or other Algerian political tendencies, rallied to the FLN straightaway. Away from the dramatic events in the Constantine region, a significant amount of political work was going on before and after 20 August 1955 to bring over to the FLN members of the UDMA, *'ulama* and PCA, as well as to rally those members of the PPA-MTLD who had not yet abandoned Messali Hadj. This work was notably led by Abane.

Abane was from the region of Kabylia and came from a modest background. A holder of the baccalaureate, he was one of the few Algerians who had had the opportunity to access a secondary education, but he was financially unable to go to university. Abane had held an administrative job before serving in the Second World War. From 1943 onwards, he was a member of the PPA and then the OS. Arrested in 1950, he was released from prison in 1955 and immediately recruited into the FLN. He was tasked with reorganising its Algiers network and bringing in other anti-colonial tendencies—not as affiliated parties, but as individuals. Abane was a skilled political operator. Extremely well read, he also had the advantage of having attended the same secondary school in Blida as a number of the men whom he sought to draw into the FLN (Rahal 2004).

Debating the nature of Algerian nationalism: gradually building the Front
By spring 1956, Ferhat Abbas had rallied to the FLN, dissolving the UDMA into it. Bringing in the UDMA membership also brought the FLN closer to French intellectuals, peace activists and liberal Christians, who were potentially influential allies in the struggle to end French rule. By this point the *'ulama* Larbi Tebessi (1891–1957) and Tawfiq al Madani had also joined the FLN, bringing with them their political connections across North Africa and the Middle East. The PCA, which had been banned by the French authorities on 21 September 1955, was trickier to dissolve into the FLN. This was not because PCA members were necessarily opposed to the goals of the FLN—on the contrary, many members, both Algerian and a few of the Europeans, very much believed in independence by this point. Rather, PCA members were more attached to their party structures than UDMA or *'ulama* members were to theirs. A number of communists took up arms in the independence struggle at an early stage—whether or not they did as individual members of the FLN (which is what the FLN claimed) or as a recognised communist grouping within the FLN called Combatants of Liberation (Combattants de la libération, CDL) (which is what the PCA claimed) continues to be debated.

The first FLN emissaries arrived in metropolitan France at the beginning of 1955, sent by Boudiaf. Their aim was to try bring under FLN control Algerians living in France. In 1954, the Algerian population in mainland France was 211,000. By 1962, this had increased to 350,000 people (Stora 1992, 143). The enduring prestige of Messali Hadj in France, who remained under house arrest until January 1959, was such that an outright attack on him was initially considered politically inadvisable. At first, the FLN limited itself to debates with supporters of the MNA in public meetings. One of the biggest bones of contention was to which organisation Algerians in France should pay their revolutionary taxes—the FLN was raising funds for its rural guerrilla, as was the MNA for the Messalist *maquis* (see Glossary) of Mohamed Bellounis (1912–58) which existed in 1955 in the region of Kabylia (>>Chap. 3, p. 104–5). Contacts between rank-and-file militants on both sides initially were close—but tensions were growing as were physical fights (Amiri 2004, 2014; Sidi Moussa 2019; in English Aissaoui 2012) (>>Chap. 3, p. 104, 136).

By late 1955, centre and left French politicians were also trying to form themselves into a Front. In Paris, new legislative elections were looming. When Prime Minister Faure called the election, he also ended the state of emergency, much to the dismay of Governor General Soustelle, and to the advantage of the FLN, who responded by committing an increasing number of attacks—800 in November 1955 and 1200 in January 1956 (Thénault 2012a, 67). In metropolitan France and amongst the European population of Algeria, there was growing support for the populist politician Pierre Poujade (1920–2003) and his message of authoritarian anti-Republicanism, rejection of taxation and extreme nationalism. This included a passionate defence of 'French Algeria' (Kalman 2013, 181). Faced with this threat to Republicanism, on 8 December 1955, a Republican Front was formed. This was a centre-left coalition which included socialists (SFIO), centrist radicals and some left-wing Gaullists such as Jacques Chaban-Delmas (1915–2000). The programme of the Republican Front was one of social reform in France, economic modernisation and 'peace in Algeria'. This ambiguous slogan could mean crushing the nationalists, or negotiating with them—or a combination of both. What this slogan was intended to mean during the election campaign was peace through more reform.

No clear winner emerged from the elections on 2 January 1956 and weeks of negotiations followed as different coalition formations sought to form a government. When the Republican Front eventually managed to do so at the end of the month, the new Prime Minister, Guy Mollet (1905–75, prime min-ister 1956–7) replaced Governor General Soustelle with Georges Catroux (<<Chap. 2, p. 46). The post of Governor General of Algeria was rebranded Minister-Resident, with the status of a cabinet member in Paris. Despite Mollet's insistence that the union between France and Algeria was unbreak-able, the settlers in Algeria were deeply suspicious of the new Republican Front government. With Tunisian and Moroccan independence scheduled for that same year, they feared that a similar offer would soon be on the table for the Algerian nationalists, swiftly followed by the government in Paris allowing the Europeans of Algeria to be chased out. Settler suspicions culminated in an attack on Mollet when he arrived in Algiers on 6 February 1956. As tomatoes rained down on him, his European assailants shouted 'Mollet to the stake', 'Mollet resign' and 'throw Catroux into the sea'. Mollet had to be extirpated from the situation by riot police (Evans 2012, 149). On hearing the news, Catroux immediately resigned, to the delight of the Europeans of Algeria. Deeply shaken by the strength of settler feeling, Mollet appointed Robert Lacoste (1898–1989) as the new Minister-Resident. In a radio broadcast on 9 February 1956, Mollet promised reform in Algeria—but underlined in the strongest terms his commitment to the destruction of the nationalist threat: 'The Government will fight, France will fight to remain in Algeria, and she will remain there. There is no future for Algeria without France' (quoted in Evans 2012, 149; see also Evans 2009).

Elsewhere in the French empire, in June 1956, the National Assembly passed the Defferre framework law (Loi cadre Defferre). This was a first step towards political autonomy in France's colonies south of the Sahara, although full independence was not necessarily envisaged. The Defferre framework law decentralised a number of powers, thus giving a degree of self-government to colonies in sub-Saharan Africa, which were renamed Overseas Territories (Territoires d'Outre-Mer, TOM). It also removed the 'two-college' voting sys-tem which privileged French citizens over French subjects. It did not apply to

Algeria, because Algeria—as provinces of metropolitan France—was under the authority of Ministry of Interior (<<Chap. 1, p. 4).

The relationship between politics and violence: investment, reform and 'Special Powers'

What 'peace in Algeria' came to mean after the formation of the Republican Front government was more repression and more reform. Crushing the nationalists and refusing to let settler self-interest stand in the way of reform any longer, the Republican Front government persisted in the politics of the 'third way'. In March 1956, the government asked the National Assembly in Paris to vote a law authorising a programme of economic, social and administrative reform and investment, but also permitting 'the most extensive powers possible to take all exceptional measures necessary to re-establish order, protect people, property and the territory' (Thénault 2012a, 68). 'Special Powers' ('Pouvoirs spéciaux'), as this law came to be known, were voted in by 455 votes against 76. PCF deputies were amongst those who voted in favour (>>Chap. 4, p. 187). Although what was happening in Algeria was officially still an 'operation to maintain order', Special Powers were typical of wartime legislation. They gave the government the power to rule by decree and avoid having to get laws voted in parliament.

The number of French soldiers sent to Algeria continued to multiply. By March 1956, the 100,000 French soldiers who had been in Algeria mid-1955 had increased to 190,000 soldiers. Just five months later, in August 1956, this number had doubled to 390,000 men (Mahieu 2001, 39–47). By the end of 1956, the ALN had 25,000 to 40,000 guerrillas (Alexander and Keiger 2002, xi). The voting of Special Powers was rapidly followed by a decree enabling civilian authorities in Algeria to delegate their powers to military commanders. This meant that the army could take over the powers of the police to arrest, detain and interrogate suspects. This was the beginning of the army becoming the French state's most powerful decision-making force in Algeria. By summer 1957, this civilian delegation of powers to the army had happened across Algerian territory (Thénault 2012a, 69).

French politicians repeatedly underlined the economic benefits of Algeria staying part of France—'investment' and 'modernisation' were recurrent themes. The new Minister-Resident, Robert Lacoste, oversaw the start of a large programme to recruit more Algerians into the administration in Algeria. Called 'exceptional promotion', this began with targeted recruitment. In 1958, binding quotas were introduced by law: between ten and 70 per cent (depending on level) of all posts in the public sector in Algeria recruited via examination had to be filled by 'French Muslim citizens from Algeria' (Shepard 2011, 313–316). Exceptional promotion sought to make the administration look more like the people it administered and improve policy-making. It was seen as the future of a reimagined French empire.

> **Debating the nature of Algerian nationalism and the terms of future debates: Lacoste promotion**
>
> 'The Lacoste promotion' is used as an insult in Algeria today, to refer to someone who acquired a post in the colonial administration as a result of the Lacoste reforms (and therefore did not join the rural or urban guerrilla) and then, because of a shortage of qualified personnel after 1962, obtained an even more senior post in the post-independence administration. The implication is that the 'Lacoste promotion' represent, at best, people who did not do their revolutionary duty, and at worst, people disloyal to Algeria who advance neo-colonial interests (>>Chap. 4, pp. 168–9). However, there is evidence of individuals in the 'Lacoste promotion' spying for the FLN, including Fadila Attia, a young secretary who passed on documents to the FLN. She was arrested and tortured by the French army before fleeing to Morocco (Vince 2015, 87).

THE MAY 1956 STUDENT STRIKE: AN FLN SHOW OF STRENGTH

The FLN needed to make big shows of force to demonstrate to the colonial authorities in Algeria, the government in Paris and the world the hold which it had on the wider population, including amongst the French-educated Algerians whom Lacoste was trying to recruit. The student strike was organised with this aim in mind. On 19 May 1956, the General Union of Algerian Muslim Students (Union générale des étudiants musulmans algériens, UGEMA) and its sister union amongst high school pupils, the Association of Muslim Algerian Student Youth (Association de la jeunesse estudiantine musulmane algérienne, AJEMA), told students to down books and boycott lessons for an indefinite period. The UGEMA issued a tract reeling off a litany of fellow students recently killed and imprisoned by the French army and police, condemning the ongoing violence inflicted on the wider Algerian population, and appealing to students to join the rural guerrilla. The tract uncompromisingly declared that 'we shall not make better corpses for having gained a diploma first!'

The UGEMA had been created in Paris in 1955, and had branches amongst Algerian students on both sides of the Mediterranean. The UGEMA was very closely allied with, but not under the total control of, the FLN. The UGEMA functioned legally until 1958, when it was banned. The students who created the UGEMA had broken away from an uneasy relationship with the National Union of Students of France (Union nationale des étudiants de France, UNEF) in France, which maintained an ambiguous position on the Algerian War until 1960, when it came out clearly in favour of self-determination. UGEMA students were in open confrontation with students of European origin at university in Algeria. The University of Algiers was a hotbed of support for keeping Algeria under French rule—Pierre Lagaillarde (1931–2014), leader of the General Association of Students of Algeria (Association générale des étudi-ants d'Algérie, AGEA), played an important role in the insurrectional events of May 1958 which brought down the Fourth Republic (>>Chap. 3, pp. 109–10), and would become a member of the Secret Armed Organisation (OAS) which violently opposed the end of French rule (>>Chap. 3, p. 133).

In a context of low Algerian literacy rates and extremely limited access to higher education, there were only 360 Algerian students enrolled at the University of Algiers in 1956—so the support of high school students was numerically more significant. However, 128 of those 360 students were study-ing medicine (Johnson 2012, 715) and Algerian medical students, along with trainee nurses and midwives would provide desperately needed medical care in rural guerrilla units (>>Chap. 3, p. 128). Students in other disciplines were needed as political commissaries, medical staff, in secretarial roles, to operate radio machinery and to make bombs. Although the FLN promoted a rather romantic image of the urban, middle-class student fighting alongside the authentic 'people'—the latter embodied by the *fellah* (peasant)—the arrival of these educated young men and women in the *maquis* was often a culture shock for all concerned. In the worst cases, students were the first to fall victim to internal purges, considered suspect as French-educated 'intellectuals'.

There were also some voices in the FLN and UGEMA leadership who argued that preserving the lives of educated young men and women, precious personnel for a future independent Algeria, was more important than sending them to fight on the frontline. As the war continued, the UGEMA increasingly sent students to continue their studies in 'friendly' countries around the world. Students also played an important role in the FLN's international lobbying, making connections with other student organisations around the world by travelling to Prague, Beijing, New Delhi, Budapest, Ibadan, Lima, Conakry, Tunis, Cairo, Moscow and Cuba, and also cities in Scandinavia, the United States and Canada. Others were sent abroad for military training in military academies based in 'friendly' countries, with the aim of leading ALN units in Algeria upon their return or delivering training in ALN camps in Tunisia and Morocco.

20 AUGUST 1956, SOUMMAM: FLN CONSOLIDATION AND FRACTURED UNITY

The Soummam Congress, named after the valley in rural Kabylia where it was held, took place on 20 August 1956, a year to the day after the Philippeville violence (<<Chap. 3, p. 77–9). There were six key delegates: Ben M'Hidi (for zone 5), Krim Belkacem (for zone 3), Ouamrane (for zone 4) and Zighoud and Lakhdar Ben Tobbal (1923–2010) (for zone 2) alongside Abane. Representatives from the zones 1 and 6 were missing, as were representatives

from the FLN in France, because of the logistical difficulties in getting to the Soummam valley.

The conference is significant for a number of reasons. Firstly, the Soummam Congress formalised the institutional structures of both the FLN and the ALN. The zones became *wilayat* (singular: *wilaya*) (Fig. 3.1). An Algiers Autonomous Zone (Zone autonome d'Alger, ZAA) was added, despite the objections of Ouamrane, who wanted to maintain control of the capital by keeping it within zone 4. The ZAA had a political wing, which produced propaganda, sought to make contact with potentially sympathetic European liberals and supported the families of imprisoned activists. It also had a military wing composed of commando cells which carried out assassinations and bomb attacks (>>Chap. 3, p. 91–6). The Soummam Congress established a centralised and standardised military hierarchy of ranks and fighting units within the ALN, with the main unit being the *katiba*—a mobile rural guerrilla unit of around 30–100 men. Despite this pyramidal structure with a clear line of hierarchical command, each *wilaya* was very much marked by the ideas and tactics of regional leaders and they were not necessarily well integrated (Meynier 2002, 383). The Soummam congress gave the FLN a parliament, the National Council of the Algerian Revolution (Conseil national de la révolution algérienne, CNRA), and an executive, the Coordination and Execution Committee (Comité de coordination et d'exécution, CCE), nominated by the CNRA. Abbas, al-Madani and Debaghine, who had recently rallied to the FLN, all found a place on the CNRA whilst Abane, Krim Belkacem and Ben M'Hidi formed the first CCE with Benyoucef Ben Khedda (1920–2003) and Saâd Dahlab (1918–2000) (both of whom were former MTLD 'centralists' (<<Chap. 2, p. 55) who joined the FLN after the 1 November attacks).

Secondly, two key principals were established at the Soummam Congress: the political had primacy over the military, and the interior (those in Algeria) took precedence over the exterior (those outside of Algeria). These principals were immediately undermined by the way in which the war was unfolding, which the FLN could only ever partly control. In February 1957, as a result of the repression which followed the eight-day strike (>>Chap. 3, p. 92), the CCE left Algiers and Algeria and thus went from being within the 'interior' to being located in the 'exterior'. Moreover, the intrigues of the '3B' (Krim Belkacem, Abdelhafid Boussouf (1926–80) and Ben Tobbal) meant that the political side of the FLN struggled to keep the military in check (>>Chap. 3, pp. 107–8, 115). The tensions between the military and the political and the interior and the exterior would be key to understanding the development, and eventual implosion, of the FLN (>>Chap. 3, pp. 142–44). They would also structure Algerian political life after 1962 (>>Chap. 4, pp. 168–9, 186).

Thirdly, the Soummam Congress set out in greater detail the official FLN vision of what a future Algeria would look like. In terms of *what* was included, Algeria would be sovereign, control all its ministries (including the army and foreign policy), possess all its territory (including the Sahara) and have all its prisoners released. The vision of *who* was included was meant to be inclusive. Rival political movements who might have ambitions to lead the anti-colonial struggle instead of the FLN were explicitly excluded—Messali Hadj and the MNA were scathingly dismissed as colonial cronies, and the PCA was characterised as incoherent and dominated by a European minority unable to accept independence. At the same time, the 'Soummam Platform' which emerged from the meeting declared: 'The Algerian Revolution is not seeking to "throw into the sea" Algerians of European origin, but rather to destroy the colonial yoke. The Algerian Revolution is neither a civil war, nor a religious war.' The stated aim was a social and democratic republic with true equality between all citizens. The platform specifically reached out to, and claimed the revolution also belonged to, Algerians of all social classes, women, liberal Europeans and the Jewish population. The latter group in particular, it was stated, should not be so quick to forget what the French state did to them under Vichy (a reference to the revocation of the Crémieux decree) (<<Chap. 2, p. 42).

This vision of an Algerian (and not just an Arabo-Muslim) Algeria was both a genuine appeal and a piece of tactical propaganda to strength the FLN's wider appeal. It was not uncontested by other members of the FLN—notably Ben Bella, who wrote an angry 27-page report questioning the new political structures, insisting that the overtures to the Jewish and European-origin populations were excessive and arguing that recognition of Egyptian support for the FLN and Algeria's pan-Arab and Muslim identity were not foregrounded enough (Meynier 2002, 192 and 196).

Fourthly, a number of key decisions were made at the Soummam Congress which would have an impact on the course of the war. There was a renewed insistence on internationalising the Algerian question and getting Algerian independence onto the UN agenda (<<Chap. 3, p. 65, 74, 77). Emphasis was placed on the importance of radio, film, the press and photographs in pursuing this goal (>>Chap. 3, pp. 93–7, 102, 115). From this point onwards, the ALN also began systemising its programme of military training. Some of this training took place in neighbouring Tunisia and Morocco, following the independence of Algeria's North African neighbours in 1956, and some was on Algerian soil. Smaller numbers were sent to the Middle East, China, the USSR and the Eastern bloc indicating that the choice to send soldiers abroad was not just a military one, but also a politically strategic one in the context of internationalisation (Arezki 2015).

> **Debating the nature of Algerian nationalism and the terms of future debates: the DAF**
>
> Most of the instructors in the ALN camps in Tunisia and Morocco, particularly to begin with, were Algerians who had left the French army, where they had received their own military training. Many of these instructors had deserted from where they had been stationed in France and West Germany in the 1950s—Algerians who were serving in the French army in Algeria would be more likely desert to join the *mujahidin* in the mountains. Desertions from the French army reached a peak in 1956. These former soldiers in the French army would come to be known by the acronym DAF (Deserteurs de l'armée française/Deserters from the French army), which acquired particularly negative connotations in the post-independence period in Algeria. It evokes those who left the French army at the eleventh hour and were possibly still representing the interests of France. This is a politicised characterisation rather than an objective analysis: all Algerian men had to do military service in the French army since the First World War (it was usually not a political choice) (<<Chap. 2, pp. 21–2, 41–2), leaving the French army in 1956 was not the 'eleventh hour', many of these men did not actually desert the French army but left at the end of their service (which may have begun before the liberation struggle took hold in 1955). There is little evidence that they were agents for France during the war. Whether they best represented the interests of Algeria and Algerians after 1962 is another question. For these reasons, Saphia Arezki (2018, 50), who has conducted the most detailed sociological study of the ALN before and after independence, does not use the term DAF. It is important to know what this term means, however, to understand the political language and codes of the post-independence period in Algeria (>>Chap. 4, pp. 168–9).

Autumn 1956: 'Ben Bella's Plane', the Suez Crisis and the French Army Increasingly Acting on Its Own Initiative

By autumn 1956, the FLN had eight offices around the world: in Cairo, Damascus, Tunis, Beirut, Baghdad, Karachi, Jakarta and New York, as well as roving representatives touring countries of all ideological persuasions. Also transmitting from Cairo was the radio station Sawt al-Arab (Voice of the Arabs), founded in 1953. For many Algerians, Sawt al-Arab was the key source of information for what was going on in the war and in the world from a non-French perspective. With the tagline 'Sawt al-Arab, calling to the Arab nation from the heart of Cairo', the radio station was a means for Egyptian President Nasser to promote an anti-imperial, pan-Arab agenda. Sawt al-Arab was highly critical of the French and allowed the FLN leaders in Cairo to use their facilities.

The FLN and Nasser nevertheless had a complicated relationship. After the 1 November 1954 attacks, Nasser had promised his unconditional support, 5000 Egyptian pounds, 28 rifles and 11 machine guns that may not even have arrived on time, although arms smuggling did take place on a larger scale after this (Connelly 2002, 74). Despite Nasser's anti-imperial stance and speeches about Arab and Muslim fraternity, his outspoken displays of support for the FLN cooled at moments when Egypt's relations with France seemed to be improving, such as in spring 1956. Moreover, the FLN did not want to be the subordinate partner—the 'little brother'—in its relationship with Egypt. In July 1956, however, Nasser's nationalisation of the Suez Canal set France and Egypt on a collision course which would have consequences for the war in Algeria.

The Suez Canal was a strategically and economically important shortcut from the Mediterranean to the Indian Ocean, opened in the nineteenth century and owned and operated by the Suez Canal Company in Paris. Both France and Britain were furious when Nasser unilaterally nationalised it. In late October 1956, Britain, France and Israel struck a secret deal to invade Egypt and topple Nasser. The invasion was a failure. Just a few weeks later, the United States, fearing that backing France and the UK might tip the whole of the Arab world into the Soviet camp (<<Chap. 3, pp. 74–77), pressured Britain and France into a withdrawal. This was experienced, particularly by France, as a humiliation.

On 21 October 1956, at the same time as France, Britain and Israel were planning their ill-fated invasion, Aït Ahmed, Ben Bella, Boudiaf, Khider and the Algerian intellectual Mostefa Lacheraf (1917–2007) had a lengthy meeting in Rabat with Mohamed V (1909–61), the king of Morocco. A further meeting was planned the following day in Tunis, bringing together Mohamed V, Tunisia's President Habib Bourguiba (1903–2000) and the FLN to discuss the situation in Algeria. The French government and army were furious about these meetings. In March 1956, Morocco and Tunisia had become independent, and both countries were keen to maintain good relations with France, for economic and political reasons. In both countries, however, there were also strong affinities with the Algerian people and the independence struggle, particularly amongst the wider population, and Mohamed V and President Bourguiba did not want to be seen as too out of step with the people of their respective countries. Both Mohamed V and Bourguiba wanted a rapid political solution to the Algerian problem.

Arriving in Tunis ahead of the planned second meeting, the head of the Moroccan government, Mbarek Bekkaï (1907–61) is reported to have declared 'Morocco and Tunisia are the wings of the Maghrib [North Africa] … When the wings are free, the body will liberate itself' (Essemlali 2011, 79). The FLN delegation, however, never made it to Tunis. On 22 October 1956, Aït Ahmed, Ben Bella, Boudiaf, Khider and Lacheraf boarded a Moroccan airline plane in Rabat to head to the meeting. The French army intercepted the plane and arrested all five men. This was without the knowledge of the head of the government, Guy Mollet, although the green light was given by Max Lejeune

(1909–55), Secretary of State for the Armed Forces. It was the first aeroplane hijacking in history (Evans 2012, 186). In the French media, it was presented as the capture of 'Ben Bella's aeroplane'—suggesting that he was the most senior member of the FLN on board. This was certainly not the case, but it reflected the message which the French wanted to drive home, that Nasser was behind the FLN, because Ben Bella was seen as particularly close to the Egyptian president. It certainly did no harm to Ben Bella's political ambitions within the FLN—sidelined by the Soummam Congress, he now became instantly recognisable. Morocco was furious and withdrew its ambassador from Paris, seeing the hijacking as a demeaning act of French interference in its affairs.

Back in Algeria, in November 1956 General Raoul Salan (1899–1984) was nominated Commander-in-Chief (>>Chap. 3, p. 109, 112). Salan and his military commanders immediately turned their attention to trying to cut off the 'water supply' so that the FLN guerrillas could no longer move like 'fish through water' (<<Chap. 3, p. 69). The initial tactic which Salan sought to use was *quadrillage*. This involved breaking territory down into grid squares and taking them back one by one. This proved to be not that effective—the FLN rural guerrillas were quick and they knew the territory better than French soldiers. It was then that the French army shifted to trying to turn the guerrilla's methods against them through counter-revolutionary warfare. This combined fast-moving patrols, supported by aerial intelligence and bombing, with 'psychological warfare' to 'win hearts and minds' of local Algerian populations (>>Chap. 3, pp. 99–101, 111, 123). A huge amount of time was spent theorising this. The basic goal, in the words of one of the French army's counter insurgency specialists, Colonel Antoine Argoud (1914–2004, a future OAS member), was: 'Protect them, involve them, control them' (Alexander and Keiger 2002, 11). To further this aim, Salan also promoted the mass displacement of rural populations into so-called *camps de regroupement* ('regrouping camps') (>>Chap. 3, p. 102) under the control of the French army.

In addition, Algeria's borders were closely guarded to prevent the movement of men and arms between Morocco and Algeria and Algeria and Tunisia. In July 1957, the Morice line, composed of mines, electrified fences, barbed wire and watchtowers began to be built along the Algerian-Tunisian border. This was reinforced by the Challe line in 1959. On the Algerian-Moroccan border the Pédron line served the same purpose (Fig. 3.1 and >>Chap. 3, p. 115). The navy enforced coastal blockades. Imports and exports were also closely watched—official authorisation was need to purchase a whole range of objects, including battery operated radios, maps, typewriters with Arabic characters and duplicating machines. The buying and selling of second hand military uniform was forbidden on Algerian territory. Customs officers had orders to check any shoes arriving which were above a size 40 (7.5 UK size). The aim was to asphyxiate the FLN/ALN. Attempts were made by the FLN and their supporters to subvert these limitations—for example, by mislabelling boots to suggest they were a smaller size—but their ability to operate militarily was increasingly circumscribed.

1957, 'The Battle of Algiers': A French Military 'Success', a FLN Political Victory

It was in the context of the rural guerrilla coming under increasing pressure that the FLN decided to launch a systematic campaign of urban terror. Hitherto, FLN actions in cities had been limited to ad hoc assassinations and reprisal attacks following executions of nationalists or specific acts of European violence against the Algerian population. These increasingly deadly acts of European violence against the Algerian population were the other factor pushing the FLN towards a more systematic campaign of urban terror. On 10 August 1956, European hardliners had planted a 30-kilo bomb on rue de Thèbes in the Casbah (the historic area of Algiers where much of the Algerian population lived), killing 15 Algerian civilians according to colonial sources, and 60 according to the FLN. The next day, Algerians participated in a number of spontaneous attacks against policemen and civilians (Meynier 2002, 322). This presented a challenge to the FLN. If the FLN was 'the people', it needed to show that it could defend the people by coordinating the response.

Launching a systematic campaign of urban terror was a nevertheless a risky strategy for the FLN. On the one hand—and this was notably the position of CCE member Ben M'Hidi (Meynier 2002, 232)—it could effectively sap French will to remain. By drawing more and more Algerians into the armed conflict, French military spending and conscription would increase, and when levels of spending and the loss of human life became intolerable, the French government would be forced to negotiate. On the other hand, Algiers was the political and military centre of Algeria with 300,000 'European' inhabitants, a much larger proportion than in Philippeville and the surrounding areas (<<Chap. 3, pp. 77–80). In urban areas, teams of guerrillas carrying out assassinations and planting bombs would be reliant on the complicity of the wider Algerian population, which risked exposing the organisation to infiltration, betrayal, arrest and dismantlement. Urban attacks carried out by the FLN nevertheless began to intensify in autumn 1956, running into their hundreds by December. They were increasingly targeting not only the police, military and the colonial administration, but also civilian targets—public places frequented by Europeans. Attacks by Europeans against the Algerian population also intensified.

The relationship between politics and violence and connecting the local, national, transnational and global: launching 'the Battle of Algiers'

In January 1957, with another discussion of 'the Algerian Question' scheduled to come up on the UN agenda (<<Chap. 3, p. 74, 77), the FLN's CCE gave the order to organise a further strike, following on from the student strike of May 1956 (<<Chap. 3, pp. 84–5). In the words of Ben M'Hidi, 'As the UN session approaches it is necessary to demonstrate that all the people are behind us and obey our orders to the letter' (Connelly 2001, 228). The strike was planned to last eight days and involve all Algerian workers in all the major towns and cities of Algeria. The start date was 28 January 1957. In anticipation, Resident Minister Lacoste, supported by Prime Minister Mollet, passed full security and police powers to General Jacques Massu (1908–2002) (>>Chap. 3, pp. 109–10, 131; Chap. 4, p. 183) and his tenth parachutist division to maintain order in Algiers. Around 8000 French soldiers took up position in the capital, surrounding the Casbah with checkpoints and barbed wire. The strike was adhered to by Algerians on a massive scale. It was then brutally broken by the French army, who rounded workers up to force them back to work and smashed shops back open. On 23 February 1957, Ben M'Hidi was arrested and killed in custody. The army unconvincingly claimed he had committed suicide. The CCE was forced to leave Algeria. The FLN/ALN bomb attacks nevertheless continued. In the words of the CCE: 'One bomb which kills 10 people and injures 50 others is the psychological equivalent of the loss of a French battalion' (Meynier 2002, 325).

The period September 1956 to October 1957 is often referred to as 'the Battle of Algiers', not least because this is the title of one of the most famous films made about the Algerian Revolution, in 1966, by Italian director Gillo Pontecorvo (>>Chap. 4, p. 167). The term is contested by some historians who argue that it suggests two equally matched adversaries whereas in reality the French army vastly outnumbered the FLN/ALN in both soldiers, weapons and institutional support (the judicial and penal systems), and this is reflected by the fact that the FLN/ALN was crushed. Indeed, the total number of actual members of FLN/ALN clandestine networks in the ZAA was probably never more than 1500 people at any one time (Meynier 2002, 326). The FLN benefitted, however, both politically and logistically, from the support and complicity of much wider swathe of the Algerian population. The term 'the Battle of Algiers' is widely used by actors on all sides of the conflict, because it is elevating for all concerned to see themselves as a part of 'a battle'.

One of the best-known aspects of 'the Battle of Algiers' is the role of Algerian women in FLN bomb networks. Once artisanal bombs had been made in clandestine workshops, women were used to transport and plant devices in European areas, notably at civilian targets such as race tracks, casinos, cafés and bars, because they aroused less suspicion. One of the most well-known commentators on this is the French Caribbean anti-colonial psychiatrist—and active FLN supporter—Frantz Fanon (1925–61). In 'Algeria Unveiled' (1965, 58) Fanon described women's veiling and unveiling as acts of resistance. He argued that before the war, women veiled to resist the gaze of the coloniser and now they were unveiling and passing themselves off as 'Westernised' women in order to better strike at the heart of colonial domination:

> Carrying revolvers, grenades, hundreds of false identity cards or bombs, the unveiled Algerian woman moves like a fish in the Western waters. The soldiers, the French patrols, smile to her as she passes, compliments on her looks are heard here and there, but no one suspects that her suitcases contain the automatic pistol which will presently mow down four or five members of one of the patrols.

This description of the role of women in 'the Battle of Algiers' has been extremely influential—Pontecorvo reproduced it on screen in *The Battle of Algiers*. It also only tells part of the story. It is true that women in the urban bomb network sometimes wore the veil to transport weapons (playing on the French assumption that veiled woman were submissive and not involved in politics), and dressed in European clothes to plant bombs (playing on the French assumption that unveiled women were Europeanised and pro-French). Fanon's focus on the veil nevertheless reproduces a colonial obsession with the physical appearance of 'the Muslim woman' which sidelines women's political opinions and motivations for joining the bomb network: 'What [these women] were disguising when they transported weapons and planted bombs was not their physical appearance or cultural identity but their political engagement' (Vince 2015, 82). Most of the women who planted bombs did not unveil in order to do so—many were students, such as Zohra Drif (b. 1934, see her 2017 memoirs in English), who already did not wear the veil. Some other members of the Algiers bomb network were of European origin, such Danièle Djamila Amrane-Minne (1939–2017) (>>Chap. 4, p. 177) and her mother Jacqueline Guerroudj (1919–2015). In 1957, Jacqueline Guerroudj was arrested and condemned to death, although not executed.

In total, women who planted bombs were probably only a few dozen—the vast majority of Algerian women, and indeed men, supported the Algiers bomb network as civilians. But they captured the imagination of the public both at the time and subsequently. In the pro-colonial press, Algerian female bombers were vilified as ungrateful wretches who had taken the benefits of a French education and then bitten the hand that fed them, probably under the influence of a no-good boyfriend. For the FLN, these women were a powerful propaganda weapon. They were young, attractive and educated—they showed that the FLN was a progressive, modern movement, not a bunch of backwards, religiously fanatical men, as French propaganda claimed. When these women were arrested, and then tortured in army custody, the FLN and their supporters used this as evidence of the barbarity, and thus illegitimacy of French rule.

> **The terms of future debates: the French army's use of torture**
> Since 2000, there has been a resurgence of interest in the practice of torture by the French army during the War of Independence, and particularly during the 'Battle of Algiers' (>>Chap. 4, p. 183). This is reflected in the publication of a wide range of testimonies and a number of academic works. In 2001, historian Raphaëlle Branche published the book of her doctoral thesis, based on extensive research in the then just-opened French military archives. She demonstrated the widescale use of torture, intensifying from 1957 onwards. From summer 1960, the practice of torture began to be unevenly reined in, as a series of scandals emerged and political pressure was applied on the French government and army to make it stop. For Branche, the use of torture was not a few 'bad apples' out of control—which is the official army position, and which was the official state position until 2018 (>>Chap. 4, p. 188). Rather, Branche demonstrates that torture was a weapon of war which was considered both essential to intelligence gathering and key to terrorising the wider population into submission (2001, in English see Branche 2014; Lazreg 2008).

Following torture, some suspects were put on trial, in military courts and then imprisoned. Other Algerians accused of supporting the FLN were interned without trial in euphemistically named *camps d'hébergement* ('accommodation camps'). At their peak in spring 1959, there were around 10,000 people in such camps (Thénault 2005). *Camps d'hébergement* were a form of preventative custody created in 1955. They were used in Algeria and in mainland France (Fig. 4.1), to round up anyone suspected of funding or providing supplies or cover for the FLN/ALN. As a form of administrative internment (i.e. there was no need to charge a suspect and go through the judicial process), suspects could be sent there indefinitely. The camps were, however, often very poorly staffed, making them fertile recruiting ground for the FLN, which sought to organise life in the camps, in often miserable conditions.

The French army's use of torture was known at the time and widely publicised by the FLN and its sympathisers. In June 1957, Henri Alleg (1921–2013), a communist journalist on the PCA newspaper *Alger Républicain*, which had been banned for its pro-independence positions, was arrested by French paratroopers in Algiers. He was subjected to horrific violence, including stimulated drowning and electric shocks. Alleg had been born into a Jewish family in London, and initially emigrated to Paris before moving to Algeria in 1939. From his cell in Barberousse prison in Algiers, Alleg wrote an account of his torture, *La Question* (*The Question* 2006 [1958]). *La Question* was secretly smuggled out and published by Editions de minuit in 1958, with a preface by philosopher Jean-Paul Sartre. For Alleg, the violence inflicted on Algerians was a shameful stain on France. Moreover, he argued, the act of inflicting this violence was corrupting a whole generation of French youth conscripted in the army. *La Question* was censored, but nevertheless played an important role in beginning to turn liberal public opinion in France against the war in Algeria (>>Chap. 3, p. 121; Chap. 4, p. 183).

In April 1957, two months before Alleg's arrest, the trial of two female members of the FLN/ALN's bomb network, Djamila Bouhired (b. 1935) and Djamila Bouazza (1938–2015), attracted international attention. Their lawyers highlighted the torture inflicted on both women in custody. Djamila Bouhired's lawyer was Jacques Vergès (1924–2013), who was from a celebrated Reunionaise anti-colonial family on his father's side and whose mother was Vietnamese. Vergès adopted the 'rupture defence' strategy ('défense de rupture'). This meant that he refused to recognise the authority of a French court to pass judgment, as he argued that it was an institution of an illegitimate colonial system. This became a common strategy of the collective of lawyers who defended FLN activists (Thénault 2012b). Bouhired and Bouazza were nevertheless both condemned to death. This only intensified the international campaign in their favour and the death penalty was not carried out. FLN representatives distributed leaflets around the world calling on people to save the two women. In Egypt, star director Youssef Chahine made a film about Djamila Bouhired (*Gamila al-Gaza'iriyya* [Djamila the Algerian], 1958). Vergès published, with Georges Arnaud, *Pour Djamila Bouhired* [For Djamila Bouhired 1957], denouncing the torture to which she had been subjected.

The terms of future debates: what happened to 'the disappeared'?
Thousands of Algerians who were taken into custody by the French army 'disappeared'—that is to say, is it likely that they were killed and their bodies dumped or hidden. In the course of 1957, the General Secretary of the Prefecture of Algiers, Paul Teitgen (1919–91), identified 3024 people who he thought had 'disappeared'—although this approximation only included people who had left a trace in the paperwork which had arrived on his desk (Klose 2013, 185). In protest, he resigned, refusing to be part of a system of torture and summary justice (Thénault 2001; in English see Klose 2013). Many of these 'disappearances' remain unsolved. In 2018, President Emmanuel Macron (b. 1977, president since 2017) formally recognised the role of the French state in the killing of one of the 'disappeared', a young communist mathematician of European origin who supported the FLN, Maurice Audin (1932–57) (>>Chap. 4, p. 188). A website was subsequently launched by the historians Fabrice Riceputi and Malika Rahal to try and match other families with relatives who went missing with available archival information: http://1000autres.org/

In 1960, the now famous 'two Djamilas' would become 'three Djamilas', when the case of Djamila Boupacha, a member of the FLN/ALN's Algiers network who had been tortured and raped in French army custody, was brought to light. Boupacha's case was publicised by her French-Tunisian feminist lawyer Gisèle Halimi (b. 1927) (>>Chap. 4, p. 183) and leading French intellectual and feminist Simone de Beauvoir. Her case was considered particularly shocking because Boupacha had been tortured after the politicians in Paris had supposedly brought the army back under control (Halimi and de Beauvoir 1962; in English see Surkis 2010). International condemnation followed. As a gesture of solidarity, world-famous artist Pablo Picasso sketched a portrait of Djamila Boupacha in December 1961.

By summer 1957, the FLN's Algiers bomb network had been almost totally dismantled by the French army, with its leaders either killed or imprisoned. The military strength of the French army might have won the battle by crushing the ALN, but ultimately, they lost the war. Under the scrutiny of an international media increasingly fascinated by the unfolding conflict, the terror of the methods employed by the French army to stop terrorism fatally undermined the French claims of its 'right to rule', as well as alienating the Algerian wider population.

A Campaign to Win over International and Metropolitan French Opinion

The publicising of French army torture by the FLN and French official denials that it was taking place on any significant scale were part of a wider propaganda war being waged to win over international public opinion. Based on the Tunisian frontier, a group of young filmmakers—Algerian, French and of other nationalities—produced a series of photographs and films seeking to promote the FLN, Algerian independence and discredit French rule (Bedjaoui 2015). In 1958, René Vautier (1928–2015) released his film *Algérie en flammes* [Algeria in flames], which was shot in the *maquis* and edited in East Germany. It depicted, in the words of the voiceover: 'the Algerian people, side-by-side with the ALN, fighting for its liberty, dignity against the brutality of French invasion and colonial domination'. The FLN gathered and publicised photographs of French atrocities. Its activists published pamphlets and booklets which were likely to win over French and international liberal and left-wing opinion. Images of women participating in the struggle were seen as particularly powerful in conveying the idea that this was a modern liberation movement bringing together a whole people. Photographs of women in military uniform bearing arms were taken, some staged, alongside images of rural women providing food and basic medical aid to rural guerrilla units. The FLN newspaper *El Moudjahid* serialised what was presented as the diary entries of a woman fighting alongside her brothers in the mountains.

FLN publications also foregrounded the role of the ALN in providing healthcare to Algerian populations with little access to medicine and doctors, plagued by hunger and infectious diseases, as a result of French army action and the long-standing absence of any infrastructure. The FLN positioned itself as a state-in-waiting, fulfilling the functions of a French state which was failing to supply basic services (>>Chap. 3, p. 103–4). In doing so, the FLN appropriated the language of humanitarianism—a language created in Western institutions—to advance the political goal of Algerian independence (Johnson 2012, 720; see also Johnson 2016). In January 1957, the FLN's CCE created its own (not officially recognised) branch of the International Committee of the Red Cross, the Algerian Red Crescent. This was based in Tangiers (Morocco) and Tunis (Tunisia). The language of humanitarianism was also used to secure funds for medicines and supplies, including from the USSR, Japan, Korea and Cuba. It was used to attract Syrian, Iraqi, Sudanese, Jordanian, Libyan, Saudi Arabian, Italian, Canadian, Chilean, Norwegian, Turkish and East German donations to ease the plight of Algerian refugees displaced in Tunisia and Morocco (Johnson 2012, 724). The Algerian Red Crescent was also involved in organising the release of French army soldiers who had been captured by the ALN. The ability to capture and release prisoners of war, and claim to be respecting the 1949 Geneva Conventions on how they should be treated, was the ultimate mark of a sovereign state (Branche 2014; in English see Branche 2018).

The French state had a much bigger budget than the FLN and was spending a lot of money to try and counter its propaganda. In 1957 alone, the French Information Center in the United States spent $450,000 dollars on full-page advertisements in the leading American newspapers—this was ten times the budget of the FLN's New York office (Connelly 2001, 229). They produced a wide range of films, aimed at domestic and foreign audiences (Denis n.d., includes links to a number of these films). This propaganda had many of the same themes as that of the FLN. It sought to convey the savagery of its adversary, but this time with lots of images of slit throats, disembowelled bodies and burnt down homes and schools attributed to FLN action. This was juxtaposed with 'our' forward-looking agenda to develop Algeria for the benefit of the wider population, but in this vision the future was French. The film *Kepi bleu* (1957) opens with pictures of new, modern tower blocks, roads, trains, ports, airports and dams and men going to work. It describes how these images of 'Western, French genius' were threatened by 'ambitious fanatics trying to destroy Western civilisation', attacking schools, homes and lives. Fraternal French soldiers (specifically soldiers in the SAS (>>Chap. 3, pp. 99–101)) are shown shaking hands with smiling locals whilst nurses provide medical care. The voiceover tells the audience that: 'Two drops of eyewash are better than all the propaganda in the world to open your eyes' (For more on film, see Pinoteau 2003; in English see Welch and McGonagle 2013). To counter FLN propaganda of 'modern-looking' women in the rural and urban guerrilla, the French military and government also made particular efforts to present Algerian women as victims of supposedly backwards 'Muslim tradition' who could only be freed through French intervention (Perego 2015).

WHO IS THE STATE? THE FRENCH STATE VERSUS THE FLN STATE-WITHIN-A-STATE

For Matthew Connelly (2002), the novelty of the FLN's achievement was winning Algeria's right to sovereignty on the international stage whilst its territory remained under French rule and no exclusively Algeria-based state or authority had been previously recognised in international law. This is the 'diplomatic revolution' referred to in the title of his book. Other scholars argue that the diplomatic achievements of the FLN internationally should not overshadow the centrality of the struggle on Algerian soil (Roberts 2004). The FLN was increasingly successful in undermining the French army and state's attempt to control the territory of Algeria. Indeed, it could be argued that throughout the colonial period, the French state only ever nominally controlled vast swathes of Algerian territory. French efforts to assert governance over under-administered rural territories or shantytowns on the edge of urban areas only began in earnest in the 1950s, when the FLN had already started to win the allegiance of large sections of the population. When people living in a given village or area went over to the FLN, these territories were 'lost' to France even if the FLN had not planted their flag in the soil. It nevertheless remained a persistent goal of successive French governments to win, or win back, the 'Muslim' population and thus bring the places where they lived under the authority of the French state. Three examples will be presented to assess how realistic this goal was between 1955 and 1961: the Social Centres (Centres sociaux), the Specialised Administrative Sections (Sections administratives spécialisées, SAS) and 'regrouping' camps (*camps de regroupement*).

Strengthening the French State in Algeria? Example 1: Centres Sociaux

Along with 'Algeria is France' and the FLN 'outlaws' were just a 'law and order' problem, 'integration' was the watchword for the French government after the 1 November 1954 attacks (Shepard 2011, 306) (<<Chap. 3, p. 71–2). It would remain a key idea for the government and policy makers until at least 1959. An idea for how 'integration' might be brought about was set in motion just after Soustelle took office as Governor General in early 1955. The Centres sociaux sought to prepare Algerians to participate in Soustelle's vision of a new Franco-Algerian nation through material development. Formally established in October 1955, they brought together people from metropolitan France and

'Europeans' and 'Muslims' in Algeria to run literacy classes, medical care and job training for Algerian men and women. By 1959, there were around 65 centres functioning across Algeria (Forget 1992, 42). At the head of the Centres was Germaine Tillion (1907–2008) who, like Soustelle, was an ethnographer and Second World War resister. Tillion also had extensive experience of fieldwork in Algeria in the 1930s, and considered that what was happening in Algeria was a rebellion resulting from illiteracy and underdevelopment. The Centres came to be viewed with suspicion by both the colonial authorities and the FLN. For the FLN, they risked undermining the nationalist message that only independence could take Algerians out of their socio-economic misery. Some members of the Centres were killed by the FLN. The colonial authorities came to suspect that the Centres had been infiltrated by the FLN, and some Centre workers were imprisoned for passing medical supplies to the FLN. Tillion herself developed contacts across the political spectrum, including with the FLN. On 15 March 1962, six Centre sociaux inspectors were assassinated by the OAS (>>Chap. 3, pp. 133–4).

Strengthening the French State in Algeria? Example 2: The SAS

On a much larger scale to the Centres sociaux, in September 1955, the Specialised Administrative Sections (SAS) were created. The SAS were civil administration bodies run by members of the army, supported by Algerian auxiliaries who spoke Arabic or Tamazight (Berber). The aim of the SAS, in the words of Soustelle, was 'to try and bridge the yawning gap between the administration and the poorer inhabitants' (Alexander and Keiger 2002, 5). By the end of 1961, there were 700 SAS established across rural Algeria, in addition to twenty Urban Administrative Sections (Sections administratives urbaines, SAU) in urban areas, notably in the Algiers Casbah. There were also the equivalents of the SAS in metropolitan France, established in areas with a high concentration of Algerians (Frémeaux 2002).

The role of a SAS was to prevent local populations supporting guerrillas by carrying out censuses, controlling the movements of inhabitants, patrolling the area, collecting intelligence and attempting to win 'hearts and minds' by offering healthcare, schooling for boys and girls and 'psychological action'. Because many men had left their villages to join the rural guerrilla, or had left to go and work in cities in Algeria or in mainland France as a result of the effect of the war on Algerian agriculture, much of the SAS's target audience was female. In any case, this fit in with the widely held belief that women were a more promising target than 'fanatical' and 'traditionalist' men. Both the French army and the government propaganda claimed that women would be emancipated from their confinement in the home and the weight of tradition through French reforms in political rights, family law, healthcare and education. In turn, it was hoped that winning over women was the key to winning over the 'Muslim family'. In 'Psychological action' sessions, which had titles such as 'France,

Protector of Children' and 'The Rebellion Brings Misery and Death', SAS officers sought to convince women that the death, disease, chronic malnutrition and repeated military intrusions into their homes which now dominated their lives was the fault of the FLN, and that improvement could only come by sticking with France.

Some of the SAS soldiers, for example, teachers conscripted into the army, were relieved to have been taken out of armed combat, and threw themselves into the task of educating boys and girls who had never previously had access to formal schooling. On the ground, in some places and in some instances, there is evidence of tensions existing between the SAS and other sections of the army—for example, in 1961, around 30 women from the villages of Timiloust and El Hadoud in Kabylia went to the local SAS headquarters to protest that seven of them had been raped by a French army *commando de chasse* ('hunting commando') (>>Chap. 3, p. 118). The SAS officer took the complaint to his superiors, and according to the archives, the perpetrators were punished—a rare example of rape being punished during the war. For other SAS officers and soldiers, the role of protector was entirely subsumed by the tasks of surveillance and control, and indeed some actively participated in torture and violence against civilian populations. In all cases, it was clear for the Algerian population that if they did not want to voluntarily participate in SAS activities designed to 'help' them, they would be made to do it anyway. As Neil Macmaster (2009, 212) puts it: 'French welfare intervention was always under the immediate or imminent sign of the gun'.

In autumn 1957, the SAS were joined by Itinerant Medical-Social Teams (Equipes médico-sociales itinérantes, EMSI). By August 1960, there were 171 EMSI units. Seeking to fulfil similar tasks to those of the SAS, but mobile rather than static and directly attached to the French army, the EMSI were composed of all-women teams of social workers drawn from the 'European' and 'Muslim' communities. They were tasked with teaching Algerian women domestic skills. Of course, Algerian women already had their own skills for cooking, cleaning and looking after their children, but for the EMSI, local practices were backwards, superstitious, and possibly harmful. The idea behind the EMSI was that by bringing Algerian women 'modern', rational domestic science, they in turn would become agents of modernity within their families and communities. This 'modernisation' of the Algerian woman and family was presented as the future of a new Algeria which was inseparable from France. This, too, was counter-revolutionary, psychological warfare, although most members of the EMSI were too preoccupied with the more banal day-to-day realities of their welfare programmes to theorise the wider implications of what they were doing. Their most political task would be getting women to vote in the 1958 referendum (Seferdjeli 2004, 2005; Macmaster 2009) (>>Chap. 3, p. 112).

Connecting the local, national, transnational and global: 'psychological action' and 'modernisation' were much-theorised strategies which established states and revolutionary movements around the world adopted in this period—but how did Algerian women in rural areas and working-class communities in France respond?

The effectiveness of the French army's psychological action is difficult to evaluate. SAS officers complained to their hierarchical superiors about shortages of funds and supplies not arriving. Many women refused to attend SAS activities or engage with the EMSI, either on principal, or from fear of FLN/ALN reprisals against those seen to be engaging with the enemy, or because the model of the modern French housewife was not one to which they aspired. Other women did bring their children for vaccinations and to get food aid. It is hard to know to what extent they did this because they were convinced by the psychological action, because they were coerced by the French army or whether they were using SAS facilities simply because their families were hungry, their children sick and they wanted them to learn to read and write.

In the vast majority illiterate and poor, these Algerian women were attuned to the ways in which they were seen as 'backwards' and 'ignorant'—by the French state and army, and indeed by the most well-meaning SAS officers and the majority of social workers. Many of these Algerian women sought to use this condescending assessment to their advantage, to evade suspicion and to secure material resources. In the village of Bouzeguene in Kabylia in 1959, one enthusiastic but naïve SAS officer recorded his disappointment that the psychological action which the previous week he thought was working so well appeared to have no effect once the SAS had no more supplies to distribute (Vince 2015, 80). When Chérifa Akache was arrested by the French army, she told them that she had 'accidentally' helped the ALN soldiers because she had confused them with the French army, and that she had no idea where her husband was (she knew that he had joined the ALN) because he had abandoned her, and she claimed that as 'her culture' dictated, she had gone back to live with her family (Vince 2015, 87). In mainland France, women in the FLN and the MNA adopted similar strategies when they were arrested in order to minimise their clandestine activities. They claimed that they had acted under duress, they used the fact that they were women and/or Algerian to insist that they did not understand what they were doing, and they depicted themselves as never leaving the kitchen and forbidden from receiving men unrelated to them at home (André 2016, 205).

Strengthening the French State in Algeria? Example 3: Camps de Regroupement and Forced Resettlement

In other severely under-administered regions where there were high levels of guerrilla activity, notably the Aures, 'forbidden zones' were created and rural populations forcibly removed into *centres* or *camps de regroupement* ('regrouping' centres or camps). Not to be confused with internment camps (where suspect individuals were detained) (<<Chap. 3, p. 94), *camps de regroupement* held entire families and villages who were not necessarily suspected of anything. As in internment camps, they were surrounded by barbed wire and under army surveillance, but the proclaimed aim was to 'protect' Algerians from the FLN. In reality, the goal was to eliminate the rural guerrillas' logistical support networks—and in that sense, their purpose was similar to internment camps. As in internment camps, the FLN was also effective at infiltrating *camps de regroupement* (Sacriste 2012).

Camps de regroupement stripped rural populations of their livelihoods—they could no longer farm their land and had little hope of finding alternative employment. They left their homes with what they could carry before the French army's aerial bombardment and shooting on sight began. The practice of 'regrouping' began to be used in the course of 1955, and was systemised, theorised and generalised across Algeria between 1956 and 1957, notably by officers who had served in Indochina who were very much influenced by counter-insurgency doctrine seeking to drain the 'water' of peasant logistical support from around the 'fish' of the guerrilla (<<Chap. 3, p. 69, 90). By 1957, *camps de regroupement* were being created across Algeria, and the practice remained in place until mid-1961. SAS officers usually ran the camps. By 1961, around a third of the rural population, or 2,350,000 people, had been 'regrouped' (Cornaton 1998; in English see Feichtinger 2017).

In the camps, security concerns took precedence over providing the trappings of a functioning administration or infrastructure. In February 1959, a young civil servant called Michel Rocard (1930–2016; prime minister, 1988–91) wrote a highly critical secret report for the government on the horrific conditions he had found there. Poor sanitary conditions were allowing tuberculosis and malaria to proliferate and the population was teetering on starvation, reduced to eating grass and plant roots. A child was dying in a camp every other day. The document was leaked in April 1959, and was published in *Le Monde* and then in a series of other national newspapers. This prompted a debate in the French National Assembly in June 1959, and criticism of France at the UN in July 1959. Publicising the deplorable conditions in the camps, and the long-term damage being wreaked on rural society, became part of the FLN's propaganda strategy.

The relationship between politics and violence: what can we learn from
Centres sociaux, **SAS and** *camps de regroupement* **about French attempts to
'really' make Algeria French?**
Both the 'third way' promoted by successive French governments (Evans
2012) and 'integration' promoted by Soustelle (Shepard 2006) (<<
Chap. 3, pp. 71–2, 83) sought to end the rebellion by building a new
Franco-Algerian society. The three examples explored here reveal how
unrealistic their chances for success were. Taking the *Centres sociaux,* the
SAS and the *camps de regroupement* together, we can see that the more
effective a programme was militarily (i.e. in stopping physical support for
the FLN), the less successful it was at 'winning hearts and minds'. The
inverse is also true: the more effective social and economic programmes
were at winning the confidence of Algerian men, women and children,
the less invested its members of staff were at pushing the political message
that Algeria should remain part of France. The *camps de regroupement*
dramatically curtailed the support which local populations could provide
to the ALN, but they also destroyed the image of a fraternal France
ensuring human development. The Centres sociaux seem to have genu-
inely built positive relationships with the Algerian people with whom
they worked, but in doing so, many of its staff were brought closer to
support, or sympathise with, the FLN position that Algeria had to become
independent.

The FLN State-Within-a-State and the War-Within-the-War

In order to reinforce its own legitimacy and control, the FLN sought to put in
place a parallel system of administration and infrastructure to that of the French
state (a state-within-state). Algerians were instructed to not just reject the SAS
and EMSI but also to refuse to pay taxes, use the legal system, vote in elections
and register births, marriages and deaths. In autumn 1956, a French intelligence report described the whole of the northern region of Batna as being
under a new FLN system of secret local councils, with FLN-designated forestry
guards, and a network of schools in the forest to teach boys and girls Arabic
(Meynier 2002, 202). The FLN created its own legal system for civil and penal
matters, with behavioural and moral codes. There was a system of FLN welfare
payments for families in which the main breadwinner was in prison, the ALN
or had been killed. These structures were replicated in urban areas. The FLN
also sought to send political commissaries into the internment camps and
camps de regroupement to bring these populations under FLN control even if
physically they were confined to the camp. The ability of the FLN to impose
itself as a state-within-a-state varied across regions, and indeed, local areas.
Complying with orders to boycott the French and colonial institutions was not

just encouraged through political awareness raising, but also enforced through violence.

The FLN violently imposed its hegemony on the MNA. In 1956, the MNA was still dominant in mainland France, especially in Metz and in Seine Maritime. Verbal exchanges between FLN and MNA members had escalated into a cycle of assassinations, with each assassination settling the score of the previous murder and prompting the next. The FLN was better armed and more war ready, and killed a number of the MNA's senior figures as well as grassroots activists. This was, in the words of Mohamed Harbi, a senior member of the FLN's French Federation (Fédération de France, FF-FLN) and later historian, a 'war within the war' (quoted in Amiri 2014, 579). By summer 1956, the FLN in France had successfully extended its influence across France and Belgium to the detriment of the MNA, although increased visibility meant that nearly all its senior leaders had been arrested. In France, the FLN's state-within-a-state model was also replicated (justice, social work, taxation), although this was trickier as the proportion of Algerians in France was obviously much lower than in Algeria, and the French state much more present. Algerian workers nevertheless contributed massively to the revolutionary tax to fund the FLN. Sylvie Thénault (2005) describes the FF-FLN as the 'genuine financial backers of nationalism', funding both the war in Algeria and political action on the international stage.

Back in Algeria, there was a MNA rural guerrilla section around Bouira, the region south of Algiers, created in 1955 by a PPA activist and former MTLD local councillor, Mohamed Bellounis (1912–58), on the instructions of the MNA leadership. The FLN accused Bellounis of complicity with the French, or at the very least, they considered that the French were turning a blind eye to his activities in order to undermine the FLN/ALN. In May 1957, Bellounis did actively seek out financial and military support from the French army. This happened in the wake of the 'Melouza massacre', the most highly mediatised FLN/ALN attack against supporters of the MNA in the course of the war.

Debating the nature of Algerian nationalism: Melouza
On 29 May 1957, all the men and boys of an entire village, numbering in their hundreds, were assassinated by ALN rural guerrillas, purportedly after they refused to rally to the FLN and instead declared Messali Hadj their leader. Although this is often referred to as the Melouza massacre, the killings actually took place at Mechta Kasba, a settlement near the village of Melouza, on the edge of the Constantine and Kabylia regions. The village of Melouza itself was in fact pro-FLN (McDougall 2017a, 224). The 'massacre of Melouza' was widely used in French propaganda, presented as a cold blooded FLN elimination of a 'pro-French village'. Yet the reasons behind the massacre were much more about local politics and personalities than about France versus the FLN or even the MNA versus the FLN. The man who ordered the killings, Saïd Mohammedi

(*continued*)

(continued)

(1912–94), who had replaced Krim Belkacem as the head of the *wilaya* 3, had, unusually, previously fought in the German army in the Second World War. Mohammedi might be seen as emblematic of a regional leader obsessed with the need to assert his authority and prove that he was 'in charge' to his superiors as much as to the local population (>>Chap. 3, p. 108). The inhabitants of Mechta Kasba, in a remote region rarely visited by strangers, were not well disposed to outsiders throwing their weight around. This was not an unusual scenario, fortunately most did not end so tragically (McDougall 2017a, 224–225; Meynier 2002, 452–453).

In reaction to the killings, Bellounis founded the National Army of the Algerian people (Armée nationale du peuple algérien, ANPA), a 2000–3000 strong force which was financially and militarily supported by the French army. This existed until July 1958. The killings in Mechta Kasba made it very difficult to bring about any rapprochement between the MNA and the FLN. At the same time, Bellounis's turn to the French army was deeply troubling for many members of the MNA leadership and rank-and-file, and contributed to discrediting the MNA. By the late 1950s, Messali Hadj found himself and the MNA, in the words of one of its London-based members, considered by wider public opinion to be 'a second division football team' (Sidi Moussa 2019, 10).

Overall, the vast majority of Algerians were convinced, rather than coerced, into seeing the FLN as the legitimate representative of 'the people' and 'the state'. This is reflected in mass adherence to the student strike (spring 1956) (<<Chap. 3, p. 84–5), the eight-day strike (January 1957) (<<Chap. 3, p. 92), and public demonstrations called by the FLN at politically important points—just before a vote went to the UN (>>Chap. 3, p. 133), or on the anniversary of 1 November, for example. Fatima Berci, who was part of the ALN's rural support network in her village in Kabylia, summarises the situation that she and her neighbours found themselves in: 'The French came, they surrounded us, they made us come out, they smashed the roofs, and then the *mujahidin*, they came and they made us rebuild their houses.' She says 'we were caught between two fires', and yet ultimately, she concludes, 'we were ready to die for our country' (Vince 2015, 59). Another rural woman, Chérifa Akache, who cooked for the ALN and as a result was arrested and tortured by the French army, is cognisant of the fact that she might not have had much choice (death was a probable outcome whatever she did), but ultimately she chose to support the ALN: 'I preferred to die a heroine for the revolution than be killed by the *mujahidin* as a traitor' (Vince 2015, 61).

For Algerian civilians, fear of the violence of the French army was not the same as fear of the violence of the ALN. The former was random and indiscriminate; the latter was targeted at people suspected of being traitors. When purges took place, paranoia and personal rivalries rather than evidence could drive the definition of 'traitor'. It is estimated that 3000 to 7000 FLN activists were killed during internal purges between 1958 and 1961 (McDougall 2017a, 225). Nevertheless, as Raphaëlle Branche (2019, 125) argues, 'contrary to what the French army thought, two forces of the same nature were not applying pressure on Algerian civilians. One came from the exterior and was clearly identified as foreign, whilst the other came from the interior and had many shared references with civilians.' In short, in the words of James McDougall (2017a, 224): 'If, by 1961, the FLN could legitimately stand as the political expression of the Algerian people, this position had been achieved by popular adhesion more than by the Front's coercion'.

May 1957–May 1958: The French Government Under Pressure—Financial Problems, the Sakiet Sidi Youssef Bombing, International Condemnation

The French government was under pressure at home and abroad. A week before the Melouza massacre in May 1957, which it sought to spin to its advantage, Guy Mollet's Republican Front government (<<Chap. 3, p. 81–3) lost a vote of confidence in the National Assembly. Already much weakened by the Suez crisis (<<Chap. 3, p. 89), it was unable to balance the books as military spending in Algeria spiralled. Mollet was replaced for a few months over summer 1957 by the government of the Radical party's Maurice Bourgès-Maunoury (1914–93), which was followed by the government of fellow Radical Félix Gaillard (1919–70) between November 1957 and April 1958. In January 1958, France had requested $655 million in credit from the United States, the International Monetary Fund (IMF) and the European Payments Union (EPU). The French government claimed that its financial problems were so great that it might not be able to launch the EEC if funds were not forthcoming. The United States was keen to promote the creation of the EEC as a bulwark against the communist bloc. It is widely suspected that Washington used this occasion to put pressure on France to reach a political solution in Algeria (Connelly 2002, 155) (<<Chap. 3, pp. 74–77).

International pressure on France further intensified the following month. On 8 February 1958, the French air force, with the authorisation of the Gaillard government, bombed the Tunisian village of Sakiet Sidi Youssef (Fig 3.1). The stated aim was to destroy an ALN camp located there, but there were significant civilian casualties. In total, 70 people were killed and 150 wounded, including children. The incident caused international outrage—even Sweden and Norway, who had so far said little about the conflict in Algeria, expressed their disapproval at the UN (Evans 2012, 231). Tunisian President Bourguiba was enraged. He blockaded the French naval base in Bizerte and closed the French consulates. The United States was also furious, fearful that France was alienating the 'moderates' in the Arab world, such as Tunisia, and pushing them into the arms of the communist bloc. Following the Sakiet bombing, American Secretary of State John Foster Dulles would repeatedly express his fear that the French army was out of control (Wall 2001, 126). The Moroccan government—as well as the rest of the Arab and Muslim world—also reacted angrily and adopted an even more explicit public position in favour of Algerian independence.

Under American pressure, Gaillard received two US envoys. One of them was Robert Murphy, who had been in extensive contact with Ferhat Abbas in 1943 (<<Chap. 2, p. 47). This prompted outrage in France and amongst settlers in Algeria as evidence of American interference in French 'internal affairs'. In addition to France's ongoing economic difficulties, Gaillard's meetings with the US envoys led to him losing a vote of no confidence in the National Assembly in mid-March 1958. The Christian Democrat Pierre Pflimlin (1907–2000) was called upon by President René Coty (1882–1962) to form a new government, which was duly approved by the National Assembly. It lasted only two weeks, from 14 to 28 May 1958.

August 1957–Spring 1958: Tensions Within the FLN— Political Versus Military, Interior Versus Exterior

The FLN had plenty of its own internal problems. There were divisions between the politicians and the military leaders, between those based within Algeria and those outside of Algeria, and within the *wilayat* and amongst the men on the frontiers (Fig. 3.1). When the CNRA (the FLN's parliament) met in Cairo in August 1957, the '3Bs' (Krim Belkacem, Boussouf and Ben Tobbal) reversed the principals established at Soummam the previous year, in which the interior had primacy over the exterior and the political over the military (<<Chap. 3, pp. 85–7). Instead, colonels and military officers now had a prominent place on the executive CCE and the legislative CNRA. The ALN's military bases in Morocco and Tunisia, first established when Algeria's North African neighbours became independent in 1956, were growing in size and importance, whilst the ALN within Algeria's borders was increasingly decimated by the French army. Abane was furious at being sidelined by the '3B', and at the growing strength of the military and the exterior. In April 1958, the FLN newspaper *El Moudjahid* reported that Abane had been killed in action—that is, by the French army—in the course of a mission. In reality, he had been murdered in Morocco in December 1957 by Boussouf's men.

Until spring 1958, the FLN's bases in Tunisia and Morocco had been relatively disorganised and various mutinies and acts of disobedience had taken place as some ALN soldiers refused to cross the electrified fences and risk the anti-personnel mines to re-enter Algeria (Arezki 2018, 137). In April 1958, Krim Belkacem created two Military Operational Committees (Comités opérationnels militaires, COM) to reassert control. The Tunisian COM (from September onwards called an Etat major/military headquarters) was established in Ghardimaou, 10 km from the Algerian border, under Saïd Mohammedi (<<Chap. 3, pp. 104–5). The Tunisian COM oversaw the interior *wilayat* in the east. The Moroccan COM/Etat major was created in Oujda (20 km from the Algerian border), and oversaw the interior *wilayat* in the west, under Houari Boumediene (1932–78, President of Algeria 1965–78).

Although there was a bigger ALN presence in Tunisia and it was easier to transport weapons over land (via Libya and Egypt) into Tunisia than by sea into Morocco, the most disciplined and best organised base was that of Boumediene. He succeeded in imposing his authority and securing the loyalty of the men in Oujda, whilst the legitimacy of Mohammedi was constantly contested in Ghardimaou (Arezki 2018, 138). Houari Boumediene (real name Mohamed Boukharouba) came from a rural family in Guelma in eastern Algeria. He had studied at al-Zaytuna University in Tunis and al-Azhar University in Egypt, and it was whilst he was in Egypt that he was selected as one of the first members of the FLN to receive military training abroad, in Alexandria, at the end of 1954. He came back to Algeria in February 1955 on a mission to smuggle arms into Algeria, but spent relatively little of the war on Algerian territory. Named by Boussouf as his successor to head the *wilaya* 5 in 1957, Boumediene would eventually become much more powerful than his former boss. Boumediene began to build Oujda into a military stronghold, which strengthened his own power within the FLN as much as it benefitted the military organisation of the FLN. Following the FLN's state-within-the-state model, the Algerian population of Oujda had their own courts, police, registry office, child benefit and taxation system and recruitment and propaganda mechanisms, with the aim of keeping the Algerian population away from the (still significant) French presence in Morocco. There were also training camps and rest camps and logistical support networks from which incursions and attacks in Algeria could be launched—although this was increasingly difficult with the electrified fences and anti-personnel mines which the French army had placed along the border (Fig. 3.1 and <<Chap. 3, p. 90). In October 1958, FLN/ALN military numbers in Morocco were estimated at 2200 (Essemlali 2011, 89). This number would continue to increase.

Debating the nature of Algerian nationalism and the terms of future debates: Oujda

It is important to explain Boumediene's base at Oujda, because in the post-independence period the place name 'Oujda' (like 'DAF' (<<Chap. 3, p. 88) would become, for those opposed to the post-1962 Algerian political system, shorthand for the idea that independence was 'stolen' from the men and women who fought and died on Algerian soil by army colonels who were not even present in Algeria during the war (>>Chap. 4, p. 168–9). President Abdelaziz Bouteflika (b. 1937, president 1999–2019), who was a close collaborator of Boumediene in the *wilaya* 5 during the war, was born in Oujda, although his family was from the western Algerian town of Tlemcen. Already during the anti-colonial struggle, leaders of the *wilayat* within Algeria often viewed both the 'frontier armies' and the politicians living outside Algeria with suspicion. They complained that whilst they were fighting, dying and living in miserable conditions in Algeria, those in the 'exterior' FLN/ALN were living in comfort (although Boumediene himself was famously austere) and not doing enough to get them arms and supplies.

13 MAY 1958: SETTLERS AND ARMY LEADERS REBEL

At the start of May 1958, international pressure on France to bring about a negotiated solution to the conflict in Algeria was stronger than ever. Pflimlin had previously indicated that he was in favour of this, and his nomination as prime minister provoked outrage amongst settler hardliners. On 13 May 1958, the day Pflimlin was officially invested with the powers of prime minister, Commander-in-Chief General Salan decided to lay flowers on a war memorial in Algiers. The gesture was in memory of three French soldiers, taken prisoner by the ALN, who the FLN had just announced had been executed, purportedly for torture, rape and murder. The flower laying ceremony was accompanied by a demonstration of 100,000 Europeans (Evans 2012, 233). It rapidly descended into a riot, incited by fervent partisans of 'French Algeria', including ex-student leader Lagaillarde and Poujadiste (<<Chap. 3, p. 82) café owner Joseph Ortiz. The American Cultural Centre was looted, as was the seat of the highest civilian authority in Algiers, the General Delegation. The police and army did not intervene.

Colonel Roger Trinquier (1908–86) and Lagaillarde decided to form a Committee of Public Safety (Comité de salut public, CSP). It was composed of 45 members, including four Algerians, as well as Lagaillade, Ortiz and the director of the newspaper *L'Echo d'Alger*, Alain de Serigny (1912–86). Local Committees of Public Safety began to spring up across Algeria. Although its stated purpose was to restore order, the CSP was a direct challenge to the authority of the civilian administration in Algeria. Arriving shortly after end of the 13 May 1958 demonstrations, General Massu took control of the CSP in Algiers, declaring from the balcony of the Minister-Resident's office: 'I, General Massu, have just formed a committee of public safety... so that in France a government of public safety may be formed, presided over by General de Gaulle' (Evans 2012, 233–234).

This call for the return of de Gaulle was not because he had proved himself to be a particularly fervent supporter of French Algeria—he wanted to Algeria to remain French much like any other member of the French political class. Rather, de Gaulle was seen as the only political and military figure with the sufficient authority and legitimacy to resolve the Algerian crisis. By seeing de Gaulle as a potential saviour, members of the CSP found common ground with de Gaulle's supporters in Paris, such as Debré, Soustelle and Chaban-Delmas, who were keen to bring back de Gaulle to put an end to what they saw as the eternal crises of the Fourth Republic (Macmaster 2009, 114).

May and early June were marked by daily parades in the centre of Algiers, and elsewhere in Algeria, organised by the CSP. The aim of the demonstrations was not only to produce a display of force against what was perceived to be the defeatist direction of the government in Paris. Through scenes of 'fraternisation', demonstrators also wanted to prove that a 'Franco-Muslim community' could exist, which in turn would be the salvation of 'French Algeria' (Rahal 2010). The organisers of the demonstrations therefore sought to very visibly include people identifiable as 'Muslims'. Much was made in the press of the presence of banners in the demonstration with slogans such as 'the Casbah replies: all present' or 'We are French and we wish to stay French', alongside images of men and women wearing turbans, veils and other distinctive items of Muslim clothing, carrying bunches of flowers in the colours of the French flag.

Another key element of these demonstrations was the unveiling of Algerian women. Throughout the colonial period, the veil had been a symbol of 'being Muslim', and 'being Muslim' was synonymous with not being fully French (<<Chap. 1, p. 7). Unveiling was presented as the symbol of both 'integration' and 'fraternity'. The Europeans of Algeria claimed that they were 'emancipating' their 'Muslim' sisters, insisting that the latter wanted to become 'kif kif les Françaises' (just like French women, in a mixture of Algerian Arabic and French). Given that, for decades, settlers had sought to block any inkling of reform which would have led to greater legal, political and socio-economic equality for Algerians (<<Chap. 2, pp. 23–4, 25, 36–8, 42, 51), this co-option of the language of 'integration' and 'fraternity' might seem surprising, but it was strategically logical. It sought to shake off suspicions expressed in the international, but also parts of the national, press that the CSP was composed of white supremacist putchists attempting to pull off a similar coup to that of General Francisco Franco in Spain in 1936. Such language and imagery also sought to bring de Gaulle himself onside, as he too was wary of such associations (Macmaster 2009, 116–117).

The relationship between politics and violence: 'fraternisation' in 1958
Algerian participation in these demonstrations—and they did participate in large numbers—has been subject to much controversy. For settlers and those in the army who struggled to accept the end of French Algeria four years later, 'fraternisation' in May 1958 was the proof that an alternative to independence had been possible, the 'Muslim' men and women in these demonstrations were presented as 'rallying' to the CSP, against the FLN (>>Chap. 4, p. 171). For the FLN at the time, and in Algerian national history subsequently, the presence of Algerians in this demonstration is hard to reconcile with the idea that by May 1958 the FLN had succeeded in establishing its hold over the Algerian population (Rahal 2010). The women who were present at unveiling ceremonies have attracted particular attention, not least because of an indefatigable obsession with the veil in France. Algerian nationalists, both at the time and subsequently, have presented these women as either forced to participate by the French army, or prostitutes paid to put on a performance.

It is impossible to definitively determine to what extent Algerians enthusiastically participated in the May 1958 demonstrations. Most Algerians were silent observers (Rahal 2010). There were some enthusiastic supporters, whether because they fervently believed in French Algeria or because they were caught up in the general euphoria which promised peace and political change. There is also plenty of evidence that Algerian participation in the demonstrations was manufactured. The CSP and the army-controlled SAU (<<Chap. 3, p. 99) in Algiers played a clear role in orchestrating the presence of Algerians, by 'persuading' them to participate. Even when explicit threat was not used, the SAU embodied colonial authority—it was hard to say no (Rahal 2010; Macmaster 2009). The 'Fifth Bureau', the army section in charge of psychological warfare and propaganda established in January 1955, had also intensively studied the indoctrination of crowds and knew how to make public demonstrations appear spontaneous when they were in fact staged. The performative nature of unveiling ceremonies is clear. We know little about most of the women who chose or were forced to unveil, but we do know about 18-year-old Monique Ameziane who participated in an organised public unveiling in Constantine on 26 May 1958. Ameziane's mother was of 'European' legal status and her father was of 'Muslim' status—in fact, he was a wealthy, pro-French administrator who had fled to France in April 1955. In his absence, his son Mouloud, Monique's brother, had allowed the family farm to become an FLN base, before it was taken over by the French army in April 1958 and turned into an infamous centre for torture (Mauss-Copeaux 2017; Einaudi 1991). Monique Ameziane had never previously worn the veil. She was told that if she participated in an unveiling ceremony she would save the life of her brother and be allowed to sit her baccalaureate exams. She duly complied (Macmaster 2009, 134–135).

September 1958: The Birth of the Fifth Republic and Some New Rights for Algerian Women

The standoff between the CSP in Algiers and the government Paris continued. On 24–25 May 1958, Salan established a further CSP in Corsica. The generals and the CSP were edging slowly towards Paris, a coup d'état appeared imminent. On 26 May, Pflimlin met with de Gaulle. Much to his surprise, the next day de Gaulle announced that he was forming a cross-party Republican government to ensure national unity. Backed into a corner, Pflimlin resigned. On 29 May, President Coty asked de Gaulle to form a government. With his government approved by the National Assembly, de Gaulle promised a new constitution (Evans 2012, 235). The Constitution of the new Fifth Republic was approved by referendum in September 1958. It concentrated significantly more powers in the hands of the president, at the expense of the National Assembly. A further referendum in October 1962 ensured that henceforth the president would be elected by universal suffrage, not by a vote of parliamentarians, further strengthening presidential power. The Fifth Republic Constitution also made all Algerians full French citizens, and notably Algerian women were given the right to vote for the first time (<<Chap. 2, p. 51) .

The FLN called on Algerians to boycott the referendum on the constitution. As part of the French army and government's campaign to show both domestic and international audiences that it was 'emancipating' Algerian women, significant efforts were deployed to get them to come out and vote— the SAS, the SAU and the EMSI were all mobilised to bring women physically to the polls, alongside a big propaganda campaign (Macmaster 2009, 273–277). For a small group of French-educated, self-defined 'French Muslim' women, who were not favourable the FLN or independence, opening up the right to vote presented new opportunities (Wadowiec 2013). Elected to the National Assembly in November 1958, Nafissa Sid Cara (1910–2002) was the first ever 'Muslim' woman to serve in a French government. The FLN dismissed these women as colonial cronies and argued that only liberation from colonial rule could bring about the emancipation of women. With its state-within-a-state system already well established, the FLN was equally dismissive of French attempts in 1959 to effectively end the Muslim personal status (see Glossary) and bring marriage under civil rather than religious jurisdiction—Algerians were already avoiding any kind of colonial administration in huge numbers (Macmaster 2009, 280–305).

De Gaulle: A Man with a Plan, Called upon to 'Save France'?

Having been on the margins of French politics since the end of the Second World War, when presented with the opportunity to come back in at the top in May 1958, de Gaulle immediately stepped into action. On 1 June he became Prime Minister, and on 4 June he went to Algeria, where his return to power was joyously greeted by the settlers, and nervously observed by the FLN and their supporters. Speaking to the euphoric crowds massed in Algiers, de Gaulle sought to reassure, impose his legitimacy on both the civilian population and the army and reach out to both 'Europeans' and 'Muslims'. In doing so, he uttered one of the most ambiguous statements in political history: 'Je vous ai compris' ('I have understood you'). Who, exactly, he had understood was deliberately left unclear. For settlers, he had understood them: he was there to re-establish order and ensure the longevity of French rule, even if that meant some limited reform—in the same speech he promised equal voting rights for all. A few days later, in Mostaganem, de Gaulle was more explicit in this aim, proclaiming not just 'Vive la République! Vive la France' as in Algiers but also 'Vive l'Algérie française!' [Long live French Algeria!], which was the rallying cry of the settler hardliners. For de Gaulle's audience in Algiers who were members or sympathisers of the FLN, it was also possible that they thought that de Gaulle had understood them, and that he had recognised the strength and legitimacy of their demands for self-determination. After all, he also promised that the 'Ten million Frenchmen [and women] of Algeria [i.e. the entire population of Algeria] would decide their own destiny'.

Connecting the local, national, transnational and global: de-centring de Gaulle

De Gaulle remains one of the most divisive political figures in French history (Jackson 2018). For his supporters, he was the great statesman, liberation leader, decoloniser, the man who saved France from both the Nazis and settler fascism. He was the man who made France great on the world stage by refusing to meekly follow Cold War cleavages and fall into line behind the Americans. For his critics, he was an authoritarian ruler who was a past master at mythologising his own special role in French history and using national crises for his own political ends. He unilaterally imposed his leadership on a politically diverse resistance movement during the Second World War. He used the Algerian War as an excuse to get rid of the Fourth Republic and bring about constitutional change which centralised power in the hands of the president (and thus in his own hands)—Mitterrand famously branded the Fifth Republic constitution a 'permanent coup d'état'. For the settlers, he betrayed them by ultimately abandoning Algeria (<<Chap. 1, pp. 12–13; >>Chap. 4, pp. 160–1, 167, 187). For many of those on the left, one of the reasons why he was willing to accept independence because he was a racist who believed that non-white Muslims could never be French. And ultimately, his authoritarian politics and stifling social conservatism were rejected by a new generation of students in May 1968.

What both supporters and detractors of de Gaulle do in these assessments is put him at the heart of the decision-making process—that is, this is a historical interpretation with an emphasis on the role of the individual

(*continued*)

(continued)

in determining the course of history (Merom 1999). Scholarly accounts have taken a long time to de-centre de Gaulle from the story. An often-reproduced analysis is that by 1959 de Gaulle had accepted the loss of Algeria and empire more broadly, or, put another way, he was no longer willing to invest the necessary men and resources to maintain it, because he no longer saw it as essential to his steadfast goals of French 'greatness', 'rank' and 'independence' (Vaïsse 1998). Instead, by the late 1950s, de Gaulle had decided that these goals could be achieved through France possessing the nuclear bomb (first tested in the Sahara in February 1960) and by making France a first amongst equals in the process of European construction after the signing of the Treaty of Rome in 1957. One of the most used quotes about de Gaulle 'changing his mind' about Algeria comes from the memoirs of Alain Peyrefitte (1925–99), who after 1962 became one of de Gaulle's most trusted ministers. He recalled de Gaulle declaring that Algeria 'undermines the position of France in the world. As long as we are not relieved of it, we can do nothing in the world. This is a terrible burden. It is necessary to relinquish it' (Connelly 2001, 234).

Less flattering assessments of de Gaulle also put him at the centre of the story. They underline the illiberal views he held which made it easier for him to accept Algerian independence—he simply did not believe in the Franco-Algerian nation which proponents of full integration were promoting (Shepard 2006). In 1959, de Gaulle declared: 'If we went ahead with integration, if all the Arabs and Berbers of Algeria were considered French, how could we stop them coming to live in France, since the standard of living is so much higher? My village wouldn't be called Colombey-les-Deux-Eglises [Colombey-the-two-Churches], but Colombey-les-Deux-Mosquées! [Colombey-the-two-Mosques]' (Tyre 2006, 276). The fascination with de Gaulle as an exceptional figure also favours a reading of the Algerian War as distinctly different in its Fourth and Fifth Republic phases.

The idea of de Gaulle as the central actor with a grand plan has been increasingly challenged. De Gaulle was not acting in a vacuum. He was dealing with the same variables as previous governments—the FLN, UN, US, USSR and Cold War context, the human and material cost of the war, the ambivalence of most of the metropolitan French public about Algeria and the anger of most settlers at the first hint of compromise. In the 1950s, European construction was not imagined as an alternative to empire, rather empire was imagined as part of European construction (>>Chap. 3, p. 130). At the level of senior civil servants, and many politicians, there were significant continuities in personnel between the Fourth and Fifth Republics. If one looks at what de Gaulle and his governments *did* from June 1958 onwards, there are remarkable continuities with the Fourth Republic: repression, reform and seeking to make alliances with 'more moderate' Algerians in order to marginalise the FLN.

The Creation of the GPRA, the Growing Power of the Military over the Political and the Exterior over the Interior

The FLN was alert to the dangers of the French government seeking out alternative Algerian interlocutors. In response to de Gaulle's return to power, the FLN sought to present itself as a government-in-waiting by creating a Provisional Government of the Algerian Republic (GPRA) in September 1958. This replaced the CCE (<<Chap. 3, p. 86). Established in Cairo, the first president of the GPRA was a politician, Ferhat Abbas, although the other key posts were held by senior military figures—Krim Belkacem was Vice-President and Foreign Minister, Lakhdar Ben Tobbal was Minister for the Interior and Abdelhafid Boussouf head of the secret services. The GPRA received immediate diplomatic recognition from Tunisia, Morocco and every Arab state except Lebanon. This was followed by China, North Vietnam, North Korea and Indonesia. In autumn 1960, Nikita Khrushchev, on a visit to the UN, embraced Krim Belkacem and declared that this confirmed the USSR's de facto recognition of the GPRA. In Beijing, Abbas made the GPRA's first formal request for Chinese volunteers to the FLN. This was symbolic gesture serving the purposes of propaganda, given the practical difficulties of bringing volunteers from China to North Africa (Connelly 2001, 221; Haddad-Fonda 2014).

The GPRA set out building networks with states in the communist world, the Middle East and Western Europe. Yet as the GPRA was increasingly successful in isolating France diplomatically, the GPRA itself was increasingly isolated within the FLN. In spring 1959, the leader of the *wilaya* 3, Colonel Amirouche (1926–59, Amirouche Aït Hamouda, almost always referred to as Amirouche) and his deputy Si Haoues (1923–59, real name Ahmed Ben Abderrezak), angry at what they saw to be the exterior's failure to supply the *wilayat* of the interior with sufficient weapons, set off from Kabylia to meet with members of the GPRA in Tunis. On the way, they were killed by French soldiers in an ambush. Ever since, rumours have circulated that Amirouche and Si Haoues were betrayed by their rivals in the FLN, as the French army unit which killed them seemed remarkably well informed about where the two men were going to be (Harbi 1980, 237). In January 1960, the FLN's parliament, the CNRA, met in Tripoli (Libya) and decided to create one unified army general staff (Etat major général, EMG). This brought the existing east and west EMGs under Boumediene's control (<<Chap. 3, p. 108) and he moved from Morocco to the EMG's new central base in Ghardimaou in Tunisia. This further loosened the GPRA's control over the ALN. The EMG was instructed to send troops into Algeria, but this was increasingly difficult because of the Pédron and Morice/Challe lines (Fig. 3.1). Losses were heavy and Boumediene eventually put a stop to sending in new soldiers. As ALN combatant numbers within Algeria shrank, the number of combatants on the borders grew. In the middle of 1960, there were 9500 ALN combatants in Tunisia, and 6500 in Morocco (Arezki 2018, 148), and these numbers would continue to increase.

October 1958, the Constantine Plan: Making Citizens Through Modernisation

On 3 October 1958, in the eastern Algerian town of Constantine, de Gaulle announced an ambitious five-year plan of social and economic reforms scheduled to run between 1959 and 1963. 'All of Algeria', de Gaulle declared, 'must have her share in what modern civilisation can and must bring to man in terms of wellbeing and dignity.' De Gaulle continued this theme in his New Year address on 8 January 1959: 'a special place is destined for the Algeria of tomorrow, pacified and transformed, developing its own personality and closely associated with France'. The Constantine Plan consisted of billions of francs of investment in industrialisation, modernising agriculture, forestry and constructing housing. It promoted increasing access to education and roles in the administration for Algerians.

The Constantine Plan was presented as a new initiative but was in fact the result of many years of government-funded studies into chronic Algerian underdevelopment and grinding poverty. The substance of the proposals which were presented in 1958 had already been formulated by 1957. 'Mise en valeur', that is to say, the idea that the metropole should invest in the colonies and in colonial subjects in order to better control them and enable them to contribute more to economic growth and national defence can be traced back to the interwar period (Thomas 2005). It was, however, after the Second World War that France started to seriously consider actually investing in its colonies on a significant scale. Not everyone in France thought that this was a good idea—the journalist Raymond Cartier, for example, regularly critiqued the burden on the French taxpayer (Naylor 2018, xxiii). Nevertheless, it became a widely held view amongst French civil servants and politicians across the left and right that that investment in the colonies was the future. In the specific context of Algeria after 1 November 1954, investment was seen as a means to prevent independence. In December 1958, senior civil servant Paul Delouvrier (1914–95), a key figure of French post-Second World War state planning, was nominated Executive Officer (Délégué général) in Algeria. This was the equivalent post of Governor General/ Resident Minister. In taking up the post, Delouvrier replaced General Salan, who had been combining this civilian role with his military position. Delouvrier was tasked with overseeing the Constantine Plan.

Part of the Constantine Plan involved dealing with the *camps de regroupement* (<<Chap. 3, p. 102). Delouvrier sought to bring them under civilian oversight and rationalise the practice of regrouping into a socio-economic plan to create 1000 model villages which would 'modernise' Algerian peasants through 'acculturation' (familiarising them with French/Western 'ways of life') (Sacriste 2012). The 1000 villages programme aimed to build modern, prefabricated homes to house nuclear families. Homes were to have running

water and villages would be equipped with roads, electricity and town halls. This new way of living was meant to change the way of life of rural Algerians, who were seen by the planners as backwards, superstitious peasants. It was envisaged they would become 'rational' citizens with 'modern' ideas about medicine and hygiene, education and family (Feichtinger 2017).

The goal of the Constantine Plan thus went well beyond socio-economic reform to fix the political problem of the rebellion—it actively sought to transform Algerian society (McDougall 2017b). The civil servants who worked on it were convinced that Muslim culture was a barrier to economic productivity. Modernisation was envisaged as the means of turning Muslim men and women into producers and consumers, and thus citizens. In the words of Jean Vibert, Director of the Plan in Algiers: '*Homo-economicus* has been born. He has replaced *homo-islamicus*, that man who accepted an extremely low level of [material] needs and who, as a result, did not feel the need to work more than was necessary' (Davis 2017, 76).

Connecting the local, national, transnational and global: modernisation
The kinds of reforms which the French government sought to introduce in Algeria from 1955 onwards need to be understood as part of a global preoccupation after the Second World War with 'development' and 'modernisation' (Cooper and Packard 1997). Different states and political systems around the world, from Western Europe to the Eastern bloc to independent states in Africa and Asia, were obsessed with planning, modernising and industrialisation in order to build 'modern' economies and societies. Ed Naylor (2018, xix) argues that 'the "modernising" dynamic was not so much a political concession to be wrested from the French authorities but rather a process of social and economic transformation already underway in colonised societies.' That is to say, the French government was not leading a modernisation agenda in Algeria (or elsewhere in its African colonies), rather it was desperately trying to catch up with and manage major changes which had already taken place: 'Rapid urbanisation, labour migration and trade unionism disrupted the stable mediocrity to which the interwar colonial state had aspired' (Naylor 2018, xix).

Most of the projects contained in the Constantine Plan were unfinished or never started. In part, this was because of the war and funding problems. It was also because the plans were too strongly associated with the French army and too insistent on coercing Algerians to 'modernise': these were 'vast programmes of social planning and engineering with violent means' (Feichtinger 2017, 51). The aspirations of the planners often simply did not match those of the people they were seeking to transform. Plans for both villagisation (Macmaster 2018) and replacing urban shantytowns with proper housing (House 2018) failed to take into account the needs and desires of the people meant to live there. In terms of the redistribution of land, by June 1960, only 28,000 of the 250,000 hectares of land which were meant to have been distributed as part of the Constantine Plan had been allocated, and no one had taken up the 460 plots ready to be occupied.

Ideas about 'modernisation' nevertheless had a significant impact. Whilst rejecting the Constantine Plan, the FLN promised an alternative which—in terms of actual measures—was quite similar: the redistribution of land, indus-trialisation and nationalisation (>>Chap. 4, pp. 157–8). The fact that newly independent states across Africa, Asia and the Middle East often continued similar 'modernisation' policies after independence reveals that nationalist leaders often came to the same conclusions as their former colonial rulers about what needed to be done to address the political and economic problems which their countries faced, and about the central role of the state as the motor of change. This reflects a consensus in the analysis of the economic issues and their proposed solutions, but with a radical difference in opinion on who had the political legitimacy to enact such programmes.

FEBRUARY–AUGUST 1959: THE CHALLE PLAN AND ITS IMPACT

Reform and repression continued to be intimately entwined. The Challe Plan— named after the army general who oversaw it, Maurice Challe (1905–79)—was a military offensive on a huge scale from February to August 1959, sweeping across Algeria from west to east to root out the ALN. By March 1959, the high point of the offensive, there were 429,000 French army soldiers in Algeria (Jauffret 2011). Key elements of the Challe Plan were aerial bombardment (including dropping napalm) massive population displacement (<<Chap. 3, p. 102) and *commandos de chasse* ('hunting commandos'). *Commandos de chasse* were highly mobile, relatively small troop units created to hunt down ALN rural guerrilla units by mimicking their tactics. They often had a large percentage of Algerians in them—in the words of Challe, 'The best *fellagha* [pejorative term for a member of the ALN] hunter is the French[man] of North African Descent' (Branche 2017, 47) (<<Chap. 3, p. 100).

The Challe Plan decimated the ALN within Algeria's borders. From its peak in January 1958 of between 60,000 and 90,000 soldiers (Jauffret 2001), by 1960 there were an estimated 8000 combatants (Meynier 2002, 304)—the rest lost to death or arrest, whilst some escaped to the ALN's camps in Tunisia and Morocco (Fig. 3.1). The impact of the Challe Plan on rural civilians was equally dramatic. With crops and livestock destroyed and massive population displacement, civilians were often starving. In the words of one rural woman, Ferroudja Amarouche:

There was nothing to eat, there wasn't any water, and even sometimes we ate grass. And the French soldiers said to us: 'There isn't even enough grass for you to eat, serves you right.' One Ramadan, there was nothing to eat, it was grass we tried to eat. And even the grass was difficult to find. [There was] nothing, nothing (Vince 2015, 35).

This in turn created a refugee crisis on a huge scale. In 1960, there were an estimated 250,000 to 300,000 Algerian refugees living on the Moroccan, Tunisian and Malian borders. Rape, both in custody and during French army raids on villages and in *camps de regroupement,* was commonplace between 1954 and 1962, and its incidence intensified during the Challe Plan (on rape and sexual violence see Branche 2002; Lazreg 2008; Vince 2010).

STORIES BY AND ABOUT SOLDIERS, AT THE TIME AND SUBSEQUENTLY: FRENCH SOLDIERS FROM METROPOLITAN FRANCE, *HARKIS, TIRAILLEURS SÉNÉGALAIS* AND SOLDIERS IN THE ALN

French Soldiers from Metropolitan France: From Conscript Ambivalence to Declining Morale; Perpetrating 'Our' Violence and Enduring the Violence of 'the Other'

French troops in Algeria consisted of professional soldiers, conscripts (*appelés*) completing their military service, and soldiers from the colonies. This latter category included both 'Europeans' and 'Muslims' from Algeria, as well as soldiers from France's other colonies. The majority of men in France who came of age during the War of Independence did their military service in Algeria. In 1955, the *rappelés*—men who had already completed their military service and were reservists—were recalled to Algeria.

There is a large body of academic work about men from France who were conscripted into the French army (Mauss-Copeaux 1998; Jauffret 2011; Brazzoduro 2012; Pervillé 2007). This is in addition to extensive oral history archives containing the testimonies of conscripts (Roche and Belgacem 2017) and soldiers' published memoirs. Some of the most senior professional soldiers in the French army who served in Algeria also published their memoirs. A common theme which emerges in the accounts of conscripts from mainland France is that none of them particularly wanted to go and fight in Algeria. They knew very little about Algeria, they did not see it as their concern, and as such they were not particularly sympathetic towards the Europeans of Algeria. Conscripts were, however, generally more sympathetic towards the Europeans of Algeria than they were towards their enemy, the FLN/ALN, and for many conscripts the FLN/ALN was indistinguishable from the wider Algerian population.

Amongst these conscripts and professional soldiers in the French army were settlers, who served both in regular French army units and in special units for Europeans from North Africa—notably in the Zouaves (>>Chap. 4, p. 186). They had a much more visceral attachment to Algeria, which generally, but not always, translated into a belief in the necessity of defending the existence of French Algeria at all costs. This would later lead some to later take up arms against the French army in the OAS (>>Chap. 3, pp. 133–4).

In mainland France, there were a number of protests against conscription and the call up of reservists. Until 1960, these protests tended to be against compulsory military service, and sometimes against war in general, rather than a specific rejection of the war in Algeria. The vast majority of soldiers did go to fight, and, like most soldiers in most wars, they fought well when they were well equipped, well-led and had built up a camaraderie with other soldiers in their unit (Jauffret 2011; in English see Jauffret 2002). The FLN/ALN developed propaganda aimed at conscripts in the French army encouraging them to desert. One pamphlet from July 1955 read: 'You need to know that Algerians look at you in the same way that yourselves, your elders and your fathers saw the soldiers of Hitler's army in a recent past' (Aït-El-Djoudi 2007, 42). There were, however, only 886 desertions recorded. One of the most high profile desertions was that of Henri Maillot (1928–56). A European-origin member of the PCA, Maillot's attachment to Algeria and the Algerian people prompted him to join forces with the independence struggle. Maillot deserted in April 1956, taking weapons with him to the ALN's rural guerrilla. He was killed in action in June. In addition to these desertions, there were 420 conscientious objectors and 12,000 French soldiers who did not present themselves for duty when called up. This disobedience represented one per cent of the total number of soldiers called up, a lower percentage than in most wars (Quemeneur 2011).

In 1960, public debate surrounding French soldiers going to fight in Algeria reached a peak, with the publication of the 'Manifesto of the 121' ('Manifeste des 121'). Signed by 121 French intellectuals and artists from various left-wing backgrounds, the Manifesto declared that the refusal to serve in the French army in Algeria was justified and that the French people had the right to support and protect the oppressed Algerian people. Moreover, it argued that 'The cause of the Algerian people, which is decisively contributing to destroying the colonial system, is the cause of all free men'. The Manifesto was published on 6 September 1960, a day after the trial of 24 *porteurs de valises* ('suitcase carriers') opened. Established by the existentialist philosopher Francis Jeanson (1922–2009), the *porteurs de valises* was a network composed of French and Algerian activists who transported funds and documents for the FLN in mainland France (Ulloa 2007; Evans 1997).

By the final year of the war, morale was steady declining amongst French soldiers: 'no-one wanted to be the last person to die in this war without a name' (Jauffret 2011, 133). Life in the army could be boring as well as dangerous, with most conscripts counting down the days until the end of their tour. By 1962, many metropolitan conscripts blamed the settlers for forcing them to waste their youth and risk their lives in Algeria, and after the creation of the OAS in early 1961, there was open conflict between the French army and the OAS.

Testimonies recounting torture carried out by the French army became commonplace in a few French newspapers and magazines from 1957 onwards (<<Chap. 3, pp. 94–5). Television and radio, which was state-owned, remained under French government control. Most of the large national newspapers and magazines also reproduced the government message that French soldiers were fighting bravely, the right military and political decisions were being taken and the vast majority of the 'Muslim' population wanted to remain French (by 1962, this official message had switched to the necessity of peace and the end of French Algeria (>>Chap. 3, p. 139)). In other, smaller, outlets, dissenting voices began to be heard—for example, in the PCF's *L'Humanité*, the satirical *Le Canard enchaîné*, the liberal Christian *Témoignage chrétien*, as well as in *L'Express, Les Temps modernes* and *L'Esprit*. Soldiers returning from Algeria were seen as particularly convincing eyewitnesses to persuade the wider French public that all was not well in Algeria (Eveno 2005; in English see Kuby 2013; McDonnell 2018). In their published accounts, soldiers described the torture, pillage, rape and violence which they had witnessed the French army committing against Algerians. They described Algerians being treated as sub-human. The war was depicted as destroying Algeria, French youth, and France. In 1959, a survey was carried out with 533 returning conscripts by the Study and Research Group on Youth Organisations and Popular Education (Groupe d'études et de recherche sur les organisations de jeunesse et d'éducation populaire), which brought together 53 organisations demanding the end of the war in Algeria. When asked what their worst memory of the war was, for 18 per cent of those questioned it was the 'humiliations', 'brutality', 'acts of violence', 'abuse' and 'torture' inflicted on the Algerian population. Some even compared what the French army was doing to the actions of the Nazis during the Second World War. A few interviewees described what they saw as too horrible to speak about (Bantigny 2007).

In oral histories with former soldiers carried out during the 1990s, such as the large-scale interviewing projects conducted by historians Anne Roche and Jean-Charles Jauffret and their students, interviewees rarely referred to torture, sexual violence or the execution of prisoners. When they did, they employed euphemistic expressions such as 'heavy handed interrogations' or 'blunders' (Jauffret 2011, 244). Those who acknowledged that torture took place rarely said that they were direct witnesses, and much less participants. Some interviewees condemned torture, others stated that the purpose of extracting vital information justified its use, others still argued that that the FLN/ALN was even more brutal (Roche and Belgacem 2017). These interviews took place before the re-emergence of the 'torture debate' in the French media from 2000 onwards (>>Chap. 4, p. 183). In interviews carried out with soldiers since this date, torture is a key theme, although interviewees nearly always present themselves as bystanders, not perpetrators. The exception to this tends to be intelligence officers who are much franker about their use of torture. An emphasis on the violence of, or fear of the violence of, the FLN/ALN remains a key theme in French soldiers' accounts (i.e. they present themselves as victims). More recent interviews are also more likely to include French soldiers expressing their sympathy with *harkis* (also seen as victims)—again, in the past two decades, the particular place of *harkis* in the war has been subject to notable French media attention (>>Chap. 4, pp. 172–4, 184, 187–8). In contrast to the plethora of memoirs of professional and conscripted metropolitan soldiers about their Algerian War, there are very few memoirs of, or academic works about, soldiers of settler origin. In part, this seems to be because they were often mixed in with metropolitan soldiers so do not have a distinct 'memory', in part it might also be because of the concerted effort after 1962 by associations of former settlers to construct an image of themselves as civilian victims of the FLN and the French army (>>Chap. 4, pp. 170–2).

Harkis: *Algerian Soldiers and Auxiliaries in the French Army: Particularly Dangerous and Particularly Useful, with Complicated Memories*

In 1960, 100,000–150,000 Algerians were enrolled in the French army (Hautreux 2011, 45). The majority of these men were enrolled into distinct auxiliary units, called *harkas*, from the Arabic word for movement. From this is derived the term *harki*. After 1962, the meaning of the term *harki* would come to be used to describe all Algerians serving in the French army (auxiliaries and regular conscripts) as well as Algerian notables seen as 'pro-French' (>>Chap. 4, p. 161). Some older generations in Algeria also use an older French term to describe North African soldiers in the French army, 'goumier'.

There were different kinds of auxiliary units in the French army. Their roles ranged from cooking, to translating, to 'self-defence' units created in villages to ward off ALN incursions. Some were SAS auxiliaries, others were in *commandos de chasse*. Some Algerians were also conscripted into the regular French army, notably in 1959, because the mobilisation of French men to fight in the Second World War in 1940 had led to a dip in the birth rate and, 19 years later, a shortage of 18 year olds (Hautreux 2013, 141). Many Algerians refused conscription. The call up to the French army could be a prompt to instead join the ALN, if they had not already done so. The difficulty of knowing exactly how many Algerians served in French army in regular units or as auxiliaries between 1954 and 1962 is reflected in the fact that estimates range from 200,000 to 400,000. François-Xavier Hautreux (2011, 45–46) has calculated that this means that between 10 and 20 per cent of the Algerian rural population was enrolled in the French army at some point during the war.

Having large numbers of Algerians in the French army was a potentially risky strategy—there was a far higher risk of these soldiers deserting, or spying for the FLN. The FLN had networks of informers and double agents amongst *harkis*, and their wives and families. 1956 was the year in which there was the highest percentage of desertions: 1.57 per cent of men in auxiliary units deserted and 4.43 per cent in regular units. These desertions were often collective, sometimes deserters took their weapons with them, and in some cases, they killed other members of their unit before they left (Hautreux 2013, 77). French army generals nevertheless considered that these risks were outweighed by the advantages: these soldiers knew the terrain, they spoke local languages and they were sometimes familiar with the families of men who had joined the ALN in the villages where they conducted operations. Whereas Algerians conscripted into the regular army served across Algeria, *harki* auxiliary units tended to stay in their region of origin: 'In a way, recruiting [Algerian] auxiliaries was like arming peasants to fight their neighbours' (Hautreux 2013, 21). It was hoped that this would have a demoralising effect on the FLN and their supporters.

The reasons why these men chose to join as auxiliaries were varied. A few of those who joined the French army were devoted to the 'motherland', such as the much-publicised Saïd 'Bachaga' Boualem (1906–82). For some, long-standing local animosities meant that if a neighbouring rival family went over to the FLN, you went over to France in order to perpetuate the feud. For others, joining the French army was an act of revenge for violence committed against family members by the FLN. Other *harkis* were former ALN rural guerrillas who were forced to join the French army after their capture. Indeed, trying to 'turn' ALN soldiers through intense 'psychological action' (i.e. threats against their families and torture) was one of the techniques which the French army had brought to Algeria from their Indochinese experience. Even if they were not 'turned', giving the impression to their fellow ALN soldiers on the outside that they had switched sides was just as useful, because it could sow destructive paranoia, infighting and purges. For most *harkis*, the main motivation for joining the French army was poverty.

The relationship between *harkis* and the wider Algerian population was complex. On the ground, many rural families had a *harki* in their family and other members of their family in the FLN/ALN. In the village of Tifelfel in the Aures mountains, women detained by the French army in a makeshift prison as collective punishment for their husbands joining the ALN describe acts of solidarity from Algerian and Moroccan 'goumiers' serving in the French army who were guarding them. These included intervening when beatings went 'too far'. But Algerian, Moroccan and French soldiers also participated in the regular rape and torture of these women (Adel 2019). For Fatima Berci in the village of Agraradj in Kabylia, Algerians in the French army were noteworthy perpetrators of acts of violence and rape: 'It was a clean war as long as there were no goumiers. The goumiers did a lot of harm' (Vince 2015, 62). We should be wary of making generalisations about the motivations and behaviour of Algerians who served in the French army during the War of Independence. After 1962, two politicised narratives about the harkis were consolidated in France (the *harkis* were French loyalists who were not sufficiently recognised) and in Algeria (the *harkis* were traitors to the nation) which have powerfully shaped both public and academic discussion (>>Chap. 4, pp. 161–5).

Tirailleurs sénégalais: *The Limits of Pan-African, Pan-Muslim Solidarity and the Messy Ends of Empire*

In February 1958, the FLN newspaper *El Moudjahid* issued a plea to sub-Saharan African politicians, urging them to take a stronger position internationally in favour of Algerian independence: 'The ministers and deputies who do not dare to energetically denounce the use of African soldiers against another colonised people allow brothers to kill each other for the great amusement of French racists' (Zimmerman 2011, 140). Politically and economically dependent on France, and socially and culturally very close to the French political class, many sub-Saharan African political leaders were cautious about criticising France, even after their countries became formally independent in 1960 (<<Chap. 3, p. 74). This was to the frustration of trade unions and student movements in sub-Saharan Africa, many of whom were actively critiquing the war in Algeria (Ginio 2016). African soldiers in the French army 'faced the opprobrium of radical youth in Dakar and Bamako' (Mann 2006, 181).

Whether this would have bothered them was questionable. Many of the sub-Saharan African soldiers in the French army in Algeria in 1954 and 1955 were already veterans of France's colonial war in Indochina. From 1956 onwards, the French army led a recruitment drive in West Africa, seeking to reinforce its numbers. That year, around 25,000 African soldiers were serving in Algeria (Mann 2006, 22). Some were volunteers (career soldiers), others were drafted. The majority served in separate units for colonial troops, although some were integrated into the regular army. The term 'tirailleurs sénégalais' ('Senegalese sharpshooters') is often generically used to describe these sub-Saharan African soldiers, a reference to the specific unit in the French army for West African (not just Senegalese) soldiers. In urban and rural areas, so-called *tirailleurs sénégalais* participated in the same kinds of operations as other troops: patrols, ambushes, searching villages and homes, rounding up 'suspect elements' and displacing rural populations into *camps de regroupement*.

Pursuing its strategy of appealing to different groups who might be susceptible to condemning colonialism and supporting the cause of independence (the Jewish population of Algeria, liberals, conscripts, etc.), the FLN targeted specific propaganda at sub-Saharan African troops. Via pamphlets and the radio, the FLN called on them to defect and return home, or even join the FLN. Their message focused on their shared suffering as colonial subjects, the ingratitude of the French army towards its colonial soldiers, and injustices committed in France's colonies in sub-Saharan Africa. Less often, there were references to the shared religion of Islam across North and West Africa (Ginio 2016, 114–116). In turn, the French army carefully monitored the military and psychological training of these soldiers, scrutinised their morale and dispensed its own propaganda, particularly concerned that Islam would prove a source of affinity between Algerians and West Africans (Ginio 2016, 121). Defections from the French army by *tirailleurs sénégalais*, were, however, vanishingly rare. The FLN's evocation of sub-Saharan African troops as fellow colonised men and brothers was a rhetorical ploy as much as a genuine belief. *Tirailleurs sénégalais* did not have a positive reputation amongst the wider Algerian population. This type of unit had participated in the repression in the region of Setif and Guelma after 8 May 1945 (<<Chap. 2, pp. 47–9). Indeed, they were considered so terrifying that 'saligani' ('Senegalese') was inscribed into Algerian oral tradition as an object of fear in popular poetry and in tales to scare small children (Sabeur 2017).

Subsequent interviews with sub-Saharan African soldiers who participated in the Algerian War in the French army suggest that did not identify with either the 'coloniser' or 'the colonised'. Rather, they saw themselves as soldiers in an army with a battle to fight. This this was military duty, not an ideological commitment. In cases where soldiers volunteered, they had done so for financial reasons. Algerians appear in their accounts not as brothers, fellow Muslims or a fellow colonised people, but rather as 'the enemy', particularly because this was an irregular war in which the adversary did not necessarily wear a uniform (Mbaye 2011; Zimmerman 2011; Ginio 2016 see also Khoulé 2011). The accounts of sub-Saharan African soldiers of their war in Algeria share many common features with those of French soldiers (and indeed those of soldiers in the ALN)—they talk about the operations in which they participated and they emphasise the violence of the enemy rather than their own violence. There are also some different elements: some veterans discuss the importance of keeping talismans (*gris gris*) as protection against death and injury, whilst others mention the use of Wolof speakers to transmit cable messages between French army units, because this was a language which was incomprehensible to Algerians if communications were intercepted (Mbaye 2011, 48).

Another specificity of the presence of sub-Saharan African soldiers in the French army between 1954 and 1962 is that their countries of origin became independent in the middle of the conflict. Undoubtedly, the Algerian War of Independence sped up French decolonisation elsewhere. For Guinean soldiers, independence came in 1958, when Guinea voted not to become part of the new 'French Community' proposed by de Gaulle to redefine France's relationship with its sub-Saharan African colonies. Ahmed Sekou Touré (1922–84), who led the 'no' vote and became Guinea's first president, was openly pro-FLN and demanded that Guinean soldiers be demobilised and repatriated. The rest of the West African soldiers were demobilised and repatriated once their countries became independent in 1960, although this was not necessarily straightaway (Zimmerman 2011) (>>Chap. 4, p. 162).

In the interviews which exist, former sub-Saharan African soldiers explicitly discuss torture and extra-judicial killings (Mbaye 2011, 45). Like French soldiers, interviewees are always bystanders and not perpetrators, but in this case, sub-Saharan African soldiers place the responsibility for these acts of violence not with just 'other soldiers', but with 'the French'. In the words of Massamba Arame Ndiaye (an ex-sergeant in a unit of *tirailleurs sénégalais*): 'It was French soldiers who did that [carried out torture] and not Africans' (Mbaye 2011, 45). The idea that sub-Saharan African soldiers did not participate in torture contradicts accounts of the time and memories of Algerian populations who came into contact with them. In one of the sets of case notes that psychiatrist Frantz Fanon included in his 1961 book *The Wretched of the Earth*, a European-origin police officer described his participation in extensive torture sessions after the arrest of suspects: 'In the end your fists are ruined. So you call in the Senegalese. But they either hit too hard and destroy the creature or else they don't hit hard enough and it's no good' (Fanon 2001, 216).

Soldiers in the ALN: Embedded in, But Also (Partly) Transforming Algerian Society

Men and women who fought in the ALN were volunteers. The overriding motivation was to liberate Algeria from French rule. But these volunteers were also selected—not everyone who wanted to join the rural guerrilla, or plant a bomb in the city, was allowed to do so. The ALN leadership needed to be sure that new recruits could be trusted, and this is why they were often tested before they were allowed to join—given a task such as stealing a weapon or even carrying out an attack. Particularly in rural areas, the ALN leadership also needed to be reasonably convinced that recruits were in sufficient physical health to deal with the conditions of guerrilla warfare, which involved constant marching over difficult terrain, exposure to harsh weather and poor nutrition, in addition to the risk of death in combat. Given the FLN/ALN was a clandestine organisation, family networks played a key role in recruitment. The student strike in May 1956 (<<Chap. 3, pp. 84–5) also sent young urban men and some women into the up into the ALN's rural guerrilla units. The whole point of revolutionary warfare, however, was that it made the people—that is, the wider civilian population—an integral part of the struggle (Djerbal 2010). The survival of the ALN was dependent on both a formal network of auxiliaries called *mousebbiline* (Djerbal 2003) and a more informal, but equally crucial, network of mostly women, and indeed children, who cooked, healed and acted as lookout or spied on the French army.

Some of the first men in the ALN had quite extensive military experience as a result of service in the French army. They would often draw on this to provide basic training to other recruits in shooting, observation, camouflage, ambushes, transmission, setting up camps and tactics (Aït-el-Djoudi 2007, 103). ALN soldiers also received a political and moral education, focusing on God, the motherland and unity (Aït-el-Djoudi 2007, 109). From April 1956, some of this training was in camps in Morocco and Tunisia, but most men in the *maquis* learnt 'on the job'. From 1959 onwards, after the first groups of rural guerrillas had been significantly depleted as a result of French army operations, their replacements were less politicised and less well trained (Branche 2019, 121). Different groups of rural guerrillas were more dispersed, and for many simply holding out became the priority.

Debating the nature of Algerian nationalism: the term *mujahidin*

In discussing what the FLN 'was', much discussion has centred on the religiously inflected terminology it used to describe the conflict and its participants. Regular soldiers could be referred to as soldiers—in Arabic *junūd* [sometimes transliterated as djunud] (singular: *jundi* [djundi]) but often they were referred to as *mujahidin* [sometimes transliterated as moudjahidine], the plural of the Arabic *mujāhid* [moudjahid], meaning holy warrior. The FLN newspaper was called *El Moudjahid*. Men and women in, or supporting, the FLN/ALN referred to each other as 'brothers' and 'sisters', a fraternal language which evoked the *umma*, the community of believers (<<Chap. 2, p. 32). Those who were killed in combat were *shuhada* (martyrs). Both 'jihad' (holy war) and 'mujahid' have become highly charged terms since the 1980s and the conflict between the USSR and the Taliban in Afghanistan, and then between the United States and the Taliban in the 2000s. The Taliban fighters are also referred to as the *mujahidin*. In the 1950s, however, the FLN was not seeking to wage a religious war, much less establish a theocratic state. Rather, the language of religion was a familiar, unifying language, as were religious rituals. Soldiers in the ALN prayed with civilians and fasted with them during Ramadan. They reproduced societal codes, for example by having separate sleeping areas for women and men in rural guerrilla units. The ALN presented themselves to local populations as liberators in a new army, but first and foremost, they also had to be seen as 'men of honour, faithful to the values of the society to which they belonged' (Branche 2019, 114).

For a long time, it was taboo to write one's memoirs in Algeria. It seemed to go against the wartime slogans 'one sole hero, the people' and 'by the people, for the people'. The popular suspicion was that the more you had to say about the war, the less likely it was that you actually participated in it. Most participants in any case could not write their memoirs as they were illiterate. From the 1990s onwards, as the wartime generation aged, the publication of memoirs nevertheless grew exponentially. These tend to be very similar to memoirs of other kinds of resistance movements and wars: there is an emphasis on recounting daring military operations in rich detail, criticising the violence of the other side and skimming over 'our' violence. When those who were on 'our' side are critiqued, it is often with an eye on what happened next—that is, the person became part of an opposing party or disliked faction in the post-independence period. Across the memoirs of men and women of different political tendencies, the core values of the war—the sacrifice of the people, the unity of purpose—are nevertheless consistently reproduced (>>Chap. 4, pp. 168–9, 175–8).

Debating the nature of Algerian nationalism: women in the ALN

In a society in which the separation of the sexes was a principle of social organisation, the presence of women both in the ALN's military operations and as part of civilian support networks was strikingly novel. In 1974, out of 336,784 officially recognised veterans, 10,949 were women (Amrane 1991, 225–227). This figure undoubtedly vastly underestimates the number of women who participated in the war. It certainly excludes the majority of women in the ALN's rural support networks. In villages where most of the men had already left (to join the ALN or to find work in France), it was rural women who received ALN soldiers when they came looking for food or cover. The official statistic on female veterans is more likely to include women who were nurses in ALN rural guerrilla units and in urban bomb networks. In towns and cities, women planted bombs and went into hiding alongside men (<<Chap. 3, pp. 91–5). There were about 2000 women in the ALN's rural guerrilla units, mostly very young (half were under 20, 90 per cent were under 30) and they mainly occupied medical roles—that is, they were nurses (Amrane 1991). For one former nurse in the *wilaya* 4, Fadéla Mesli (later a deputy in the Algerian Constituent Assembly): 'We had two struggles to lead, the struggle against colonialism, and the struggle in our families. A woman who lived amongst men, there were dangers, there were our customs. We led two revolutions, one against colonialism, the other against taboos, and I would say that the latter was even more difficult' (Vince 2015, 96–97).

Talking about their experiences many years later, women who were in the ALN's rural guerrilla units are very clear that they were treated with the utmost respect by their brothers-in-arms, who respected their contribution and treated them like sisters, not potential wives or sexual conquests. The stories of rural women who were part of the support networks are similar—they say that treated those who came from the mountains like their sons, in turn they were considered to be the *mujahidin*'s 'mothers' and 'sisters' (Vince 2015; Seferdjeli 2012; Amrane 1991). Yet in captured FLN/ALN documents held in the French army archives, there are examples of ALN soldiers being sanctioned by their superiors for rape, and some local leaders were desperate to get rid of the women in their units, complaining that the 'laws of nature' were getting in the way of fighting (Vince 2015, 90–91). The 'asexual' nature of life in rural guerrilla units is also thrown into question by the fact that the ALN started to regulate marriage between male and female combatants. Significantly, however, when female former combatants today do talk about sexist behaviour or sexual harassment, they always blame this on 'false' or 'eleventh hour' *mujahidin*. Morally reprehensible behaviour is presented as connected to political illegitimacy. The subtext is that 'true' *mujahidin* would not behave in such a way (Vince 2015, 107–110) (>>Chap. 4, p. 177).

16 SEPTEMBER 1959 OR THE MANY POTENTIAL ENDS OF EMPIRE

Many historians—among them Benjamin Stora in his 2010 book *Le Mystère de Gaulle* (The de Gaulle mystery)—point to a televised speech made by de Gaulle in autumn 1959 as the key moment when de Gaulle publicly indicated that had changed his mind about Algeria. On 16 September 1959, to general surprise, de Gaulle uttered for the first time the word 'self-determination', and in doing so recognised the right of the Algerian majority to choose its political future. De Gaulle presented three options for the future of Algeria: secession, Frenchification or a federal relationship. He argued that secession, a total separation, would be a political and economic disaster for Algerians leading to communist dictatorship. Frenchification would necessitate making Algeria an indistinguishable part of France and Algerians French, which he judged unrealistic. De Gaulle's preferred choice was a federal relationship, in which Algeria was ruled by Algerians, but with close, interdependent ties with France in key areas such as the economy, education, defence and foreign policy. Yet 16 September 1959 was not the starting point of a straight line to the signature of the final peace agreement, the Evian Accords, in March 1962.

The relationship between politics and violence: possible alternative ends to empire?

Today, the majority of historians would agree that the form which the end of empire took in Algeria (and indeed across Africa)—that is to say, the transfer of power from empires to a series of nation-states—was neither inevitable nor carefully planned by European states. Challenging teleological readings of decolonisation (i.e. reading history backwards with the assumption that everything is leading up to the final outcome) has been pioneered by Frederick Cooper (2005, 2014). Drawing upon his work, a number of historians have paid close attention to alternative endings of empire in Algeria which French politicians and civil servants imagined might be possible in the late 1950s and early 1960s. These included 'Eurafrique' (Eurafrica), partition and a fully integrated Franco-Algerian nation. These alternative endings—or rather transformations—of empire also need to be understood as part of a longer history of colonial states thinking about, and colonised peoples urgently pressing for, political and socio-economic change.

Eurafrique *(Eurafrica)*

Contrary to the long-held idea that France chose to *replace* its empire by invest-ing in European construction—that is to say, it swapped one embodiment of international greatness and rank for another—European construction was inti-mately *intertwined* with the reimagining of empire (Brown 2017; Shaev 2018). *Eurafrique* (Eurafrica) was a nebulous term which began to emerge in the 1920s. It referred to the potential for Europe and Africa to form one unit politically, economically, socially and culturally in order to promote mutual development. After the Second World War, *Eurafrique* was pitched as an alter-native to the end of empire and the creation of sovereign nation-states, it was 'an economic and political bloc for the preservation of France's geopolitical position' (McDougall 2017b). For many French civil servants and politicians, France and Algeria were imagined together as part of *Eurafrique*. Algeria became part of the EEC with the signing of the Treaty of Rome in 1957. The Common Market and the Constantine Plan both began at the same time, and dealt with some of the same issues, notably how to bring together very differ-ent economic contexts and political and social structures, and balance eco-nomic and political concerns. As Muriam Haleh Davis (2018, 48) underlines: 'in the 1950s, empire was both a model for, and an integral component of, European integration'.

Partition

In 1961, Peyrefitte published an essay titled *Faut-il partager l'Algérie?* (Should Algeria be partitioned?). In this report, filled with maps sketching out potential new borders, he proposed partition as means to end the conflict and move towards peaceful cohabitation and association, with a zone created from Algiers to Oran under French rule, where the 'Europeans' of Algeria and pro-French 'Muslims' would live, with the rest of Algeria's 'Muslims' under the rule of the FLN. French bureaucrats looked around the world for comparisons, often sim-plifying very complex situations in Ireland, Palestine, India, Cyprus, Yugoslavia and Berlin, which they might draw upon in the formulation of their plans (Asseraf 2018).

Eurafrique + *Partition* = *Common Organisation of the Saharan Regions*

At the intersection of ideas about Eurafrica and partition was the Common Organisation of the Saharan Regions (Organisation commune des regions sahariennes, OCRS). In the course of the Algerian War of Independence, the Sahara had grown in political and economic importance. Oil was first discovered in 1956 and the first atomic bomb test took place in Reggane in February 1960 (Fig. 2.1). Formally established in 1957, the OCRS united the Saharan regions of Algeria, Mauritania, Niger and Chad, with the stated aim of their 'development [*mise-en-valeur*], economic expansion and social promotion'. Representatives of all the member countries were involved in administering the organisation, but France remained the dominant player. The OCRS was a new kind of political/administrative/socio-economic entity. Neither nation-state nor empire, it only covered parts of the territory of each of the countries involved. It aimed to enable France to maintain its strategic and economic interests in the region, and at the same time be a blueprint for a new kind of transnational, trans-Mediterranean Franco-African relationship built on mutual benefit and exchange (Sèbe 2010; Suggitt 2018). The functioning of the organisation was already complicated by the independence of Mauritania, Niger, Mali and Chad in 1960, and the differing attitudes of these nation-states' new political leaders towards participating in the OCRS, or not. The FLN had always insisted that the Sahara was an integral part of Algerian territory, and the OCRS died as an organisation and as an idea with Algerian independence.

JANUARY–FEBRUARY 1960: THE 'WEEK OF THE BARRICADES' AND GROWING SETTLER UNEASE WITH THE POLITICAL DIRECTION TAKEN BY THE GOVERNMENT IN PARIS

Having acclaimed de Gaulle's return to power, the European population of Algeria was increasingly angry with the political direction being taken in Paris. This anger was shared by some army generals. In January 1960, General Massu was transferred back to mainland France for publicly criticising de Gaulle's management of the conflict. In response, from 24 January to 1 February 1960, the European population of Algiers blocked a number of major roads in the city in the 'week of the barricades' ('la semaine des barricades'). When gendarmes were sent to break up the barricades, there were violent confrontations, resulting in 14 gendarmes and eight demonstrators being killed. Two of the key organisers of the week of the barricades were Lagaillarde and Ortiz, who had previously played a central role in the 'May Days' of 1958 (<<Chap. 3, pp. 109–10). They were joined by Jean-Jacques Susini (1933–2017), president of the General Association of Students of Algeria (AGEA). De Gaulle refused to budge, public opinion in mainland France was unsympathetic to the Europeans involved in the protest and the movement petered out (Evans 2012, 270–275).

The relationship between politics and violence: impossible alternative ends to empire?

Studying all these alternative ends of empire has been very useful in challenging the long-held assumption (in reality a post-hoc rationalisation) that it was inevitable that decolonisation would result in an Algerian nation-state and a French nation-state recentred on metropolitan France, within the territorial boundaries which are the lines on the map today. However, how realistic were these alternatives? The fundamental issue was that the FLN would not have accepted any of them. The FLN was vehemently opposed to the OCRS and any kind of partition which threatened to undermine Algeria's unity and territorial integrity. On 5 July 1961, following five days of general strike, there were massive demonstrations of Algerians against partition. The FLN was living in the shadow of a number of what they saw as disastrous partitions, from the partition of Palestine and the creation of the state of Israel in 1948 to secession in the Belgian Congo in 1960. In the Congo, independence under Patrice Lumumba (1925–61) was rapidly followed by the secession of mineral-rich Katanga, an area where Belgium maintained troops, and the assassination of Lumumba in January 1961 (Asseraf 2018, 102). All of these alternative ends of empire would have necessitated French state violence on a huge scale to make them happen. This in turn would have fatally undermined the new models of more equal governance which they were seeking to achieve. Like 'integration' (<<Chap. 3, pp. 72, 98–9, 110), these were 'impossible' endings (McDougall 2017b). In a curious coda, the first President of Algeria, Ben Bella, expressed a mild and fleeting interest in *Eurafrique* after independence. In December 1962, keen to secure all possible sources of funding for the new Algerian state, he wrote to the president of the EEC Council to ask if Algeria would still be included in the programmes of the European Community (Brown 2017, 199).

UN RESOLUTION 1573 IN DECEMBER 1960, THE 8 JANUARY 1961 REFERENDUM ON SELF-DETERMINATION

On 1 December 1960, the French government announced that a referendum on self-determination in Algeria would take place on 8 January 1961. Ten days later, on 11 December 1960, a huge wave of demonstrations began across Algeria in support of the FLN and independence, which were loosely organised by the FLN (Meynier 2002, 466). Men, women and children took to the streets, and notably took to the streets of 'European areas' in the cities and towns of Algeria, waving the Algerian flag and chanting 'Long live the FLN', 'Long live the GPRA', 'Abbas in power', 'Free Ben Bella' and 'Independent Algeria' (Rigouste 2017).

The demonstrations were timed to coincide with another UN vote on the 'Algerian Question'. On 19 December 1960, after years of lobbying by the FLN and their international supporters, UN resolution 1573 received a majority of votes (63 to eight) at the General Assembly. The resolution recognised 'the passionate yearning for freedom of all dependent peoples and the decisive role of such peoples in the attainment of their independence', 'the right of the Algerian people to self-determination and independence' and 'the territorial integrity of Algeria'. The additional motion for a UN-supervised referendum failed to pass by only one vote.

Less than a month later, men and women across metropolitan France, its overseas territories and Algeria voted overwhelmingly in favour of self-determination, by 75 per cent to 25 per cent. In mainland France, the majority of voters were increasingly weary of the protracted conflict. In Algeria, after 1958, 'European' votes were no longer worth more than 'Muslim' votes, which meant that the Europeans of Algeria were outnumbered (<<Chap. 3, p. 112). The 'no' vote, rejecting self-determination, won by a large margin in areas where there was a European majority, such as the centre of Algiers and in the city of Oran. In cities, many Algerian voters followed the FLN orders to boycott the vote—as they did not recognise the legitimacy of the French state to organise such a poll—but elsewhere in the country Algerians did participate in the referendum, and voted 'yes'.

January 1961: The Creation of the OAS, 23 April 1961—The Generals' Putsch

In response to the result of the 8 January 1961 referendum, the Secret Armed Organisation (Organisation Armée Secrète, sometimes translated as Secret Army Organisation, OAS) was founded. The goal of the OAS was to keep Algeria French by all means judged necessary, including violence. The OAS was created in Madrid because three of its founders—Lagaillarde, Ortiz and Susini—had fled to Franco's Spain to avoid trial following the 'week of the barricades'. They were joined by the (now retired) former commander-in-chief in Algeria, General Salan, following a failed military putsch which he was involved in alongside other senior figures in the French army on 23 April 1961. One of Salan's co-conspirators was another former commander-in-chief, General Challe. After the putsch failed, Challe surrendered, but other participants joined the OAS. The OAS was hoping to prompt mass desertions from the French army. However, the majority of both senior and rank-and-file soldiers (who were mostly conscripts, not professional soldiers) were either loyal to the French army or adopted a wait-and-see attitude.

Beyond their passionate belief in French Algeria, their rejection of the direction de Gaulle had taken in his Algeria policy and their hatred of the FLN, the military and civilian members of the OAS were ideologically diverse, and there were plenty of internal rivalries. Some members were Catholic traditionalists, some were fascists. Others—such as Jacques Soustelle and Georges Bidault (1899–1983)—were centre-right politicians who rejected what they saw as a radical redefinition of what 'France' meant and what it meant to be French. Bidault, a leading figure in the Second World War French resistance and former Prime Minister (in 1946 and 1949–50), argued that the 'amputation of a French province' was 'illegal, unconstitutional and illegitimate' (McDougall 2017a, 230). Characterised, both at the time and subsequently, as a reactionary, fascist movement, the OAS sought to counter this image by presenting itself as the defender of Republican principles using the language of the one and indivisible Republic proclaimed in the constitution, the idea that citizenship could not be revoked, and evoking assimilation and secularism (Shepard 2006, 90). Its name was a reference to the 'Armée Secrète' of the French resistance during the Second World War (Dard 2014, 641). But it was not clear what kind of Algeria it was fighting for—one which would stay within the Fifth Republic? A Federation? Or a kind of settler independence where white minority rule would continue, as in Rhodesia (Evans 2012, 291)?

The OAS began by carrying out assassinations against French politicians and civil servants whom it considered in favour of Algerian independence and individuals suspected of being in the FLN. It also produced pro-French Algeria propaganda (leaflets, posters, graffiti and pirate radio programmes). Although its slogan was 'The OAS strikes where it wants and when it wants', in Algeria the organisation was only ever really established in the cities of Oran, Algiers, Constantine and Bône (Annaba) (see Fig. 2.1), where there was a concentrated European population. Despite having a number of fascists and anti-Semites in their ranks, the OAS made a concerted effort, in some cases successful, to recruit amongst the Jewish population of Algeria. Despite plenty of evidence of its anti-Arab racism, it even recruited a handful of Algerians. Its hard core of full-time members was never more than 1000 (Dard 2014, 641). The OAS nevertheless benefited from the complicity and the support of significant sections of the European population of Algeria, who were encouraged to participate in public demonstrations of support by banging pots and pans at their window, or honking 'Al-gé-rie fran-çaise' on their horn (three short beeps and two long ones) (Branche 2007, 328). From the ceasefire onwards, there was also increasingly widespread participation by the European population of Algeria in OAS acts of violence (Thénault 2008) (>>Chap. 3, pp. 141–2).

17 OCTOBER 1961 IN A LONGER CONTEXT: 'THE BATTLE OF FRANCE'

Along with the referendum on self-determination, the creation of the OAS and the Generals' Putsch, a date which today would be on any timeline of the Algerian War in 1961, particularly those produced in France, is 17 October. Indeed, having long been ignored, 17 October today has particular visibility in French public histories of the conflict. As night fell on 17 October 1961, 30,000 unarmed Algerians—men, women and some children—converged on the centre of Paris from the shantytowns and slum housing where the majority of them lived. Organised by the FF-FLN, the demonstrators were objecting to the application of a curfew on Algerian workers, imposed twelve days earlier, which forbade them from leaving their homes between 8.30 pm and 5.30 am. They were also marching in favour of independence and against police brutality. At a number of points in the city, the demonstrators were violently attacked by the police and by the Auxiliary Police Force (Force de police auxiliaire, FPA) (>>Chap. 3, p. 137). An estimated 50 to 200 Algerians were beaten to death and shot by the police, with a number of bodies thrown into the Seine. Around half of the demonstrators were arrested. A week later, more than 14,000 protesters were still being held in improvised detention centres. Many of them had been tortured (Cole 2003, 116). Thousands were expelled to Algeria.

On 20 October 1961, Algerian women and the French wives of Algerian men, came out to demonstrate again, in protest at what had happened three days previously and in support of those still detained. There were a number of small scale protests by French workers and intellectuals. Accounts of police violence against Algerians were published in the French and international press. *France Observateur* included some of the photographs taken by Elie Kagan, who had captured images of Algerians being rounded up as well as photographing dead and injured demonstrators (Gordon 2015, 344). The demonstration and its aftermath were quickly hushed up by the police and the government, who refused to admit the extent of the violence or the number of deaths, officially acknowledged as two people. The official French position was that the police were acting in self-defence and FLN-MNA rivalries were largely to blame for the violence.

The terms of future debates: 17 October 1961
When 17 October 1961 first re-emerged in public and scholarly debates in the 2000s, the focus was on the number of Algerians who had been killed: a low number was seen evidence of 'reasonable' police force, and a high number proof of a police 'massacre'. More recent scholarship has moved away from the numbers debate and situated 17 October in a longer history of the French police beating and killing Algerians. Historians have argued that what happened on 17 October 1961 needs to be understood as part of a *system*, which combined 'specialised' policing of Algerians in France and counter-revolutionary warfare, not an isolated event where things got out of control. This was not simply an extension of the violence in Algeria into the metropole. Rather, the ongoing war in Algeria intersected with a long-established history of policing North Africans in mainland France in targetted ways (Blanchard 2011). Moreover, under the orders of the Paris Prefect (head) of police Maurice Papon (1910–2007), Paris witnessed its own particular development of counter-insurgency theory and methods (House and Macmaster 2006; Amiri 2004; Prakash 2013).

'The Battle of France', as Lindi Amiri (2004) has termed the struggle between the French state and the FLN on metropolitan soil, also needs to be understood within the history of the FLN in mainland France, which was not just an offshoot or replica of the FLN organisation in Algeria. By 1958, the FLN was the dominant Algerian nationalist organisation in France, although the popularity of the MNA persisted in the metropole far more tenaciously than it did in Algeria. In June 1958, police reports estimated that the FLN in France had around 9000 militants, the MNA 4000 and about a third of the 329,000 Algerians in France were making regular financial contributions (paying the 'revolutionary tax') to the FLN and the MNA, with the FLN collecting nine-tenths of the total (Aissaoui 2012, 235). In spring 1958, following the arrest of a number of the FF-FLN's key leaders, the Federal Committee (Comité fédéral) of the FF-FLN had left France for Cologne in West Germany (Federal Republic of Germany, FRG). West Germany, however, was not necessarily a safe haven for the FLN. The French security services created a front called the 'la main rouge' (the red hand)—publicly believed to be a breakaway group composed of former French army parachutists, police and right-wing militants—as a cover for operations against the FLN. Notably, a series of bomb attacks and assassinations targeted its weapons supply chain (Von Bülow 2007).

In summer 1958, the decision was taken by the FLN to open a 'second front' in France with the aim of diverting French military and police attention from Algeria (although in fact troop numbers in Algeria would increase). A series of attacks were carried out against French targets, notably assassinations of policemen and attacks against infrastructure, such as setting oil depots on fire (Aissaoui 2009, 146). It was, however, a challenge to organise the war in France from Cologne. For the FF-FLN, the 17 October 1961 demonstration aimed to be a public display of force, showing the hold the FLN had over the Algerian population of Paris. It also sought to prove the organisational power of the FF-FLN leaders in Cologne and local leaders still in Paris, in relation to other parts of the FLN structure. Tensions between the different branches of the FLN were mounting as independence seemed increasingly likely. Indeed, the demonstration was called in defiance of GPRA orders (House and Macmaster 2006, 5).

Unlike in Algeria, the repression of the FLN in mainland France was not conducted by the army, but by the police and gendarmes. French police, gendarmes and the French state had a long history of singling out 'North Africans' (Algerians tended to be subsumed into this broader category) as a 'problem' population. They were seen as particularly prone to criminality and thus required 'specialised' forms of surveillance, control and social work intervention. As a result, there was also history of confrontation between the French police and Algerians in France. This ranged from street scuffles and localised riots following arrests (Blanchard 2012a; in English Howard 2013) to clashes between Algerian workers and police during trade union demonstrations (Blanchard 2012b). Police brutality was commonplace. In July 1957, the state of emergency already in force in Algeria was extended to mainland France. One of the main impacts was that internment (detention without trial) could henceforth be widely used.

In March 1958, just as the FF-FLN's Federal Committee was leaving Paris, Papon was nominated the Prefect of Police in the capital. Between 1949 and 1951 and then 1956 and 1958, Papon had been Prefect (appointed governor) of the Constantine region. He had also been General Secretary to the Resident General of Morocco between 1954 and 1955. In Paris, Papon began to work on developing methods to 'substitute repressive action with preventative action' (Prakash 2013, 502–503). These drew on military practices in Algeria, themselves based on ideas developed in Indochina about counter-insurgency, which incorporated mass repression and psychological action. In short, Papon introduced 'forms of state terror, which would normally be circumscribed to the military theatres of operation in North Africa, into the metropolitan capital' (House and Macmaster 2006, 15). SAS officers provided guidance on the establishment of the Technical Assistance Service for French Muslims of Algeria (Service d'assistance technique aux français musulmans d'Algérie, SAT-FMA), the SAS equivalent in mainland France. The SAT filed thousands of reports on Algerians and their political tendencies to identify potential suspects. The Auxiliary Police Force (FPA) was created in December 1959, composed of Algerian auxiliaries (*harkis*) led by French army officers assigned to the police. The FPA played a key role in leading operations to raid homes in Algerian areas looking for FLN activists, supporters and weapons. This was a source of significant tension between the police and the Algerian and wider North African population. Papon was responsible for imposing the curfew which prompted the 17 October 1961 demonstration, and for the conduct of the policing operation on that night. It was also because of Papon—and his earlier participation in another war—that in 1998, the memory of 17 October 1961 would resurface in French public debate (>>Chap. 4, p. 179).

8 FEBRUARY 1962: CHARONNE

In late 1961, what was capturing public attention in metropolitan France was not police brutality against Algerians but rather the increasing number of acts of violence committed by the OAS. By the start of 1962, the OAS was carrying out daily attacks on the French mainland. Bombs were set off outside government ministries, and intellectuals and journalists seen as sympathetic to the FLN were assassination targets (Evans 2012, 309). The French left (trade unions, communists, the non-communist left and students) began to organise a growing number of demonstrations against the war, against the OAS and in favour of peace in Algeria. Explicit support for Algerian independence was still not forthcoming from many on the French left. As Jim House and Neil Macmaster (2006, 17) argue: 'The registers of anti-fascism, anti-racism, and humanitarianism, and the theme of "Peace" in Algeria (as opposed to "Independence"), were constant fall-back solutions of the left during the period 1961–2 that either masked or displaced the political demands Algerians were making for independence'. On 8 February 1962, the PCF and trade unions organised a demonstration against OAS violence. In the course of the demonstration, scuffles with the police broke out. Eight people, including three women and a teenage boy, who sought refuge in the Charonne metro station were crushed and beaten to death following police charges. A ninth person later died in hospital.

The terms of future debates: Charonne and the PCF

'Charonne', as the demonstration and killings on 8 February 1962 would come to be known, prompted an immediate public reaction. A general strike took place across the Paris region, and hundreds of thousands of people marched through the capital, and in other major French cities. What happened on 8 February 1962 was a much more familiar kind of repression for the French left that what had happened to Algerian demonstrators on 17 October 1961. From its beginnings in the 1920s, the PCF had struggled to find a place for, and effectively mobilise, the Algerian population of France. Its political direction was undermined from the outset by 'the lack of reflection on the links between colonialism and the immigrants' political consciousness' (i.e. it struggled to combine working-class politics with anti-colonial politics). It was also caught between 'the denunciation of colonialism and participation in the apparatus of the state'—most famously, with PCF deputies in the National Assembly voting to give 'Special Powers' to the army in Algeria in 1956 (Izambert 2008, 109) (<<Chap. 3, p. 83). Protests surrounding Charonne, in contrast, could be situated in the long and proud revolutionary tradition of the people of Paris standing up to police violence, and losing their lives as a result. Charonne enabled the PCF in France to situate itself as an opponent of the Algerian War and supporter of independence—a position which it has maintained until the present—despite a much more complicated past (>>Chap. 4, p. 187).

THE IDEA THAT 'ALGERIA IS FRANCE' SHIFTS FROM MAINSTREAM CONSENSUS TO MINORITY BELIEF

When the FLN carried out its first attacks in November 1954, there was a broad consensus, from across the French political spectrum (Gaullists, Christian Democrats, Radicals, Socialists, trade unionists and most communists in France), and amongst most civil servants and journalists, that Algeria was, and should remain French. FLN representatives struggled to get the 'Algeria Question' on the UN agenda, let alone voted on. Five years later, this had dramatically changed. The reaction in metropolitan France to the settlers' week of the barricades in early 1960 had been unsympathetic. UN resolution 1573 had passed in December 1960. The results of the January 1961 referendum on self-determination were emphatic. The Generals' Putsch of April 1961 had failed, whereas a similar kind of manoeuvre had worked in 1958. There was increasing public outrage at the actions of the OAS, however much the organisation claimed to be defending the Republic. In short, 'By the early 1960s a late-blooming metropolitan consensus embraced an argument that ever since has functioned as fact: Algeria was not France, but a colony, and thus it deserved and would obtain independence' (Shepard 2006, 89).

Negotiations, Concessions and Internal Tensions

On 20 May 1961, a first round of negotiations started between the FLN's GPRA and the French government at Evian-les-bains, a French spa town on the border with Switzerland. This followed a number of false starts and years of both sides sending out tentative feelers. It was also preceded by the assassination of the socialist mayor of the town, Camille Blanc, on 31 March 1961 by the OAS, because he had accepted the presence of FLN representatives in his town. To get to the point of negotiations, the French government had conceded more than the FLN. In a speech on 23 October 1958, de Gaulle offered the FLN what he termed 'the peace of the brave' ('la paix des braves'), encouraging the FLN/ALN to lay down their weapons—with honour and dignity—but without negotiation. The FLN refused. De Gaulle had threatened diplomatic rupture with any country which recognised the GPRA, and still countries went ahead and recognised the FLN's provisional government. His prime minister, Debré, was a fervent believer in French Algeria, and this was now clearly coming to an end, one way or another. Even when de Gaulle publicly accepted the principle of self-determination in September 1959, he refused to recognise the FLN as the sole representative of the Algerian people. He attempted to use the release of Messali Hadj earlier that year to put pressure on the FLN, by implying that he had alternative interlocutors amongst Algerians. Messali Hadj in turn refused to play this game. De Gaulle long maintained hope that a 'third force'—composed of more 'compliant and moderate'—Algerian representatives could be found to negotiate with (House and Macmaster 2006, 4). But it was increasingly difficult to deny the FLN's claim that it alone embodied the Algerian people.

Talks thus opened at Evian-les-bains in May 1961 after de Gaulle finally accepted that France would only negotiate with the FLN's GPRA, and that a ceasefire would not be in place before talks began. At this point, the French negotiators nevertheless maintained that the Sahara was a French creation which should be kept under French control to preserve France's economic and strategic interests—this led to the breakdown of this first round of negotiations. In September 1961, de Gaulle conceded that Algeria would become independent with the Sahara as an integral part of its territory, enabling negotiations to recommence. For Byrne (2010, 225), the Evian Accords, when they were finally signed on 18 March 1962, were a 'failure of de Gaulle's original war aims'.

The FLN negotiators sent to Evian were also under pressure. These men were the delegates of the GPRA and tensions between the GPRA, the EMG on the border and the ALN *wilayat* fighting inside Algeria were running high. The GPRA accused Boumediene and the EMG of not sufficiently supporting the internal resistance, whilst Boumediene and the EMG accused the GPRA of being corrupt and incompetent. The *wilayat* of the interior considered that it was being ignored by both. The GPRA was well aware of the risk of being accused of 'selling out' Algeria and squandering the sacrifice of those who had died in the liberation struggle if they struck a deal which was viewed to be bad. Political solutions in general were viewed with suspicion within the nationalist movement—at so many points in the recent past going down the legalistic pathway had led to the dead end of French broken promises (Meynier 2002, 615–634; in English Evans 2012, 302 and 310–312). In August 1961, the President of the GPRA, Abbas, became the most high-profile political casualty of the GPRA's desire to not be seen as too moderate when he was replaced by Ben Khedda. The GPRA was also aware of the potential, if it struck a good deal for Algeria and Algerians, that this would make them popular and strengthen their position in the internal power struggles within the FLN.

The growing violence in Paris in early 1962 provided the final push for concluding the peace negotiations. Talks reopened a few days after the Charonne killings, on 11 February 1962. A final round of talks then began in Evian-les-bains on 7 March 1962. The peace agreement—henceforth known as the Evian Accords—was signed on 18 March and a ceasefire came into force on 19 March 1962. The news was greeted by scenes of joy across Algeria. The Evian Accords, and thus Algerian independence, were ratified in mainland France by referendum on 8 April 1962: 91 per cent of voters chose 'yes' and three per cent 'no', with a voter turnout of 75 per cent. Algerian independence under the terms of the Evian Accords was ratified in a referendum in Algeria on 1 July 1962: 99.7 per cent of voters voted 'yes', with 92 per cent voter turnout. Independence was declared on 3 July. 5 July would be designated as the official date of Algerian independence, marking 132 years to the day since French boots first landed on Algerian soil.

The GPRA negotiators had secured all of the FLN's primary war aims—Algeria was independent and its territorial integrity respected. The Evian Accords set out a transition period in which power would pass to a Franco-Algerian joint body, the Provisional Executive (Executif provisoire), headed by a former president of the Algerian Assembly, Abderrahmane Fares (1911–91), who was seen as a 'compromise figure' between Algerians and 'Europeans' (Thénault 2012a, 281). The Provisional Executive was based in the small coastal town of Rocher Noir (Boumerdes), 29 km to the east of Algiers. It had its own 40,000-strong 'local force' (Force locale), composed primarily of Algerian conscripts in the French army and auxiliaries (i.e. *harkis*), who were tasked with overseeing the ceasefire and organising the final referendum. The Accords also set out a blueprint for future Franco-Algerian relations, based on collaboration. Under the terms of the Evian Accords, France maintained privileged access to Algerian oil and gas, they kept the Mers-el-Kebir and Bou Sfer military bases for 15 years, their nuclear testing sites remained and the legal protection of European legal, property and cultural rights (i.e. the French language) were guaranteed. Inhabitants of Algeria had the possibility to choose French or Algerian nationality in the next three years. All of these provisions would be undermined in the ten years following independence. The new Algerian state changed its nationality law (>>Chap. 4, p. 158) and nationalised land, businesses, property, and oil and gas, whilst those *harkis* who sought to make France their home after 1962 were not treated as Frenchmen like any other (>>Chap. 4, pp. 161–5).

The Evian Accords were a short-lived victory for the GPRA. If de Gaulle failed in his war aims, he nevertheless remained president until 1969. The GPRA, in contrast, secured the FLN's war aims and was marginalised in the course of the next few months. The EMG aggressively attacked the agreement and its negotiators—they criticised the passing of power to the Provisional Executive and not to the GPRA, they condemned the concessions to the Europeans of Algeria and the ongoing French military presence. This was a tactic for the EMG to destabilise the GPRA more than a disagreement about the content of the Evian Accords (Meynier 2002, 631).

Implosion and Festivities

The Evian Accords prompted an explosion of OAS violence, furious at what they saw as the French government's betrayal of the Europeans of Algeria and determined to make the ceasefire fail. As the Algerian referendum on the peace agreement approached on 1 July—and thus independence inevitable—OAS violence reached its paroxysm. The OAS and their supporters popularised the slogan 'the suitcase or the coffin', first pronounced by Ortiz in December 1959 (McDougall 2017a, 229), convincing the majority of the European population of Algeria that there was no future for them in independent Algeria and precipitating their departure. Hospitals, libraries, town halls, ports and the Algerian population in general became a target for OAS bombs and fires. This was a 'scorched earth' policy motivated by the desire to leave nothing functioning for the new independent Algerian state (Branche 2007, 332). The OAS also targeted the French army, who in turn fought to bring European areas, notably those in Algiers and Oran, under French control.

The terms of future debates: Rue d'Isly, 26 March 1962
On 26 March 1962, the French army opened fire on Europeans protesting at the army encirclement of the Bab el Oued area of Algiers, killing 54 people and wounding 140. The army operation in Bab el Oued had been to capture OAS militants who were entrenched in the neighbourhood, following deadly OAS attacks on Algerians and the French army (Evans 2012, 313–316). The 'Rue d'Isly Massacre' would become sacrosanct in the memory of many former settlers, embodying what they saw as the French state's betrayal of them (>>Chap. 4, p. 171).

Within the FLN there was a political imperative, and indeed orders, to maintain the ceasefire. At the same time, particularly on the ground, there was a desire to respond in kind to OAS violence against Algerians. This response was not necessarily particularly well aimed at actual members of the OAS. In some areas, the European population as a whole came to be considered a legitimate target for kidnappings and assassinations. Much of the violence between, on the one hand, Algerians and, on the other hand, Europeans and those Algerians considered to be pro-French was the product of local dynamics which entered into a spiral of hate, fear and vengeance. Towards the end, this escaped the control of any organisation. Fouad Soufi's fine-grained study of the unfolding violence in Oran in 1962 (2000) demonstrates this very clearly, from a car bomb on a busy street in the Algerian quartier of Ville-Nouvelle in the middle of Ramadan on 28 February 1962 (killing around 35 Algerians) to the killing of around 100 people (around a quarter of whom were European) following independence celebrations on 5 July 1962, when shots of an unknown origin were fired into the crowd. In settler memory, 5 July 1962 in Oran is an emblematic date, which for them represents Algerian violence against Europeans, and the French army's failure to prevent this.

After the Evian Accords and the ceasefire between the French army and the FLN/ALN, the FLN and the French army became objective allies against the OAS. Meanwhile, the FLN was imploding. In the days before independence was declared, the CNRA—meant to be the FLN's parliament—voted its programme for post-independence Algeria (the June 1962 Tripoli programme) but then collapsed as a result of infighting about who should take power. By summer 1962, two rival coalitions had formed, which would come to be known as the 'Tlemcen group' and the 'Tizi Ouzou group', the names deriving from the cities where they established their strongholds. This confrontation was not really about different ideas or visions of independent Algeria. It was about who would take power. The Tlemcen group consisted of Boumediene and the EMG (frontier army) allied with the *wilayat* of the Aures (1), Oran (5), the Sahara (6) and some officers in North Constantine (*wilaya* 2) (see Fig. 3.1). Upon his release from prison on 18 March 1962, Ben Bella joined this alliance, as did Bitat and Khider, released at the same time. Abbas also joined this group, resentful at his previous ousting as president of the GPRA.

The 'Tizi Ouzou group' was composed of members of the GPRA, including its president, Ben Khedda, as well as the now less influential '3Bs' (Krim Belkacem, Ben Tobbal and Boussouf), the *wilayat* of Kabylia (3) and Algiers (4), the head of the *wilaya* 2, Salah Boubnider (1929–2005), sections of the FF-FLN (*wilaya* 7) and historic leaders Boudiaf and Aït Ahmed (both of whom had been on the hijacked plane with Ben Bella and were also recently released from prison). The alliances formed were by default—you joined the group you disliked the least—not based on shared ideology, or even affinity—which is why the fact that Boumediene would overthrow President Ben Bella three years later in a coup on 19 June 1965 should not come as a surprise.

Both the Tlemcen group and the Tizi Ouzou group sought to demonstrate their legitimacy through the presence in their ranks of 'historic leaders' (<<Chap. 2, p. 55) and soldiers of 'the interior' who had fought on Algerian soil. Beyond arguments about legitimacy, however, the Tlemcen group had an undeniable military advantage because it had the frontier army. By March 1962, this consisted of nearly 22,000 men on the Tunisian border and nearly 10,000 on the Moroccan border. In contrast, there were only 12,000 FLN/ALN soldiers in the mountains and urban centres (Mohand Amer 2010, 71; see also Mohand Amer 2014).

Ben Bella, and the frontier army in Morocco, entered Algeria and went to Tlemcen on 11 July 1962. In August, a tenuous and short-lived compromise was reached between the two groups, agreeing that elections to a Constituent Assembly would take place in September. In the end, the Tlemcen group decided who would be on the electoral lists. The Provisional Executive prepared to transfer power to the 'Political Bureau' ('bureau politique') of the Tlemcen group, not the GPRA (and thus not to the Tizi Ouzou group). As the frontier army arrived in Constantine, fighting broke out between the frontier army and the *wilaya* 2. In Algiers, the *wilaya* 4 refused to accept any authority but its own. At the start of September 1962, Ben Bella marched on Algiers with his men to impose the authority of the Political Bureau. Fighting broke out with members of the *wilaya* 4. Amongst the population of Algiers, there was little enthusiasm for continuing the conflict. Demonstrators took to the streets chanting 'seven years, that's enough'. The crisis of summer 1962 ended on 5 September 1962 with a ceasefire between the Political Bureau and the *wilaya* 4. The Tlemcen group had won. When Hocine Aït Ahmed created his oppositional rural guerrilla, the Front for Socialist Forces (Front des forces socialistes, FFS) in 1963, there was little appetite amongst most for continuing the struggle and it soon petered out.

Debating the nature of Algerian nationalism and the terms of future debates: why we need to know about the implosion of the FLN in summer 1962

This rather complicated story of infighting is important to understand for two reasons. Firstly, 'the FLN' did not 'win' in 1962, a faction of the FLN, within which the military was very powerful, did. Of the 'nine historic leaders' of 1954, only two, Ben Bella and Bitat, played a role in post-independence politics. Ben Boulaïd, Ben M'Hidi and Didouche had been killed by the French army in the course of the war. Aït Ahmed, Boudiaf and Krim Belkacem were not on the winning side in summer 1962 and would go into exile, shortly afterwards to be joined by Khider who cut ties with Ben Bella in 1963. Khider would be assassinated in Madrid in 1967, and Krim Belkacem in Frankfurt in 1970, and it is strongly suspected that this was on the orders of the Algerian state. Secondly, the infighting of

(*continued*)

(continued)

summer 1962 would be key in establishing one of the most enduring oppositional narratives in post-independence Algeria: the idea that independence was 'stolen' from democratic politicians and the *mujahidin* who fought and died on Algerian soil by undemocratic military men who did not actually fight in the war and after independence set about building a single-party state which served their own interests. Like all foundational myths, this does have a factual basis, but this has been exaggerated for political purposes. As we have seen, there were *mujahidin* from the 'interior' on both sides, although it is true that the *wilayat* which saw the fiercest fighting during the war were those most opposed to the Tlemcen group. There were also politicians on both sides. The most enthusiastic proponent of secular democracy, Abbas, joined the Tlemcen group. There were military men on both sides. Although it is true that there were more civilian politicians in the Tizi Ouzou group, military men Krim Belkacem, Ben Tobbal and Boussouf, who were on the side of the Tizi Ouzou group, had previously been responsible for reversing Abane's attempts to ensure the primacy of the political over the military (<<Chap. 3, p. 107). Summer 1962 was not then, a coup d'état against democracy. Nevertheless, the idea of 'independence stolen' by 'the Oujda clan' (<<Chap. 3, p. 109), the 'DAF' (<<Chap. 3, p. 88), the Lacoste promotion (<<Chap. 3, p. 84) and the 'marsiens' (a play on words combining 'March' [*mars* in French] and 'Martians' [aliens] to describe eleventh-hour resisters who joined the FLN in March 1962) was politically extremely useful. It allowed oppositional leaders after 1962 to celebrate the shared values of the independence struggle (unity, common purpose and sacrifice) which were universally accepted across Algerian society, whilst at the same time turning these same values against those in power, by arguing that they had betrayed them (>>Chap. 4, pp. 168–9, 178, 186).

Amid this infighting and score-settling there were also festivities on a huge scale—men, women and children dancing in the street, parading through European areas, staying out all night, celebrating independence. There was also intense local-level organising to keep food supply chains open, notably during the OAS violence when it was dangerous to leave 'Muslim areas' in many cities with a large European population, such as Oran. Algerians organised the production of identity cards ready for the vote to ratify independence. They planned the return to Algeria of tens of thousands of refugees in Morocco and Tunisia. They set up schools and located teachers so that as many Algerian children as possible could return to, or start for the very first time, an education in September 1962.

CONCLUSION: THE REMAKING OF ALGERIA AND FRANCE

This chapter began by arguing that the Algerian War/Algerian Revolution was fought across three interconnected arenas. There was a military confrontation between a regular army and rural and urban guerrillas, a political struggle between two diametrically opposed visions of what Algeria was (an integral part of France or a separate nation-state) and a battle between the French state and the FLN to secure international support. The outcome of the war—Algerian national independence in a sovereign state—was the result of the interplay between all of these different sites of struggle. By late 1959, the FLN/ALN within Algeria had been decimated. That does not mean that this was a military victory for the French army. By treating the entire civilian population as potential enemy combatants, the methods used to dismantle the nationalist political and military organisation had played a key role in galvanising popular support for the FLN/ALN, and for independence, both amongst Algerians and on the international stage. The FLN succeeded in proving that Algeria was not France, and in the end the French state accepted this in its own self-interest, to the detriment of the Europeans of Algeria. That was not before, however, extensive effort and huge sums of money had been expended to try and make Algeria *really* French—politically, legally, socio-economically and culturally. However, it was not just that 'integration' or 'the modernising mission' were *undermined* by the violence of the French army, the police, the OAS or the FLN. For this radical rethinking of French Algeria to be *implemented in the first place*, the Algerian population would need to be subdued through the use of violence. Herein lies the inherent contradiction of the 'modernising mission' and 'integration' led by the late colonial state: 'implementing the new-found determination to make Algeria truly "French" meant exercising a degree of coercion not seen since the end of the nineteenth century wars of conquest' (McDougall 2017b). Even if this second conquest had been successful, the destruction and resentment it would have provoked would have only ever kept Algeria French temporarily.

Behind these overarching explanations of why the FLN 'won' and why France 'lost' are much messier day-to-day experiences. Stories of confusion, chance and fear as well as unwavering belief, fearlessness and fatalism. Stories of changing allegiances, least-bad choices, adroit manoeuvring and mistakes. Stories of day-to-day survival. Few would deny today that a war took place in Algeria, the terms 'events' and 'operations' have largely fallen out of mainstream usage. Whether or not a 'revolution' took place continues to be debated (<<Chap. 1, p. 2). Many (particularly French) historians are still reluctant to use the term. They argue that the struggle was primarily against a foreign occupier, this was not an overturning and reimagining of the structures of Algerian society (Meynier 2002, 158–159). This unwillingness to label 1954–62 a 'revolution' perhaps stems from an unfavourable comparison between the *al-thawra al-jazāʾiriyya* (the Algerian Revolution) and the French Revolution of 1789 or the Russian Revolution of 1917, finding that Algeria does not measure

up to the French or Russian overthrow of autochthonous established orders—particularly because the FLN did not have any elaborate programme for what would happen after independence. Yet 'revolutions' can be defined in different ways. For Connelly (2002), the War of Independence was a 'diplomatic revolution' because it radically changed the way in which international politics was done. A nationalist liberation movement could gain political legitimacy before it had territorial sovereignty. For Daho Djerbal (2010, 68), the revolutionary nature of the conflict was connected to the use of revolutionary warfare, which brought about a gradual fusion between the people and its army as the vast majority of the Algerian people became implicated in the struggle.

Building upon this latter argument, James McDougall (2017a, 233) underlines the importance of focusing less on how 'revolutionary' the FLN's programme and ideology were and more on how the war itself revolutionised Algerian society, 'mobilising long-standing codes and structures of social solidarity into a new, assertive, militant sense of political community'. Little was expected of, and even less was given by, the colonial state to Algerians. In contrast, the new Algerian state was expected to fulfil all the needs and expectations of the people who had fought to bring it into existence. Whether or not the post-independence state would do this was another question, but the expectation existed as did a language to articulate these demands, a language of sacrifice, martyrdom, one sole hero the people, by the people for the people, anti-colonialism and freedom from foreign interference. The turning upside down of the established order can also be understood as not just about overthrowing political, economic and social structures, but also about symbolic disruptions. When, in summer 1962, Algerians paraded through the streets in European areas, this was a turning upside down of the established order. When women broke with societal norms about the separation of men and women and joined rural guerrilla units, when they stayed out all night to dance in the streets in the days following the declaration of independence, this was also a turning upside down of the established order (Vince 2015, 102–104). Whether or not these changes would be durable does not determine whether they were 'revolutionary' or not.

The end of 'French Algeria', as the subtitle of Todd Shepard's 2006 work suggests, involved 'the remaking of France' (for a succinct introduction, see also Shepard 2016). Shepard encourages us to take seriously attempts by some French policymakers and politicians in the 1950s to give genuine substance to the notion of 'integration' and apply race-blind liberty, equality and fraternity across the French empire. The 1958 constitution made all Algerians full French citizens and thus embraced the idea of a multi-ethnic French citizenship stretching beyond the territory of metropolitan France. Just four years later, what it meant to be French was radically redefined: France now meant 'the hexagon' (the geographical shape of metropolitan France, largely ignoring the French overseas departments in the Caribbean, Indian Ocean and Pacific Ocean), and non-whites and Muslims could not be imagined as 'natural' or obvious French citizens. As a counterpoint to Shepard's argument, it is probable that the intense levels of violence needed to make a transcontinental, universalist, progressive Republic a reality would have fatally undermined it from the outset. The abandonment of this vision was 'not simply a betrayal of the imperial Republic's history and values: it was, rather more simply, the reluctant recognition of its impossibility' (McDougall 2017b). Nevertheless, if we remain at the level of what it was possible for some politicians and policymakers in France to imagine, rather than what would ever have been tolerable in Algeria to Algerians, we can agree that 1962 marked a radical reassessment of what it meant to be French, within dramatically reduced geographical boundaries.

REFERENCES

Adel, Khedidja. 2019. La prison des femmes de Tifelfel. Enfermement et corps en souffrance [The Women's Prison of Tifelfel. Imprisonment and Suffering Bodies]. *L'Année du Maghreb* 20 (1): 123–158. https://doi.org/10.4000/anneemaghreb.4674.

Ageron, Charles-Robert. 1997. L'insurrection du 20 août 1955 dans le Nord-Constantinois: de la résistance armée à la guerre du peuple [The 20 August 1955 Insurrection in the North-Constantine Region: From Armed Resistance to People's War]. In *La Guerre d'Algérie et les Algériens, 1954–1962* [The Algerian War and the Algerians, 1954–1962], ed. Charles-Robert Ageron, 27–50. Paris: Armand Colin/Masson.

Aissaoui, Rabah. 2009. *Immigration and National Identity: North African Political Movements in Colonial and Postcolonial France.* London and New York: Tauris Academic Studies.

———. 2012. Fratricidal War: The Conflict Between the Mouvement National Algérien (MNA) and the Front de Libération Nationale (FLN) in France During the Algerian War (1954–1962). *British Journal of Middle Eastern Studies* 39 (2): 227–240. https://doi.org/10.1080/13530194.2012.709701.

Aït-el-Djoudi, Dalila. 2007. *La guerre d'Algérie vue par l'ALN 1954–1962: l'armée française sous le regard des combattants algériens* [The Algerian War Seen by the ALN 1954–1962: The French Army as Seen by Algerian Combatants]. Paris: Autrement.

Alexander, Martin S., and John F. V. Keiger, eds. 2002. *France and the Algerian War 1954–62: Strategy, Operations and Diplomacy.* London: Frank Cass.

Alleg, Henri. 2006 [1958]. *The Question.* Trans. John Calder. Lincoln: University of Nebraska Press.

Amiri, Linda. 2004. *La bataille de France. La guerre d'Algérie en metropole* [The Battle of France. The Algerian War in the Metropole]. Paris: Robert Laffont.

———. 2014 [2012]. La Fédération de France du FLN, acteur majeur de la guerre d'indépendance [The Federation of France of the FLN, Major Actor in the War of Independence]. In *Histoire de l'Algérie à la période coloniale* [History of Algeria During the Colonial Period], ed. Abderrahmane Bouchène, Jean-Pierre Peyroulou, Ouanassa Siari Tengour, and Sylvie Thénault, 576–582. Paris: La Découverte.

Amrane, Djamila. 1991. *Les Femmes algériennes dans la guerre* [Algerian Women in the War]. Paris: Plon.

André, Marc. 2016. *Femmes dévoilées: Des Algériennes en France à l'heure de la décolonisation* [Unveiled Women: Algerian Women in France at the Hour of Decolonisation]. Lyon: ENS Editions.

Arezki, Saphia. 2015. La formation militaire des combattants de l'ALN aux frontières de l'Algérie et à l'étranger [The Military Training of ALN Combatants on the Borders of Algeria and Abroad]. In *La guerre d'Algérie revisitée: nouvelles générations, nouveaux regards* [The Algerian War Revisited: New Generations, New Perspectives], ed. Aissa Kadri, Moula Bouaziz, and Tramor Quemeneur, 231–242. Paris: Karthala.

———. 2018. *De l'ALN à l'ANP. La construction de l'armée algérienne 1954–1991* [From the ALN to the ANP: The Construction of the Algerian Army 1954–1991]. Algiers: Barzakh.

Arnaud, Georges, and Jacques Vergès. 1957. *Pour Djamila Bouhired* [For Djamila Bouhired]. Paris: Editions de minuit.

Asseraf, Arthur. 2018. 'A New Israel': Colonial Comparisons and the Algerian Partition That Never Happened. *French Historical Studies* 41 (1): 95–120. https://doi.org/10.1215/00161071-4254631.

Bantigny, Ludivine. 2007. Temps, âge et generation à l'épreuve de la guerre: la mémoire, l'histoire et l'oubli des appelés en Algérie [Time, Age and Generation Under the Strain of War: Memory, History and Forgetting Amongst Conscripts in Algeria]. *Revue historique* 641: 165–179. https://doi.org/10.3917/rhis.071.0165.

Barkaoui, Miloud. 1999. Kennedy and the Cold War Imbroglio: The Case of Algeria's Independence. *Arab Studies Quarterly* 21 (2): 31–45.

Bedjaoui, Ahmed. 2015. Sixty Years of Algerian Cinema. *Black Renaissance/Renaissance Noire* 15 (1): 126–139.

Blanchard, Emmanuel. 2011. *La police parisienne et les algériens (1944–1962)* [The Parisian Police and Algerians (1944–1962)]. Paris: Nouveau Monde.

———. 2012a. La Goutte d'Or, 30 juillet 1955: une émeute au coeur de la métropole coloniale [The Goutte d'Or, 30 July 1955: A Riot in the Heart of the Colonial Metropole]. *Actes de recherche en sciences sociales* 195: 98–111. https://doi.org/10.3917/arss.195.0098.

———. 2012b. 14 juillet 1953: repression coloniale, place de la Nation. *Histoire coloniale et postcoloniale* [14 July 1953: Colonial Repression, Place de la Nation, Extracts from Blanchard 2011]. https://histoirecoloniale.net/14-juillet-1953-repression.html. Accessed 1 June 2020.

Branche, Raphaëlle. 2001. *La Torture et l'armée pendant la Guerre d'Algérie, 1954–62* [Torture and the Army During the Algerian War]. Paris: Gallimard.

———. 2002. Des viols pendant la Guerre d'Algérie [Rape During the Algerian War]. *Vingtième siècle* 75: 123–132. https://doi.org/10.3917/ving.075.0123.

———. 2007. FLN et OAS: deux terrorismes en guerre d'Algérie [FLN and OAS: Two Terrorisms in the Algerian War]. *European Review of History/Revue européenne d'histoire* 14 (3): 325–342. https://doi.org/10.1080/13507480701611597.

———. 2014. The French Military in Its Last Colonial War: Algeria, 1954–1962, the Reign of Torture. In *Interrogation in War and Conflict: A Comparative and Interdisciplinary Analysis*, ed. Simona Tobia and Christopher Andrew, 169–184. London and New York: Routledge.

———. 2017. 'The best Fellagha Hunter Is the French of North African Descent': Harkis in French Algeria. In *Unconventional Warfare from Antiquity to the Present*

Day, ed. Brian Hughes and Fergus Robson, 47–66. Cham, Switzerland: Palgrave Macmillan.

———. 2018. Parallel Ambiguities: Prisoners During the Algerian War of Independence. In *The Civilianization of War*, ed. Andrew Barros and Martin Thomas, 100–115. Cambridge: Cambridge University Press.

———. 2019. Combattants indépendantistes et société rurale dans l'Algérie colonisée [Combatants for Independence and Rural Society in Colonial Algeria]. *Revue d'histoire* 141: 113–127. https://doi.org/10.3917/vin.141.0113.

Brazzoduro, Andrea. 2012. Postcolonial Memories of the Algerian War of Independence, 1955–2010: French Veterans and Contemporary France. In *France and the Mediterranean: International Relations, Culture and Politics*, ed. Emmanuel Godin and Natalya Vince, 275–303. Oxford: Peter Lang.

Brown, Megan. 2017. Drawing Algeria into Europe: Shifting French Policy and the Treaty of Rome (1951–1964). *Modern and Contemporary France* 25 (2): 191–208. https://doi.org/10.1080/09639489.2017.1281899.

Byrne, Jeffrey James. 2009. Our Own Special Brand of Socialism: Algeria and the Contest of Modernities in the 1960s. *Diplomatic History* 33 (3): 427–447. https://doi.org/10.1111/j.1467-7709.2009.00779.x.

———. 2010. 'Je ne vous ai pas compris': de Gaulle's Decade of Negotiation with the Algerian FLN, 1958–1969. In *Globalising de Gaulle: International Perspectives on French Foreign Policies, 1958–1969*, ed. Christian Nuenlist, Anna Locher, and Garret Martin, 225–250. Lanham, MD: Rowman and Littlefield.

———. 2016. *Mecca of Revolution: Algeria, Decolonization and the Third World Order*. Oxford: Oxford University Press.

Chakrabarty, Dipesh. 2010. The Legacies of Bandung: Decolonisation and the Politics of Culture. In *Making a World After Empire: The Bandung Moment and Its Political Afterlives*, ed. Christopher J. Lee, 45–68. Athens, OH: Ohio University Press.

Cole, Joshua. 2003. Remembering the Battle of Paris: 17 October 1961 in French and Algerian Memory. *French Politics, Culture and Society* 21 (3): 21–50. https://doi.org/10.3167/153763703782370251.

Connelly, Matthew. 2001. Rethinking the Cold War and Decolonization: The Grand Strategy for the Algerian War for Independence. *International Journal of Middle East Studies* 33 (2): 221–245. https://doi.org/10.1017/S0020743801002033.

———. 2002. *A Diplomatic Revolution: Algeria's Fight for Independence and the Origins of the Post-Cold War Era*. Oxford and New York: Oxford University Press.

Cooper, Frederick. 2005. *Colonialism in Question: Theory, Knowledge, History*. Berkeley: University of California Press.

———. 2014. *Citizenship between Empire and Nation: Remaking France and French Africa 1945–1960*. Princeton and Oxford: Princeton University Press.

Cooper, Frederick, and Randall M. Packard, eds. 1997. *International Development and the Social Sciences: Essays on the History and Politics of Knowledge*. Berkeley, CA: University of California Press.

Cornaton, Michel. 1998. *Les camps de regroupement de la guerre d'Algérie* [Regrouping Camps and the Algerian War]. Paris: L'Harmattan.

Dard, Olivier. 2014 [2012]. Qui ont été les membres de l'OAS? [Who Were the Members of the OAS?]. In *Histoire de l'Algérie à la période coloniale* [History of Algeria During the Colonial Period], ed. Abderrahmane Bouchène, Jean-Pierre Peyroulou, Ouanassa Siari Tengour, and Sylvie Thénault, 640–643. Paris: La Découverte.

Davis, Muriam Haleh. 2017. 'The Transformation of Man' in French Algeria: Economic Planning and the Postwar Social Sciences, 1958–1962. *Journal of Contemporary History* 52 (1): 73–94. https://doi.org/10.1177/0022009416647117.

———. 2018. North Africa and the Common Agricultural Policy: From Colonial Pact to European Integration. In *North Africa and the Making of Europe: Governance, Institutions and Culture*, ed. Muriam Haleh Davis and Thomas Serres, 43–66. London: Bloomsbury.

Denis, Sébastien. n.d. Parcours thématique: Les médias audiovisuels dans la guerre d'Algérie [Thematic Pathway: Audiovisual Media in the Algerian War (includes a number of French propaganda films to watch online)]. https://fresques.ina.fr/independances/parcours/0003/les-medias-audiovisuels-dans-la-guerre-d-algerie.html. Accessed 1 June 2020.

Djerbal, Daho. 2003. Mounadiline et mousebbiline. Les forces auxiliaires de l'ALN dans le Nord-Constantinois [Mounadiline and mousebbiline. Auxilary Forces of the ALN in the North-Constantine Region]. In *Des Hommes et des femmes en guerre d'Algérie* [Men and Women in the Algerian War], ed. Jean-Charles Jauffret, 282–296. Paris: Autrement.

———. 2010. Les effets des manifestations de décembre 1960 sur les maquis algériens [The Effects of the December 1960 Demonstrations on the Algerian Maquis]. *NAQD* (supplement 2): 63–92. https://doi.org/10.3917/naqd.hs2.0063.

Drif, Zohra. 2017. *Inside the Battle of Algiers: Memoir of a Woman Freedom Fighter* [French Title: *Mémoires d'une combattante de l'ALN*]. Trans. Andrew Farrand. Charlottesville and Virginia, VA: Just World Books.

Einaudi, Jean-Luc. 1991. *La Ferme Améziane: Enquête sur un centre de torture pendant la Guerre d'Algérie* [The Améziane Farm: Investigation into a Torture Centre During the Algerian War]. Paris: L'Harmattan.

Essemlali, Mounya. 2011. Le Maroc entre la France et l'Algérie (1956–1962) [Morocco Between France and Algeria (1956–1962)]. *Relations internationales* 146: 77–93. https://doi.org/10.3917/ri.146.0077.

Evans, Martin. 1997. *The Memory of Resistance: French Opposition to the Algerian War (1954–1962)*. Oxford: Berg.

———. 2009. Guy Mollet's Third Way: National Renewal and the French Civilising Mission in Algeria. *French History & Civilization* 2: 169–180. https://h-france.net/rude/wp-content/uploads/2017/08/vol2_Evans_Final_Version_2.pdf. Accessed 1 June 2020.

———. 2012. *Algeria: France's Undeclared War*. Oxford: Oxford University Press.

Eveno, Patrick. 2005. Paroles de soldats en guerre d'Algérie [Words of Soldiers in the Algerian War]. *Les Temps des medias* 4: 127–136. https://doi.org/10.3917/tdm.004.0127.

Fanon, Franz. 1965 [1959]. *A Dying Colonialism* [French Title: *L'An V de la Révolution algérienne*]. Trans. Haakon Chevalier. New York: Grove Press.

———. 2001 [1961]. *The Wretched of the Earth* [French Title: *Les Damnés de la terre*]. Trans. Constance Farrington. London: Penguin.

Feichtinger, Moritz. 2017. 'A Great Reformatory': Social Planning and Strategic Resettlement in Late Colonial Kenya and Algeria, 1952–63. *Journal of Contemporary History* 52 (1): 45–72. https://doi.org/10.1177/0022009415616867.

Forget, Nelly. 1992. Le Service des Centres Sociaux en Algérie. [The Social Centres Service in Algeria]. *Matériaux pour l'histoire de notre temps* 26: 37–47. https://www.persee.fr/doc/mat_0769-3206_1992_num_26_1_404864. Accessed 1 June 2020.

Frémeaux, Jacques. 2002. Les SAS (Sections administratives spécialisées) [The SAS (Special Administrative Sections)]. *Guerres mondiales et conflits contemporains* 208: 55–68. https://doi.org/10.3917/gmcc.208.0055.

Gaulle, Charles de. 1958. Discours du plan de Constantine, le 3 octobre 1958. Charles de Gaulle, paroles publiques. https://fresques.ina.fr/de-gaulle/fiche-media/Gaulle00022/discours-du-plan-de-constantine-le-3-octobre-1958.html. Accessed 1 June 2020.

Ginio, Ruth. 2016. *The French Army and Its African Soldiers: The Years of Decolonization.* Lincoln, NB: University of Nebraska.

Gordon, Daniel A. 2015. Le 17 octobre et la population française. La collaboration ou la résistance? [17 October and the French population. Collaboration Or Resistance?]. In *La guerre d'Algérie revisitée: nouvelles générations, nouveaux regards* [The Algerian War Revisited: New Generations, New Perspectives], ed. Aissa Kadri, Moula Bouaziz, and Tramor Quemeneur, 339–350. Paris: Karthala.

Haddad-Fonda, Kyle. 2014. An Illusory Alliance: Revolutionary Legitimacy and Sino-Algerian Relations, 1958–1962. *Journal of North African Studies* 19 (3): 338–357. https://doi.org/10.1080/13629387.2013.870039.

Halimi, Gisèle, and Simone de Beauvoir. 1962. *Djamila Boupacha.* Paris: Gallimard.

Harbi, Mohamed. 1980. *Le FLN, mirage et realité des origines à la prise du pouvoir (1945–1962)* [The FLN, Mirage and Reality from Its Origins to Taking Power (1945–1962)]. Paris: Editions Jeune Afrique.

Hautreux, François-Xavier. 2011. Quelques pistes pour une meilleure compréhension de l'engagement des harkis (1954–1962) [Some Indications for a Better Understanding of Why Harkis Joined Up]. *Les Temps modernes* 666: 44–52. https://doi.org/10.3917/ltm.666.0044.

———. 2013. *La guerre d'Algérie des Harkis, 1954–1962* [The Algerian War of *Harkis,* 1954–1962]. Paris: Perrin.

House, James. 2018. Shantytowns and Rehousing in Late Colonial Algiers and Casablanca. In *France's Modernising Mission: Citizenship, Welfare and the Ends of Empire,* ed. Edward Naylor, 133–163. London: Palgrave Macmillan.

House, James, and Neil Macmaster. 2006. *Paris 1961: Algerians, State Terror, and Memory.* Oxford: Oxford University Press.

Izambert, Caroline. 2008. The Example of a Communist Paper Aimed at Algerian Immigrants: *L'Algérien en France* (1950–1960). In *Migration and Activism in Europe Since 1945,* ed. Wendy Pojmann, 99–110. Basingstoke: Palgrave Macmillan.

Jackson, Julian. 2018. *A Certain Idea of France: The Life of Charles de Gaulle.* London: Penguin.

Jauffret, Jean-Charles. 2001. Une armée à deux vitesses en Algérie (1954–1962): réserves générales et troupes de secteur [A Two-Speed Army in Algeria (1954–1962)]. In *Militaires et guerrilla dans la guerre d'Algérie* [The Military and the Guerrilla in the Algerian War], ed. Jean-Charles Jauffret and Maurice Vaïsse, 21–37. Brussels: Complexe.

———. 2002. The War Culture of French Combatants in the Algerian Conflict. In *The Algerian War and the French Army: Experiences, Images and Testimonies,* ed. Martin S. Alexander, Martin Evans, and John F.V. Keiger, 101–116. Basingstoke: Palgrave Macmillan.

———. 2011 [2000]. *Soldats en Algérie: expériences contrastées des hommes du contingent* [Soldiers in Algeria: The Contrasting Experiences of Men of the Contingent]. Paris: Autrement.

Johnson, Jennifer. 2012. 'Humanise the conflict': Algerian Health Care Organisations and Propaganda Campaigns, 1954–62. *International Journal of Middle East Studies* 44 (4): 713–731. https://doi.org/10.1017/S0020743812000839.

———. 2016. *The Battle for Algeria: Sovereignty, Health Care, and Humanitarianism.* Philadelphia, PA: University of Pennsylvania Press.

Kalman, Samuel. 2013. *French Colonial Fascism: The Extreme Right in Algeria, 1919–1939.* Basingstoke: Palgrave Macmillan.

Khoulé, Cheikh Ahmadou Bamba. 2011. Les tirailleurs sénégalais dans la guerre d'Algérie: la transmission de la mémoire à travers les descendants [*Tirailleurs sénégalais* in the Algerian War: The Transmission of Memory to Descendants]. MA Dissertation Université Cheikh Anta Diop de Dakar.

Klose, Fabian. 2013. *Human Rights in the Shadow of Colonial Violence. The Wars of Independence in Kenya and Algeria.* Trans. Dona Geyer. Philadelphia, PA: University of Pennsylvania Press.

Kuby, Emma. 2012. A War of Words Over an Image of War: The Fox Movietone Scandal and the Portrayal of French Violence in Algeria, 1955–1956. *French Politics, Culture and Society* 30 (1): 46–67. https://doi.org/10.3167/fpcs.2012.300103.

———. 2013. From the Torture Chamber to the Bedchamber: French Soldiers, Antiwar Activists, and the Discourse of Sexual Deviancy in the Algerian War (1954–1962). *Contemporary French Civilization* 38 (2): 131–153. https://doi.org/10.3828/cfc.2013.7.

Lazreg, Marnia. 2008. *Torture and the Twilight of Empire: From Algiers to Baghdad.* Princeton, NJ: Princeton University Press.

Mack, Andrew. 1975. Why Big Nations Lose Small Wars: The Politics of Asymmetric Conflict. *World Politics* 27 (2): 175–200. https://doi.org/10.2307/2009880.

Macmaster, Neil. 2009. *Burning the Veil: The Algerian War and the 'emancipation' of Muslim Women, 1954–62.* Manchester: Manchester University Press.

———. 2018. From Tent to Village *Regroupement*: The Colonial State and Social Engineering of Rural Space, 1843–1962. In *France's Modernising Mission: Citizenship, Welfare and the Ends of Empire*, ed. Edward Naylor, 109–131. London: Palgrave Macmillan.

Mahieu, Alban. 2001. Les effectifs de l'armée française en Algérie (1954–1962) [Numbers in the French Army (1954–1962)]. In *Militaires et guérillas dans la guerre d'Algérie* [Soldiers and Guerrillas in the Algerian War], ed. Jean-Charles Jauffret and Maurice Vaïsse, 39–47. Brussels: Complexe.

Mann, Gregory. 2006. *Native Sons: West African Veterans and France in the Twentieth Century.* Durham, NC: Duke University.

Mauss-Copeaux, Claire. 1998. *Appelés en Algérie. La Parole confisquée* [Conscripts in Algeria. The Confiscated Word]. Paris: Hachette.

———. 2011. *Algérie, 20 août 1955. Insurrection, repression, massacres* [Algeria, 20 August 1955. Insurrection, Repression, Massacres]. Paris: Payot.

———. 2017. *Hadjira. La ferme Ameziane et au delà* [Hadjira. The Ameziane Farm and Beyond]. Paris: Les Chemins du présent.

Mbaye, Cheikh Anta. 2011. Les tirailleurs sénégalais dans la guerre d'Algérie (1954–1962) [*Tirailleurs sénégalais* in the Algerian War (1954–1962)]. MA Dissertation, Université Cheikh Anta Diop, Dakar.

McDonnell, Hugh. 2018. Complicity and Memory in Soldiers' Testimonies of Decolonisation in *Esprit* and *Les Temps modernes*. *Memory Studies*. https://doi.org/10.1177/1750698018784130.

McDougall, James. 2017a. *A History of Algeria*. Cambridge: Cambridge University Press.
———. 2017b. The Impossible Republic: The Reconquest and the Decolonization of France, 1945–1962. *Journal of Modern History* 89 (4): 772–811. https://doi.org/10.1086/694427.
Merom, Gil. 1999. A 'Grand Design?' Charles de Gaulle and the End of the Algerian War. *Armed Forces and Society* 25 (2): 267–288. https://doi.org/10.1177/0095327X9902500205.
Meynier, Gilbert. 2002. *Histoire intérieure du FLN 1954–1962* [The Internal History of the FLN]. Paris: Fayard.
Mohand Amer, Amar. 2010. La crise du Front de libération nationale de l'été 1962: indépendance et enjeux de pouvoir [The Crisis of the National Liberation Front of Summer 1962: Independence and Power Stakes]. PhD Thesis, Université Paris Diderot.
———. 2014. Les wilayas dans la crise du FLN de l'été 1962. [The *Wilayas* in the FLN Crisis of Summer 1962]. *Insaniyat* 65–66: 105–124. https://doi.org/10.4000/insaniyat.14796.
Naylor, Edward, ed. 2018. *France's Modernising Mission: Citizenship, Welfare and the Ends of Empire*. London: Palgrave Macmillan.
Perego, Elizabeth. 2015. The Veil Or a Brother's Life: French Manipulations of Muslim Women's Images During the Algerian War, 1954–62. *Journal of North African Studies* 20 (3): 349–373. https://doi.org/10.1080/13629387.2015.1013942.
Pervillé, Guy. 2007. La guerre sans nom: appelés et rappelés en Algérie (1992) [The War Without Name: Conscripts and Reservists in Algeria]. http://guy.perville.free.fr/spip/article.php3?id_article=96. Accessed 1 June 2020.
Pinoteau, Pascal. 2003. Propagande cinématographique et décolonisation. L'exemple français (1949–1958) [Cinematographic Propaganda and Decolonisation. The French Example]. *Vingtième siècle. Revue d'histoire* 80: 55–69. https://doi.org/10.3917/ving.080.0055.
Prakash, Amit. 2013. Colonial Techniques in the Imperial Capital: The Prefecture of Police and the Surveillance of North Africans in Paris, c. 1925–1970. *French Historical Studies* 36 (3): 479–510. https://doi.org/10.1215/00161071-2141118.
Quemeneur, Tramor. 2011. Refuser l'autorité? Etude des désobéissances de soldats français pendant la Guerre d'Algérie [Reject Authority? A Study of Disobedience by French Soldiers During the Algerian War]. *Outre-mers revue d'histoire* 370–371: 57–66. https://www.persee.fr/doc/outre_1631-0438_2011_num_98_370_4533. Accessed 1 June 2020.
Rahal, Malika. 2004. La place des réformistes dans le mouvement national algérien. [The Place of Reformists in the Algerian National Movement]. *Vingtième siècle* 83: 161–171. https://doi.org/10.3917/ving.083.0161.
———. 2010. Les manifestations de mai 1958 en Algérie ou l'impossible expression d'une opinion publique "musulmane". [The Demonstrations of May 1958 in Algeria Or the Impossible Expression of a 'Muslim' Public Opinion]. In *Mai 1958: Le retour du général de Gaulle* [May 1958: The Return of General de Gaulle], ed. Jean-Paul Thomas, Gilles Le Béguec, and Bernard Lachaise, 39–58. Rennes: Presse Universitaires de Rennes.
Rigouste, Mathieu. 2017. Algeria's Independence: The Forgotten Protests That Forged a Nation. *Middle East Eye*. https://www.middleeasteye.net/big-story/algerias-independence-forgotten-protests-forged-nation. Accessed 1 June 2020.

Roberts, Hugh. 2004. Sovereignty: The Algerian Case. *Diplomatic History* 28 (4): 595–598. https://doi.org/10.1111/j.1467-7709.2004.00439.x.

Roche, Anne and Alice Belgacem. 2017. "Je vous le raconte volontiers, parce qu'on ne me l'a jamais demandé": Autobiographies d'appelés en Algérie ['I'll Happily Tell You About It, Because No One Ever Asked': Autobiographies of Conscripts in Algeria]. *Bulletin de l'AFAS* 43. https://doi.org/10.4000/afas.3027. This article draws on an oral history archive with French Soldiers (in French): http://phonotheque.mmsh.huma-num.fr/. Accessed 1 June 2020.

Sabeur, Khaled Chérif. 2017. Les tirailleurs sénégalais à travers quelques extraits inédits de poèmes populaires kabyles [Tirailleurs sénégalais in Some Unpublished Extracts of Popular Kabyle Poetry] [Conference Paper]. The Algerian War of Independence: Global and Local Histories, 1954–62 and Beyond. https://oxfordalgeriaconference2017.files.wordpress.com/2017/05/talks_participants_oxfordalgeriaconference2017.pdf. Accessed 1 June 2020.

Sacriste, Fabien. 2012. Surveiller et moderniser. Les camps de "regroupement" de ruraux pendant la guerre d'indépendance algérienne [Surveillance and Modernisation. The 'regrouping' Camps of Rural Popularions During the Algerian War of Independence]. *Métropolitiques.eu*. https://www.metropolitiques.eu/Surveiller-et-moderniser-Les-camps.html#nh5. Accessed 1 June 2020.

Sèbe, Berny. 2010. In the Shadow of the Algerian War: The United States and the Common Organisation of Saharan Regions (OCRS), 1957–62. *Journal of Imperial and Commonwealth History* 38 (2): 303–322. https://doi.org/10.1080/03086531003743999.

Seferdjeli, Ryme. 2004. French 'Reforms' and Muslim Women's Emancipation During the Algerian War. *Journal of North African Studies* 9 (4): 19–61. https://doi.org/10.1080/1362938042000326272.

———. 2005. The French Army and Muslim Women During the Algerian War. *Hawwa* 3 (1): 40–79. https://doi.org/10.1163/1569208053628537.

———. 2012. Rethinking the History of the Mudjahidat During the Algerian War: Competing Voices, Reconstructed Memories and Contrasting Historiographies. *Interventions: International Journal of Postcolonial Studies* 14 (2): 238–255. https://doi.org/10.1080/1369801X.2012.687902.

Shaev, Brian. 2018. The Algerian War, European Integration, and the Decolonisation of French Socialism. *French Historical Studies* 41 (1): 63–94. https://doi.org/10.1215/00161071-4254619.

Shepard, Todd. 2006. *The Invention of Decolonization. The Algerian War and the Remaking of France.* Ithaca and London: Cornell University Press.

———. 2011. Thinking Between Metropole and Colony: The French Republic, 'Exceptional Promotion' and the 'Integration' of Algerians, 1955–1962. In *The French Colonial Mind. Volume 1: Mental Maps of Empire and Colonial Encounters*, ed. Martin Thomas, 298–232. Lincoln, NE: University of Nebraska.

———. 2015. *Voices of Decolonization: A Brief History with Documents.* Boston and New York: Bedford/St Martin's.

———. 2016. The birth of the Hexagone and the Erasure of France's Supranational History. In *Vertriebene and Pieds-Noirs in Postwar Germany and France: Comparative Perspectives*, ed. Manuel Borutta and Jan Jansen, 53–69. Basingstoke: Palgrave Macmillan.

Sidi Moussa, Nedjib. 2019. *Algérie. Une autre histoire de l'indépendance* [Algeria. Another History of Independence]. Paris: PUF.

Soufi, Fouad. 2000. Oran, 28 février 1962, 5 juillet 1962. Deux événements pour l'histoire, deux événements pour la mémoire. [28 February 1962, 5 July 1962. Two Events for History, Two Events for Memory]. In *La Guerre d'Algérie au miroir des décolonisations françaises: en honneur de Charles-Robert Ageron* [The Algerian in the Mirror of French Decolonisations: In Honour of Charles-Robert Ageron], 635–676. Paris: SFHOM. A version of this text is available online: https://histoirecoloniale. net/Oran-1962-par-Fouad-Soufi-1-l.html. Accessed 1 June 2020.

Stora, Benjamin. 1992. *Ils venaient d'Algérie. L'immigration algérienne en France, 1912–1992* [They Came from Algeria. Algerian Immigration in France, 1912–1992]. Paris: Fayard.

———. 2010. *Le Mystère de Gaulle. Son choix pour l'Algérie* [The de Gaulle Mystery. His Choice for Algeria]. Paris: Robert Laffont.

Suggitt, Kelsey. 2018. Impossible Endings? Reimaging the End of the French Empire in the Sahara, 1951–1962. PhD Thesis, University of Portsmouth.

Surkis, Judith. 2010. Ethics and Violence: Simone de Beauvoir, Djamila Boupacha, and the Algerian War. *French Politics, Culture and Society* 28 (2): 38–55. https://doi. org/10.3167/fpcs.2010.280204.

Thénault, Sylvie. 2001. *Une drôle de justice: les magistrats dans la guerre d'Algérie* [A Funny Kind of Justice: Magistrates in the Algerian War]. Paris: La Découverte.

———. 2005. Personnel et internes dans les camps français de la guerre d'Algérie: entre stéréotypes coloniaux et combat pour l'indépendance [Personnel and Internees in French Camps During the Algerian War: Between Colonial Stereotypes and the Fight for Independence]. *Politix* 69: 63–81. https://doi.org/10.3917/ pox.069.0063.

———. 2008. The OAS in Algiers in 1962: A Story of Terrorist Violence and Its Agents. *Annales. Histoire, Sciences Sociales* 63 (5): 977–1001. https://www.cairn. info/article.php?ID_ARTICLE=ANNA_635_0977. Accessed 1 June 2020.

———. 2012a [2005]. *Histoire de la guerre d'indépendance algérienne* [History of the Algerian War of Independence]. Paris: Flammarion.

———. 2012b. Defending Algerian Nationalists in the Fight for Independence: The Issue of the 'rupture strategy'. *Mouvement Social* 240. https://doi.org/10.3917/ lms.240.0121.

Thomas, Martin. 2002. Defending a Lost Cause? France and the United States Vision of Imperial Rule in French North Africa, 1945–1956. *Diplomatic History* 26 (2): 215–130. https://doi.org/10.1111/1467-7709.00308.

———. 2005. Albert Sarraut, French Colonial Development and the Communist Threat, 1919–1930. *Journal of Modern History* 77 (4): 917–955.

Tyre, Stephen. 2006. From Algérie française to France musulmane: Jacques Soustelle and the Myths and Realities of 'Integration', 1955–1962. *French History* 20 (3): 276–296. https://doi.org/10.1093/fh/crl010.

Ulloa, Marie-Pierre. 2007. *Francis Jeanson: A Dissident Intellectual from the French Resistance to the Algerian War*. Trans. Jane Marie Todd. Stanford, CA: Stanford University Press.

Vaïsse, Maurice. 1998. *La Grandeur: Politique Etrangère du Général de Gaulle* [Greatness: The Foreign Policy of General de Gaulle]. Paris: Fayard.

Vaïsse, Maurice, and Jean-Claude Jauffret, eds. 2001. *Militaires et guérrillas dans la guerre d'Algérie* [Soldiers and Guerrillas in the Algerian War]. Brussels: Complexe.

Vautier, René. 1958. *Algérie en flammes* [Algeria in Flames]. East Germany: DEFA. Archives numériques du Cinéma Algérien [Youtube Channel]. https://www.youtube.com/watch?v=fnSrGUDksVo. Accessed 1 June 2020.

Vince, Natalya. 2010. Transgressing Boundaries: Gender, Race, Religion, and 'Françaises Musulmanes' during the Algerian War of Independence. *French Historical Studies* 33 (3): 445–474. https://doi.org/10.1215/00161071-2010-005

Vince, Natalya. 2015. *Our Fighting Sisters: Nation, Memory and Gender in Algeria, 1954–2012.* Manchester: Manchester University Press.

Von Bülow, Mathilde. 2007. Myth Or Reality? The Red Hand and French Covert Action in Federal Germany During the Algerian War, 1956–61. *Intelligence and National Security* 22 (6): 787–820. https://doi.org/10.1080/02684520701770626.

Wadowiec, Jaime. 2013. Algerian Women and the Rights of Man: Islam and Gendered Citizenship in French Algeria at the End of Empire. *French Historical Studies* 36 (4): 649–676. https://doi.org/10.1215/00161071-2294910.

Wall, Irvine M. 2001. *France, the United States and the Algerian War.* Berkeley, CA: University of California Press.

Welch, Edward, and Joseph McGonagle. 2013. *Contesting Views: The Visual Economy of France and Algeria.* Liverpool: Liverpool University Press.

Westad, Odd Arne. 2006. *The Global Cold War: Third World Interventions and the Making of Our Times.* Cambridge: Cambridge University Press.

Zimmerman, Sarah Jean. 2011. Living Beyond Boundaries: West African Servicemen in French Colonial Conflicts, 1908–1962. PhD Thesis, University of California.

Zoubir, Yahia. 1995. U.S. and Soviet Policies Towards France's Struggle with Anticolonial Nationalism in North Africa. *Canadian Journal of History/Annales canadiennes d'histoire* 30 (3): 439–466.

CHAPTER 4

Legacies, 1962–2020

THE BOUNDARIES OF TWO NEW NATION-STATES

The People's Democratic Republic of Algeria

The Algerian War/Algerian Revolution was a foundational event for both Algeria and France. In Algeria, the conflict gave birth to a new nation-state and a new politico-military elite forged through the anti-colonial struggle and the internal conflicts of the nationalist movement. On the world stage, and well into the 1970s, Algeria was considered 'the Mecca of Revolution'. This was a description coined by the Bissau-Guinean and Cape Verdean anti-colonial leader, Amílcar Cabral (1924–73): 'Christians go to the Vatican, Muslims go to Mecca, revolutionaries go to Algiers' (Byrne 2016, 3). After independence, Algeria provided political and military support for liberation movements elsewhere in the world, including nationalists fighting against Portuguese colonial rule in Angola, Mozambique, Bissau Guinea and Cape Verde, Nelson Mandela in apartheid South Africa and the Palestinian Liberation Organisation. The Black Panthers at one point had a base in Algiers, and leaders of the Cuban revolution Ché Guevara and Fidel Castro came to stay. In the middle of the Cuban Missile Crisis in October 1962, President Ben Bella took an aeroplane from his meeting with John F. Kennedy in the US directly to Cuba and a celebratory encounter with his 'brother' Fidel Castro (Byrne 2016, 140). This was a reflection of Algerian confidence on the world stage, breezily flouting the rules of Cold War blocs and dominant powers as it positioned itself as a Third Worldist (see Glossary) leader.

Within Algeria, the war accelerated rural to urban migration and the decline of traditional forms of social organisation centred around the village or family group. At least half of the seven million-strong rural population of Algeria had been uprooted during the war. Two thirds of these 3,500,000 people had been forcibly displaced by the French, the other third had fled to Algerian cities and the Tunisian and Moroccan borders to escape the violence of the war. The

© The Author(s) 2020
N. Vince, *The Algerian War, The Algerian Revolution*,
https://doi.org/10.1007/978-3-030-54264-1_4

country's economy and infrastructure had been severely damaged, and the departure of the majority of the European population in the course of spring and summer 1962 meant major shortages in personnel to run the administration, schools, hospitals, telecommunications, the energy supply and trains. The majority of the Algerian population was illiterate. For at least the first decade of independence, Algeria would rely heavily on technical experts, teachers and doctors sent from other countries. As across the world, 'modernisation' was the watchword (<<Chap. 3, pp. 116–18). Algeria invested heavily in education, healthcare and industrialisation through large-scale state planning. Although Algeria diversified its foreign partners by seeking out aid and trade packages from the United States, China, Yugoslavia and the USSR, France remained the major actor.

Arguments about what it meant to be Algerian persisted (<<Chap. 2, pp. 34–5, 54–5; Chap. 3, p. 67, 87). Algeria's new rulers presented themselves as Arab, African and revolutionary and adopted a socialist economic programme. The constitution of 1963 made Islam the religion of state, and Arabic the sole official and national language. All political parties, apart from the FLN, now a party rather than a wartime front, were banned. The 1963 Nationality Code, one of the most hotly contested pieces of legislation in the early years of independence, limited Algerian nationality to those whose father and grandfather possessed Muslim personal status (see Glossary) in the colonial era—that is to say, 'being Algerian' in 1963 was what had made you 'not fully French' in 1865. Exceptions were made for the small minority of Europeans who had actively supported the FLN. Many in this small group took Algerian nationality and stayed in Algeria. This included Claudine Chaulet (1931–2015), who in the 1960s and 1970s led research into agrarian reform at the Ministry of Agriculture, her husband Pierre Chaulet (1930–2012), a professor of medicine and senior government advisor, and Eveline Safir Lavalette (1927–2014), who was a deputy in the National Assembly in the 1960s (Fontaine 2016). In a nod to, but not entirely conforming with, the provisions of the Evian Accords (<<Chap. 3, pp. 140–1), the Nationality Code established that the rest of the European population of Algeria could choose Algerian nationality within three years of 1962 as long as they had been resident for 10 years (if born in Algeria) or 20 years (if not born in Algeria) and had not committed 'crimes against the nation' (i.e. fought against the FLN).

Making the Muslim personal status the key marker of Algerian citizenship was the formal end of the idea of a multi-community Algeria. A multi-community Algeria had been envisaged in the Evian Accords and FLN propaganda during the war had repeatedly affirmed that Europeans 'of goodwill' and Jews, who were presented as part of the autochthonous Algerian population, had their place in independent Algeria, as citizens like any other. In reality, the idea of a multi-community Algeria was long dead, if it had ever existed as a realistic possibility. The hostility of the majority of those with 'European' legal status to living in an independent Algeria where minorities had no special standing was deeply engrained. The violence of the war had only exacerbated this—the actions of the French army, European militias, the OAS and the FLN had pitched the 'European' and 'Muslim' communities against each other like never before. Between 1960 and 1962, 75 per cent of the 'European' population of Algeria (of settler and Jewish origin) left for mainland France—some 774,000 people (Scioldo-Zürcher 2010; in English see Scioldo-Zürcher 2016).

Amongst these 774,000 people were the Jews of Algeria. By early 1963, approximately 120,000 of the estimated 140,000-strong Jewish population of Algeria (<<Chap. 1, p. 8) had left. Recent work has challenged the long-held view that the Jewish departure from Algeria was inevitable, part of a dismal picture of the place of Jews in Muslim-majority societies in the 1950s and 1960s which made migration to the newly created state of Israel inexorable (Slyomovics and Stein 2012). Most of the Jewish population of Algeria migrated to France, not Israel. That does not mean that the Jews of Algeria would 'naturally' attach themselves to France, either. New historiographical approaches have intertwined the history of the Jewish presence in Algeria into broader accounts of Algerian and colonial societies, notably through fine-grained studies of urban neighbourhoods. This work has revealed the diversity and complexity of community relations, in which religion was only one factor in shaping affinities (Eldridge 2012). Nevertheless, the majority of the Jewish population, like the majority of the settler population, did leave Algeria in 1962. They left for the same reasons: they were suspicious of the FLN and/or of the Algerian population in general as a result of violence or the fear of violence, they feared that the FLN would build a 'Muslim state', or they were attached to a 'colonial spirit' which meant they did not want to be ruled by 'Arabs' (Le Foll Luciani 2015; in English see Hammerman 2018). In 1962, for the purposes of French public policy, the Jews of Algeria were subsumed into the category of 'European repatriates' (see Glossary). For the 8000 Jews of the Sahara, notably those living in the city of Ghardaïa in the M'zab valley, who had not been given French citizenship under the 1870 Crémieux decree and had been treated as 'indigenous people' like the 'Muslim' population, this meant the French state hastily naturalising them en masse in 1961 (Stein 2012).

That is not to say that independent Algeria was a hostile environment for Europeans or Jews once the violence of spring and summer 1962 had passed. With waves of foreign technical advisors, teachers and doctors arriving in Algeria after independence, many Algerian cities were very cosmopolitan, and those who stayed or went to Algeria after 1962 often look back on this period with fond memories of warm inter-community relations (Simon 2011). But after 1963, in the same way as in French policy-making after 1962 it was impossible to imagine someone who was non-white and Muslim as a 'natural' or 'obvious' French citizen, it became more difficult to imagine someone of European or Jewish origin as a 'natural' or 'obvious' Algerian citizen.

The French Republic

Todd Shepard (2006, 2016) has argued that the Algerian War of Independence was the catalyst for a radical reimagining of France as a white European nation-state rather than a multi-ethnic empire. This is strikingly illustrated by the very different treatment given to 'Europeans' (descendants of settlers and most of the Jewish population) and 'Muslims' (*harkis* and their families)—two sub-categories of French citizen which were no longer meant to exist after 1958 (<<Chap. 3, p. 112, see Glossary 'Europeans' and 'Muslims')—as they began to arrive in metropolitan France in 1962.

The majority of the Europeans of Algeria were not born in France (<<Chap. 1, p. 4, 8). For a large number, notably those of Spanish or Italian origin, and of course, the Jewish population, France had never been the home of their ancestors. What made them 'repatriates' was not any prior attachment to French land or family connections but rather their status as beneficiaries of the rights and protections of full French citizenship since the nineteenth century. It was because they had been French in Algeria that they could become repatriates in metropolitan France. For many, leaving Algeria was a brutal uprooting. Testimonies often employ the biblical term 'exodus'—also used to describe French civilians fleeing the advancing German army in 1940. A common theme of photographs from spring and summer 1962 is that of tearful families on ships bound for Marseille, surrounded by their worldly belongings, already looking back nostalgically to Algiers or Oran. Yet the emphasis in the many accounts of this period written by repatriates on personal catastrophe, culture shock and what they see as their abandonment by the French state has masked another story—that of a mostly well-organised response by the French administration, which, in an era of already sustained development of the welfare state, began to prepare for these new arrivals from the late 1950s onwards (Scioldo-Zürcher 2010). Backed by legislation and funding which had cross-party support, repatriates were provided with financial assistance to travel to France. They were then given priority for social housing and received help with employment and access to welfare payments in order to facilitate their social, economic and professional integration.

In part, this was an attempt to neutralise anger towards the government felt by the European population of Algeria, who had already shown their inclination for rebellion in the events of May 1958 which brought down the Fourth Republic (<<Chap. 3, pp. 109–10), the 'week of the barricades' in January 1960 (<<Chap. 3, p. 131) and the Generals' Putsch in April 1961 (<<Chap. 3, pp. 133–4). The French of Algeria did not benefit from a positive image in metropolitan France, either amongst government officials or in the media. In July 1962, the socialist major of Marseille, Gaston Defferre (1910–86), bemoaning the constant stream of arrivals in his city's ports, infamously expressed the wish that the repatriates leave Marseille as soon as possible and 'try to readapt somewhere else'. The repatriates were highly politicised and authorities in France were worried about their sympathy, both real and potential, for the OAS (<<Chap. 3, pp. 133–4, 141–2).

Rapidly, however, this popular image of hot-headed colonial diehards was replaced by one in which repatriates were pitched as victims who had lost everything, and Frenchmen and women whom the state had a duty to assist (Scioldo-Zürcher 2010, 155). Those who had been employed in the public sector in Algeria were guaranteed the same or equivalent job and grade in metropolitan France, the self-employed were given loans to help re-establish themselves, and large private sector employers were encouraged to follow the example set by the state and employ Europeans arriving in France from Algeria as a priority. These material measures were reasonably successful. For many, however, they did little to assuage a sense of loss and difference. In 1962, Enrico Macias released the single 'Adieu mon pays' [Farewell my country]. Macias (b. 1938) is the son of the celebrated Jewish musician Cheikh Raymond (1912–61), a key figure in the Andalusian musical tradition who had been murdered by a 'young Muslim gunman' in 1961 (Evans 2012, 10). In 'Adieu mon pays', Macias sang 'J'ai quitté mon pays/J'ai quitté ma maison/Ma vie, ma triste vie/Se traîne sans raison [I left my country/I left my home/My life, my sad life/Drags on meaninglessly'].

The Harkis: Between the New French and Algerian Nation-States

The national solidarity which was offered to the 'Europeans' of Algeria as Frenchmen and women was in stark contrast to that offered to 'Muslims' who tried to come to France after the Evian Accords. Those *harkis* (See Glossary) who were in service on 20 March 1962 were offered three choices: join the regular French army, return to civilian life with a bonus or take a six-month reflection period. Out of 40,500 *harkis* in active service at this point, 21,000 took the discharge with bonus and 15,000 left without asking for anything— meaning nearly nine out of 10 *harkis* went back to their homes. 1000 joined the regular French army, and 2000 opted for the period of reflection. At this point, only 1500 requested to come to France with their families (Moumen 2010, 49). These figures only concern those men who were actually in a 'harka' unit (i.e. were in an auxiliary unit of the French army). Since 1962, the term 'harki' has come to refer to a much wider group of people, also including those who were conscripts in the regular French army, administrators and elected representatives seen as 'pro-French' and the families of these men—wives, children and even grandchildren born many years after the end of the war.

As more *harkis* (understood in the broadest sense) were—or felt—threatened in Algeria they sought to leave for France. Between 1962 and 1965, around 42,000 people were transferred to camps in France by the French military authorities, and an estimated 40,000 others arrived without passing through a camp (Moumen 2010, 57). Those who made it to the barracks of a French army unit still stationed in Algeria were most likely to get transferred, but there was reluctance at the highest level of the French government to evacuate *harkis* and their families. The only official explanation given was that they were susceptible to sympathise with the OAS. There were a range of other reasons which were not made public. In the immediate term, the French government refused to anticipate or prepare for the arrival of the *harkis* because it feared that being seen to actively encourage large numbers of people whom it had ceased to claim as 'French' to move to France risked undermining a fragile peace process. In the longer term, the *harkis* and their families were considered socially undesirable in France. The vast majority were illiterate. They were potentially a source of tension if placed in too close proximity with the rest of the Algerian population in France. Moreover, as France reinvented itself as a European nation-state and no longer an empire, they became ethnically and culturally 'alien'. Whilst in theory *harkis* and their families were repatriates just like any other, in practice they were never 'just' repatriates and were referred to as 'Muslim repatriates', 'repatriates of North African origin' or 'refugees'. In contradiction with the provisions of the Evian Accords, on 21 July 1962 it was declared that French citizens with 'local status' (i.e. 'Muslims') had to voluntarily declare their wish to (continue to) be French and be physically present on metropolitan French soil when they did so.

As numerous studies published from the 1990s onwards make clear, those *harkis* who made it to France encountered miserable conditions. They were parked in camps (Larzac, Rivesaltes, Bias and Saint-Maurice-l'Ardoise) in isolated rural areas in the south of France, often behind barbed wire (Fig. 4.1). None of these camps were new—they all had previous existences as military training centres or internment camps for Jewish and Spanish refugees, German and Italian prisoners of war or supporters of the FLN (Miller 2013; see also Moumen 2012). In 1964, these *harkis* and their families were joined by some Guinean soldiers who had fought in the French army in Algeria, accompanied by their wives and children. These soldiers had—unlike the majority of Guineans—voted to remain in the French Community in the 1958 Referendum and chosen to stay in the French army when their country became independent (<<Chap. 3, pp. 124–6). Neither Guinean President Sekou Touré nor the French military wanted them (Mann 2006, 142). The movements of families in the camps were closely controlled and children received only a limited on-site education. Supposedly temporary, many families remained there for decades. In 1981, there were still 3560 families—the equivalent of 28,500 people—living in such camps (Eldridge 2009, 93).

The violence to which the *harkis* were subjected in Algeria in spring and summer 1962 remains a subject of intense historical and political controversy. For some historians and activists, who often come from within the *harki* community, the *harkis* were victims of a 'massacre'. For these historians and activists, this massacre resulted from the combination of two factors. Firstly, the desire for revenge on the part of nationalists and civilian populations in Algeria, for their own wartime suffering, or motivated by baser urges to seize the property and livelihoods of *harkis* and their families. Secondly, the criminal indifference of the French authorities towards people who had served them. In Algerian official history, the *harkis* are dismissed as a Franco-French problem: the French army cynically recruited them in an attempt to crush the nationalist

Fig. 4.1 Metropolitan France, including some of the camps used to intern Algerians suspected of being in the FLN and later 'accommodate' *harkis*

movement and if the French state did not want to take responsibility for them at the end of the war, the *harkis* only had themselves to blame as traitors to the nation and collaborators with the enemy. In Algerian official history, the term 'massacre' is rejected, and it is claimed that if a few *harkis* were subject to reprisal attacks then these were isolated incidents spontaneously carried out by long-suffering local populations. The Algerian official line is that *harkis* were either pardoned, or, if they were tried for wartime crimes, this was through a legal framework with punishments such as a prison term or a temporary loss of civil rights.

What these apparently radically opposed interpretations of the fate of the *harkis* after 1962 both imply is that the *harkis* and their families were French loyalists. Yet as we have seen (<<Chap. 3, pp. 122–3), individuals' and families' motivations and actions during the war were much more heterogeneous, ambiguous and difficult to classify than simply being 'for the FLN' or 'for

French Algeria'. At least initially, if we refer to the statistics above, nine out of ten *harkis* went home—they saw their place in independent Algeria.

The lack of reliable records in a period of major population displacement and conflict between many different rival groups makes it difficult to lay to rest controversies about the number of *harkis* killed. Piecing together the fragments of archives which are available, it seems that between the ceasefire in March 1962 and the declaration of independence in July 1962, violence against *harkis* was scattered and sporadic. The most intense violence came after independence was declared, with kidnappings, assassinations and executions after 'trials' run by 'people's courts'. This was not ordered from the top of the FLN-EMG-GPRA (i.e. there was not a coordinated 'massacre' in the singular), but nor was it entirely anarchic and led by uncontrollable angry crowds. There is evidence that some incidences of violence were coordinated by some members of the newly formed Algerian army (Armée nationale populaire, ANP) or local police forces (Moumen 2011). The figure often repeated by *harki* associations is that 150,000 people were killed. What is less often stated is that this figure is based on a 1963 report from the district of Abkou (Kabylia), where a former French administrator estimated that around 2000 *harkis* had been killed. When 2000 is multiplied by the 72 districts of Algeria at the time (with no discussion of how representative Akbou was of the rest of Algeria), and rounded up, the figure of 150,000 is reached (Moumen 2011; in English see Cohen 2006). Historians' estimates range from 15,000 to 30,000 people (Stora 2005, 24) to 60,000–75,000 people (Eldridge 2009, 92).

With the focus on how many *harkis* were killed in Algeria by Algerians, and the French state's poor treatment of those *harkis* who made it to France, little attention has been paid to those who remained in Algeria after 1962 and were not killed, despite this being the situation of the majority of former *harkis*. This is hardly surprising. The question of the *harkis*—and more precisely who was/is a *harki*—continues to be politically explosive in Algeria. A key theme in contemporary Algerian oppositional discourse is that Algeria's woes can be explained as a result of the grip on power of *harkis* and their descendants, who stole independence from the 'true *mujahidin*' (see Glossary) in summer 1962 and have been wearing the cloak of historical legitimacy under false pretences ever since. In short, in Algeria, 'harki' is an insult and a metaphor more than it is a label to accurately identify a specific group of people.

The majority of Algerians who had been auxiliaries in the French army (i.e. actual *harkis*, to use the specific meaning of the term) who remained in Algeria after 1962 came from poor peasant backgrounds. One can well imagine that survival would involve keeping very quiet about their past. In some families, some siblings or cousins would have fought for the FLN/ALN whilst others were *harkis*. Participating in the war on opposing sides generally did not supersede family ties after independence. Family members in the FLN/ALN could shield their relatives from potential mob violence, arrest, imprisonment or the confiscation of property (Daum 2015). Equally, the new Algerian authorities were keen to avoid anarchical blood-letting—beyond any humanitarian considerations, disorderly violence threatened the stability of the nascent Algerian state. Some of those who had formerly worked with the French did better than others. 'Harkis' (to use the term generically) who had military experience (i.e. who had risen up the ranks in the French army and therefore were not actually auxiliaries) or who had been low level colonial administrators (again, not former auxiliaries) were more likely than illiterate peasants to find their place in an independent Algeria with a desperate need for skilled personnel.

THE ALGERIAN WAR/ ALGERIAN REVOLUTION AS AN EVER-PRESENT PAST? THE INFLUENCE AND LIMITATIONS OF PSYCHOANALYTICAL APPROACHES TO THE LEGACIES OF THE WAR

The Algerian War of Independence is still widely seen as a set of events (violence, torture, attempts at winning 'hearts and minds', population displacement) which ended in 1962, only to be subsequently, and painfully, repressed, revisited, relived and reproduced on both sides of the Mediterranean. In part, this is the result of the enduring popularity of the application of ideas drawn from psychoanalysis to understanding the legacies of the war and colonialism more broadly. Benjamin Stora's work remains seminal in such interpretations. In his 1991 *La Gangrène et l'Oubli*, Stora insisted on the gangrenous effects of occultation and the need to collectively 'come to terms' with the past:

> Franco-Algerian relations were forged in violence, by the imposition of the colonial system and by a seven-year war which enabled Algeria to acquire independence. This is why, thirty years later, time has not appeased passions. [...] From 1962 onwards, the Mediterranean, whose name in Arabic, *al-bahr al-abyad al-moutawassat* means 'the white sea in the middle', became a fracture line, an imaginary blue 'wall'. The violent divorce has unceasingly fed tensions, obsessions and fantasies from one shore to the other. (Stora 1991, 317)

Much of the work on the memory of the Algerian War has been inspired by Henry Rousso's pioneering analyses of how memories of Nazi occupation and the collaborationist Vichy regime have shifted in France since the end of the Second World War. Mirroring the stages of memory outlined by Rousso in *The Vichy Syndrome* (1991 [1987]), the 'memory' of the Algerian War in France has generally been divided into four periods by scholars: amnesia (1962–mid-1970s), challenges to amnesia (late 1970s–1980s), the return of the repressed (1990s) and obsession (2000s onwards). However, a growing number of works on the legacies and memories of the war have begun to move away from such psychoanalysis-influenced categorisations.

Connecting the local, national, transnational and global: an alternative framework for thinking about the legacies and memories of the Algerian War/Algerian Revolution

In the broader field of memory studies, scholars have underlined that nations do not 'remember' in the same way as individuals. Nations can forget less glorious aspects of the national past with no ill effects. Past events do not irrepressibly erupt into the nation's consciousness—they have to be activated and purposefully brought to public attention by individuals and groups. Rather than the Algerian War/Algerian Revolution being repressed, revisited, relived and reproduced—as if it is a fixed object—it is instead refracted through more recent events, repackaged for new contexts and repurposed for present needs. Thus instead of amnesia, challenges to amnesia, the return of the repressed and obsession, four alternative categories will be used here: (1) 1962–mid-1970s: post-war practicalities and establishing the moral basis for material demands; (2) mid-1970s–early 1990s: identity politics: making one's place in the story of the nation; (3) 1990s: the transnational memory turn: crimes against humanity, genocide, reparation, apology and law-making; and (4) mid-2000s onwards: the colonial/anti-colonial past as political code and strategic weapon.

The idea is not that we pass neatly from one period to another and that previous concerns and ways of thinking about and 'using' the war evaporate, but rather that each new stage is superimposed on the next and different demands and languages come to the fore. The advantage of this categorisation is that it works in an Algerian context as well as a French one, whereas the psychoanalysis-influenced categories were always much more focused on what was going on in France. This is *not* to argue that the memory of the Algerian Revolution in Algeria has developed in the same way as the memory of the Algerian War in France. Indeed, the often-used term 'Franco-Algerian memory wars' is in many ways a misnomer. As will be demonstrated, memories of the war in Algeria and in France have developed in different contexts and have served different purposes, meaning that they have their own codes and controversies which make 'memory wars' only rarely cross-Mediterranean. What this alternative categorisation allows us to do is to locate French and Algerian memories not in relation to *each other*, but rather see them both as connected to a wider, *global* political, legal, socio-economic and cultural context.

1962–MID-1970s: POST-WAR PRACTICALITIES AND ESTABLISHING THE MORAL BASIS FOR MATERIAL DEMANDS

For both Algeria and France, material demands and legal issues (tying up the 'loose ends' of the war) were primary preoccupations in the first decade after 1962. Accompanying the March 1962 Evian Accords in France were two presidential decrees issued by de Gaulle, amnestying acts committed in support of, and in order to repress, the 'Algerian insurrection'. This led to the release of around 15,000 prisoners held by the French authorities in Algeria, and around 5000 held in France, the vast majority of whom were Algerian support- ers of the FLN. The amnesties also meant that French administrators and members of the military could not be subject to legal proceedings related to torture, rape, extrajudicial killings and 'disappearances' (<<Chap. 3, pp. 94–6, 100, 119, 121, 123; >> Chap. 4, p. 183, 188). The March 1962 amnesty was complemented by a series of other decrees in France in 1964, 1966 and 1968. These amnestied Frenchmen and women who had joined the FLN in France (<<Chap. 3, p. 120) and former members of the OAS (Gacon 2005). As we have seen, a legislative and financial arsenal was established to meet the arrival of the 'European' repatriates).

In Algeria, the Ministry of Mujahidin was created in 1962, with the primary purpose of representing the interests of war veterans and the widows and orphans of the war dead. Veterans began to gather the necessary evidence to obtain a 'mujahid' card, which in turn would facilitate access to employment, small busi- ness ownership or a return to education, amongst other benefits. Orphanages were set up for children who had lost their parents. Indeed, orphans were con- sidered one of the major social issues of the immediate post-independence years. Whilst *Le Vent des Aurès/Rih al awras* [The Winds of the Aures] (Mohamed Lakhdar-Hamina, CNC-ONCIC 1966) and *The Battle of Algiers* (Gillo Pontecorvo, Casbah Films-Igor films, 1966) are often seen as emblematic of the first wave of Algerian post-independence cinema, providing epic, heroic accounts of the Algerian people's liberation struggle, the first feature-length film made in independent Algeria, funded by the Algerian state, was actually set in a post- independence orphanage. Jacques Charby's *Une si jeune paix* [Such a young peace] (CNC-ONCIC 1964) told the story of a football match between orphans which degenerated into a fight, as the children replayed the street battles which they had witnessed between the FLN and the OAS.

In France, amnesties were part of a process of glossing over the fractures of the war. A divisive conflict which had fractured France domestically, damaged her international image, and resulted in the loss of an integral part of her terri- tory, was submerged within a Gaullist narrative of successful—as in intentional and carefully planned—African decolonisation, riding on the 'tide of history' (Shepard 2006, 89). According to de Gaulle and his supporters, he had suc- ceeded in extricating France from the Algerian quagmire where a series of pre- vious governments had miserably failed (<<Chap. 3, pp. 113–4). The fact that de Gaulle had come to power in 1958 on the understanding that he would do the exact opposite was not mentioned (<<Chap. 3, p. 139). The war—which was still officially referred to as 'operations to maintain order in North Africa' until 1999—had little public visibility. This did not mean that 'French Algeria' had been forgotten. A small number of repatriate associations—most promi- nently, the National Association of the French of North Africa, Overseas and their Friends (Association nationale des Français d'Afrique du Nord, d'outre- mer et de leurs amis, ANFANOMA)—were established from the late 1950s

onwards. Their primary goal was to offer administrative support to repatriates and make practical demands of the French state rather than articulate a 'repatriate' version of the war which would challenge the Gaullist line. Nevertheless, the very existence of these associations was an essential prerequisite for the emergence of a '*pied-noir* memory' from the 1970s onwards. As Claire Eldridge argues (2016, 48): 'the link established by associations between material support and acceptance into the [French] national community became a potent mobilisation tool that was used to bind individual *rapatriés* [repatriates] together into a constituency with a strong sense of common purpose and entitlement.' Small-scale memorialisation, with the support of local politicians, also began from 1962 onwards: for example, putting a memorial in local cemeteries, to mark the fact that repatriates could no longer go to visit the graves of their relatives buried in Algeria.

Debating the nature of Algerian nationalism: 'true' and 'false' *mujahidin*
In Algeria, the official version of *al-thawra al-jazā'iriyya* (the Algerian Revolution) was designed to unify the Algerian people after independence, legitimise those political and military figures who took power in summer 1962 and justify the political directions which they took. The story told was one which 'the people' came together as one, under the leadership of the FLN, to reclaim their land and their Arabo-Islamic identity. Former members of the '*ulama* and their descendants were particularly influential in shaping the Arabo-Islamic aspect of the narrative (<<Chap. 2, pp. 32–5). Armed struggle was glorified, and political activity was marginalised, reflecting the dominant place of the Algerian army in the post-independence political system, and the marginalised status of many members of the former GPRA and the FF-FLN (<<Chap. 3, pp. 142–4). Messali Hadj's role in the emergence of Algerian nationalism (<<Chap. 2, pp. 29–32) was ignored. Political legitimacy stemmed not from democratic processes, but through being able to demonstrate one's veteran status. Whilst the *mujahidin* fighting and dying on Algerian soil were glorified, it was not mentioned that the key figures who took power had themselves spent much of the war on the Tunisian and Moroccan borders. Those who rejected the political, economic and cultural direction of the post-independence state were stigmatised as acting in the interests of France, being part of *hizb fransa* (literally, the party of France).

At the same time, the post-independence Algerian state has never had a monopoly on using the war as a source of political legitimacy. Sharing in the idea promoted in official history that the war brought together the Algerian people in a collective struggle for noble ideals, opponents of the country's post-independence leaders (such as Hocine Aït Ahmed, Ferhat Abbas and Mohamed Boudiaf) were quick to declare that those who took power in summer 1962 had betrayed these values and the

(*continued*)

(continued)

Algerian people. Abbas entitled his 1984 memoirs *L'indépendance confisquée* [Independence confiscated]. Popular criticism of those in positions of power described them as DAF (<<Chap. 3, p. 88), *marsiens* (<<Chap. 3, p. 144), *harkis*, the Oujda clan (<<Chap. 3, p. 109) and the Lacoste promotion (<<Chap. 3, p. 84) to discredit them. A commonly held view of those who opposed the political system after 1962 was that if true *mujahidin* had taken power, independent Algeria would be a better place. This somewhat conveniently ignores that plenty of true *mujahidin* did hold positions of power, and as a general rule, true combatants can also do bad things.

Far away from the centre of power, rural women composed poems in which they recounted the war in their own words, celebrating local heroes and heroines (Bamia 2001; Slyomovics 2014). They also sought—often unsuccessfully—to have their own veteran status recognised or acquire a war widow's pension, and began to develop critical views of a state which they saw as having failed to fulfil its 'blood debt' (see Glossary) towards them (Vince 2015, 236–239). The war was less visibly present in the public landscape in Algeria in the first decade of independence than it would become in subsequent years. Certainly, the Algerian state rapidly established a series of national days which marked key moments in the war (1 November, 5 July). It enshrined its version of the revolution in the 1963 Constitution and renamed streets and schools, replacing the names of colonial conquerors with those of nationalist heroes and heroines. But large-scale memorial projects—such as Algiers' Monument to the Martyr (*maqam al-shahid*)—would have to wait until the 1980s (>>Chap. 4, p. 178). The National Centre for Historical Studies, attached to the Ministry for the Interior and which would coordinate the writing of a state-sanctioned history, was only created in the mid-1970s (Remaoun 1994). In part, this was because Algeria's leaders had more pressing issues to deal with than commemoration in the first years of independence. In part, too, this indicates that there was not yet an agreed official line on what to 'do' with the war. Algeria's leaders simultaneously had confidence in the attachment of Algerians—unlikely to forget the war anytime soon—to a narrative of collective, anti-colonial unity, and, at the same time, they were anxious about where commemoration might stop once it began in earnest. What old rivalries—political, regional or personal—might be stirred if statues started to be erected to some figures and not others? But above all, this period of more low-key commemoration, in comparison to the more ostentatious celebrations which would follow, reflects the fact that during the 1960s and early 1970s Algeria had, alongside the wartime slogans of 'by the people, for the people' and 'one sole hero, the people', another, much more forward-looking, narrative of national construction. Appealing to both the wartime generation and those too young to have participated in the war, this was a vision of a radiant future which would be achieved by combatting illiteracy, poor housing, ill health and underdevelopment. Despite ongoing arguments about the 'winners' and 'losers' of independence, this was not a period of definitively dashed hopes, even for those on the 'losing' side of the infighting of summer 1962, but rather one of the unfinished revolution.

MID-1970s–EARLY 1990s: IDENTITY POLITICS—MAKING ONE'S PLACE IN THE STORY OF THE NATION

The Invention of the Pieds Noirs

Post-May 1968 France (and indeed the rest of the West) saw a turn to 'post-material values'. This is the idea that meeting material demands—a decent wage, housing, healthcare and education—were not enough for human fulfilment, individuals and groups also needed to be able to freely define and live their identity. The 1970s saw the birth second wave feminism, the gay liberation movement and anti-racist movements. The shift to this politics of identity also facilitated the public emergence in France of alternative narratives to the Gaullist version of decolonisation. Different groups sought to make their account of events part of the French national story, and in doing do make what they saw as their distinctive characteristics an integral part of French national identity.

The first identity-orientated repatriate association was Cercle algérianiste (Algerianist circle). Created in 1973, its stated aim was 'to save an endangered culture' and its logo featured a *hamsa* (the hand of Fatima, a popular symbol of prosperity and luck for Muslims and Jews across the Middle East and North Africa) and two black feet ('pieds noirs'). The origin of the name 'pieds noirs' is uncertain—for some it is a reference to being born on African soil, others claim that this is what the autochthonous population called the French soldiers landing in Algiers in 1830 when they saw their black boots. The activities of associations such as the Cercle algérianiste included study groups, exhibitions and book prizes (and an increasing number of testimonies began to be published), as well as mounting petitions and writing letters to elected representatives. Some associations also continued to campaign for amnesties for OAS members not yet covered by the amnesty legislation in place.

Whilst this extensive production gives the impression that time stopped for these associations in 1962, they have always been less about plunging back into the past, and more about inventing a new 'pied-noir identity' in the present. After all, in colonial Algeria, those with 'European' status were heterogeneous—they were religiously diverse (Catholic, Jewish, secular), they came from a wide range of socio-economic backgrounds (from large landowners to poor urban labourers) and they held different political views (<<Chap. 1, p. 4, 7–8). It was at the point at which the majority of them arrived in France in

1962, and through the shared experience of displacement, that they all became repatriates and the label 'pieds noirs' came into general usage. As Eric Savarese puts it in his aptly titled *L'invention des pieds noirs* [The invention of the pieds noirs] (2002, 120–121; in English see Savarese 2006), after 1962 the very fact of not existing in Algeria made the construction of a *pied-noir* community in France possible.

That is not to say there is a single *pied-noir* memory, and there are often deep rivalries between different associations. However, there are a number of key elements in their accounts of colonial Algeria, and its end, which are reproduced across repatriate associations. Algeria is depicted a lost paradise, where through the sweat of their brows, pioneers from Europe 'made the desert bloom' and led a 'civilising mission', building roads, hospitals and schools. Europeans are presented as getting on well with their 'Muslim' neighbours, until the FLN poison set in, and the Gaullist betrayal senselessly brought this idyll to an end. Exile to France was deeply painful, carried out in precipitation and panic—the expression 'the suitcase or the coffin' has become embedded in *pied-noir* mythology, encapsulating the claim that they had no real choice in 1962 (Eldridge 2016, 106). For this idealised view of colonial Algeria to work, a 'liberating amnesia' (Savarese 2002, 164) is necessary, selectively forgetting the deep inequalities of the colonial system, the domination and impoverishment of the Algerian people and the violence of the OAS (and notably the role of the OAS in popularising the expression 'the suitcase or the coffin' (<<Chap. 3, p. 141). Algerians have very little place in these *pied-noir* narratives and there is no serious consideration of whether those who had benefited from full French citizenship since the nineteenth century would have wanted to live in an Algeria in which there was majority rule and they were no longer a privileged minority. Post-1962 Algeria barely exists in these accounts—place names are always given in their colonial iterations and if the post-independence state is mentioned it tends to be through the lens of its perceived failings. The spirit is often very much that of French singer Michel Sardou, who in 1979 penned a song entitled 'Ils ont le pétrole, mais c'est tout' (They've got petrol, but that's it), vaunting France's 'Latin paradise' in response to Algerian nationalisation of French-owned petrol companies in February 1971.

Pied-noir associations have different political tendencies (Comtat 2009). Many are nostalgic, a few seek to make links with Algeria and Algerians in a spirit of reconciliation, others are overtly racist and with clear connections to the French far right. Generally speaking, by the mid-1970s, these associations were no longer focused on securing material support to help repatriates integrate into French society. Instead, they had turned their attention to demands for compensation (a demand which would be in part met by two laws in 1970 and 1978) and specific recognition for their distinctiveness. The association Unitary Rally and Coordination for Repatriates and the Dispossessed (Rassemblement et coordination unitaires des rapatriés et spoliés, RECOURS), founded in 1976 by Jacques Roseau (1938–93), was particularly effective at identifying individual politicians from different parties who might be sympathetic to advancing *pied-noir* interests locally and nationally. In return, RECOURS mobilised tactical voting in favour of these candidates. RECOURS was also in favour of closer links between the French and Algerian states. Other *pied-noir* organisations were much more hostile to any hint of Franco-Algerian cooperation. Justice Pied-Noir (1975–6) perpetrated a number of attacks on Algerians living in France, including bombing Air Algeria and an immigrant hostel housing Algerian workers (Scioldo-Zürcher 2012, 486). In 1993, Rouseau was murdered by three rival *pied-noir* men.

One the concerns central to the campaigns of many associations was defining the official chronology of the war. This could bring them into conflict with associations representing soldiers in the French army who had served in Algeria. The National Federation of Veterans of Algeria, Morocco and Tunisia (Fédération nationale des anciens combattants en Algérie, Maroc et Tunisie, FNACA) was created in 1958 to represent the interests of French war veterans. It lobbied for the war to be recognised as a war and for its participants to obtain the status of combatants. The latter demand would be satisfied in 1974, the former in 1999. The FNACA have also campaigned for 19 March, the day of the ceasefire in 1962, to be designated a day to commemorate military and civilian victims of the war. This happened for the first time in 2012 (Narayanan 2014). This date is anathema to *pied-noir* associations, for whom 19 March not only symbolises their defeat, but also marks the beginning of what they see as some of the worst violence inflicted against them—for example, in Algiers on 26 March or in Oran on 5 July 1962 (<<Chap. 3, p. 141). On 19 March 1988, when French army veterans organised a demonstration as part of their campaign to obtain official commemoration of 19 March, repatriate associations organised a counter-demonstration, accusing FNACA members of being 'fellagas' (the pejorative term used to describe ALN fighters) and 'communist assassins' (Savarese 2002, 136).

Representing mainly conscript soldiers, and therefore less ideologically engaged in the colonial project, the FNACA certainly did not reflect the views of all members of the army. Many senior military figures sustained close links with *pied-noir* associations, and lest it be forgotten, a number of generals and senior army officers had been key members of the OAS. Much of the French army leadership was convinced that they had won the war militarily but had been sold out by the politicians. Persuaded that their experiences in Indochina (where France lost) and Algeria (where France lost again) made them experts in counter insurgency and psychological warfare (<<Chap. 3, p. 90, 100, 102), many senior veterans of the Algerian War went on to provide strategic and tactical training to armies in the US and South America.

Harkis: *From Loyalist Symbol to Second-Generation Demands*

Until the mid-1970s, the 'case' of the *harkis* was appropriated by *pied-noir* associations and the section of the former 'Muslim' elite which had remained fervent supporters of 'French Algeria', notably 'Bachaga' Saïd Boualem.

Following a long career in the French army, Boualem became a National Assembly deputy in 1958 and rose to the role of vice-president of the Assembly until 1962. Upon independence, the French state facilitated his permanent move to France, with a large entourage, and there he penned his biography, entitled *Mon pays la France* [My country, France] (1962). Unlike the vast majority of the *harki* population in France, Boualam was literate and well-connected politically and with the media. Alongside *pied-noir* associations, he elaborated a politically useful story in which he used the fact that the *harkis* lived in miserable conditions in French camps as the ultimate evidence of the terrible Gaullist betrayal of 'French Algeria'. Neither Boualam nor the *pied-noir* associations paid much attention to the voices or experiences of the *harki* men, women and children for whom they claimed to speak.

Harkis came to national prominence in 1975, following a series of demonstrations and riots in the Bias and Saint Maurice l'Ardoise camps (Fig. 4.1), in protest against living conditions and the lack of job opportunities. A new wave of associations was formed, but their leaders still tended to come from families of 'Muslim' notables who had been supporters of French Algeria rather than actual former auxiliaries in the French army. M'hamed Laradji, founder of the Confederation of French Muslims Repatriated from Algeria (Confédération des Français musulmans rapatriés d'Algérie, CFMRAA), who had been a *qadi* (local administrator) in colonial Algeria, is a case in point (Choi 2016, 105). These associations struggled to sustain momentum, and still found themselves in an unequal, subordinate partnership with *pied-noir* associations, although they would benefit from the compensation laws of the 1970s and 1980s. In 1989, the *harkis* had their first stamp dedicated to them by the French post office, with the slogan 'Tribute to the *harkis*, soldiers of France'.

It was not until 1991, when there was another series of *harki* protests, that a new generation of *harki* memory activists emerged. From just 40 *harki* associations in 1973 to 400 in 1991, there were an estimated 540 by the early 2000s (Eldridge 2009, 95). Most of these were led by the adult children of *harkis*. Historians, filmmakers and writers, these women and men had the tools at their disposal to tell a different story to that promoted by the *pieds noirs*, who depicted *harkis* as martyrs of French Algeria. They also often had a desire to move away from the far-right connections of the first *harki* associations. For Mohand Hamoumou (b. 1956), the founder of the Association for Justice, Information and Reparation for *harkis* (Association justice, information et réparation pour les harkis, AJIR) and Fatima Besnaci-Lancou (b. 1954), founding member of *Harkis* and human rights (Harkis et droits de l'homme), the *harkis* did not enrol out of patriotism. Economic misery, pressure from the French army or the violence of the FLN are put forward as much more likely motivations. That said, the issue of choice is not dwelled upon by these associations, nor is the question of the acts of violence which *harkis* might have participated in during the war. Instead, this new generation of activists argued that *harkis* were victims of a colonial system which cynically enrolled them and then dumped them when they were no longer useful (Sims

2016). For Hamoumou, *harkis* were 'Arab martyrs of French Algeria' (Branche 2005, 58). The central topic and focus for commemorative activities for these *harki* activists was life in the camps from 1962 onwards—and after all, this was all many children of *harkis* had directly experienced. Like the *'pied-noir* identity', the *'harki* identity' was thus a post-1962 creation on French soil (Fabbiano 2008). The children of *harkis* brought together fragments of stories transmitted to them by their parents and their own experiences of growing up in a camp, as well as borrowing from and reacting against previous paternalistic, self-serving elite appropriations of the *'harki* story': 'Reappropriating the past was thus seen as a way for the second generation not only to obtain retrospective historical justice but also to situate their own identity in the present' (Eldridge 2009, 103). A law passed on 11 June 1994 officially recognised the debt of the French Republic to *harkis* for their sacrifices. It set out a range of welfare payments and help with housing to which *harkis* in France and their families were entitled.

17 October 1961: A Date for Second-Generation Algerians in France

The third group of memory activists which began to emerge in France in the late 1970s was led by the children of Algerian migrants to France. Their parents might have fought with or supported the FLN, or not played an active role in the conflict, but this second generation was born in France and they were unlikely to return to Algeria as their parents had once imagined they would. Confronting the institutional racism and everyday discrimination and violence which they were faced with in France thus became a priority. These memory activists coalesced around demanding official recognition of the atrocities committed on 17 October 1961 against FLN demonstrators (<<Chap. 3, pp. 134–7). The parents of many of these second-generation activists had participated in this demonstration, but not necessarily transmitted their memories to their children. Descendants of Algerians were often more likely to find out about 17 October through the memoires of French anti-colonial activists (House and Macmaster 2006, 19).

The choice of 17 October 1961 was significant. It had no place in French official history, but nor did it have a place in Algerian official history as many senior members of the FF-FLN had been marginalised shortly after the end of the war—hence the retreat into strategic silence by the demonstration's participants. From 1968 onwards, 17 October was given the title 'national day of emigration' in Algeria, but this was not a national holiday and the purpose was to mark the achievements of Algerians abroad, and the hold of President Boumediene over them, rather than integrate the date into the history of the nationalist movement (Cole 2003). The date could thus belong to Algerians in France, and especially to their children born in France, who were both French and Algerian. Indeed, 17 October could resonate beyond those with a connection to Algeria as a powerful example of state-sanctioned, racist police violence and official cover-up. Jim House (2001, 361) argues: 'Neither formalised, closed or institutionalised, the memory of 17 October was available to be used by Algerians and other racialised groups as a strategic resource in their opposition to racism in France from the early 1970s onwards.'

In 1990, the association In the name of memory (Au nom de la mémoire) was created by the journalist Samia Messaoudi, the filmmaker Medhi Lallaoui and the historian Benjamin Stora to promote public knowledge about workers' history (including the history of immigration), urban history and colonial memory in France, through exhibitions, film, fiction and working with teachers and the Ministry of Education. One of its first activities was a commemoration of the thirtieth anniversary of 17 October 1961, organised with the anti-racist organisation Movement against Racism and for Friendship between Peoples (Mouvement contre le racisme et pour l'amitié entre les peuples, MRAP). On the thirtieth anniversary of 17 October in 1991, 10,000 demonstrators followed the same route as those of the 17 October 1961 march, under the banner 'No to racism, no to forgetting. For the right to memory'. Since then, there have been a plethora of films, books, fiction and songs about 17 October, from Léila Sebbar's 1999 novel *La Seine était rouge* [The Seine was red] to Yasmina Adi's documentary *Ici on noie les Algériens* [Here we drown Algerians] (2011) to Michael Haneke's *Caché* [Hidden] (2005) and the rapper Médine's (b. 1983) song *17 octobre* (2006).

Alternative Histories with a Shared Core: A Culturally Plural, Amazigh (Berber) Algeria, Feminist Anti-colonial Nationalism and Good Muslim Algerians

In Algeria, the official version of the Algerian Revolution in which the people united behind the FLN to recover Algeria's Arabo-Islamic identity was increasingly challenged by the late 1970s and early 1980s. Left-wing activists sought out forms of nationalism different to those of the FLN, or rather the branch of the FLN which took power in 1962. They accused this faction of the FLN of encouraging the development of a narrow, cultural nationalism and building an authoritarian state which had inhibited the emergence of a more plural Algerian identity and democratic political culture. As Nedjib Sidi Moussa (2014) argues in relation to the resurgence of interest in Messali Hadj, the ENA, PPA-MTLD and MNA from the 1980s onwards, 'Talking about Messalists is a means to interrogate pluralism in Algeria, its possibilities and its limits, before and after the colonial moment.' The origins of 'feminist' and 'pro-Berber/pluralist' versions of the nationalist past (to use a very crude shorthand) can also be found in the late 1970s and early 1980s. For social and religious conservatives, meanwhile, the post-independence state had not sufficiently decolonised, and they sought to wrest the legacy of the *'ulama* from state-sponsored history (<<Chap. 4, pp. 168–9) in order to also develop their own story of the past, present and future of Algerian nationalism.

A Culturally Plural, Amazigh (Berber) Algeria

In 1980, a planned conference on Kabyle poetry by Mouloud Mammeri (1917–89) was banned by the Algerian authorities. Just 15 years previously, Mammeri had penned, in French, the epic novel about the Algerian Revolution *L'Opium et le Bâton* (The opium and the stick), which received state funding to be turned into a film. His conference on poetry in Tamazight (Berber) was less pleasing to the Algerian state. The cancellation was the spark which set off the 'Berber Spring'. This was a series of protests and riots in which cultural and linguistic oppression (the only official and national language of Algeria since independence was Arabic) were magnified by socio-economic misery in the Tamazight-speaking region of Kabylia.

One of the ways in which demands for cultural recognition and political change were articulated was through the language of the past. In the 1970s, alongside publishing grammars of the Tamazight language and studies of Kabyle culture, activist scholars began to re-examine nationalist history. Some argued that if 'Kabyle' figures in the nationalist movement had been listened to more, or marginalised less, notably at the moment of so-called Berber crisis within the PPA-MTLD of 1949—now relabelled the 'anti-Berber crisis'—a more democratic and secular nationalist movement would have developed (Ouerdane 1987, 45). Labelling the internal conflicts of 1949 'the Berber crisis' is an over-simplification (<<Chap. 2, pp. 54–5). Nevertheless, in 1949 Messali Hadj and his supporters had sought to discredit their opponents by labelling them 'Berberists', accusing them of promoting minority ethnic, linguistic and regional values at the expense of nationalist unity. Decades later, adopting the same interpretation of the crisis as primarily religious and cultural (rather than political), but this time writing from the side of those who fell afoul of Messali Hadj, self-designated Berber activists pitched 1949 as the historical origin of their contemporary struggles, the moment when the opportunity to create a culturally and politically plural Algeria was lost. This version of the past conveniently forgot that a number of key figures in the FLN from Kabylia did not necessarily identify as 'Kabyles' or 'Berbers' first and foremost, and were not necessarily more democratic than their Arabic-speaking counterparts.

Instead, this was a politically useful alternative nationalist history, in which 'Berbers', or more specifically 'Kabyles', were presented as embodying a more democratic form of Algerian nationalism (Benkhaled and Vince 2017). The 'Kabyle' origin of many of Algeria's anti-colonial heroes was also foregrounded, as was the contribution of men, women and children of the region to the liberation struggle, where some of the fiercest fighting took place. The arrival of the Arabs in Algeria in the seventh century was presented as form of invasion and colonialism just like that of the French, whereas in official history, the term 'Arab invasion' is never used. Lalla Fatma N'Soumer (1830–63), who led resistance against the French conquest in Kabylia in the nineteenth century was celebrated alongside another Berber female warrior and religious leader, Kahina (Dihya), who led resistance against the Arab conquest in the region centuries previously. Not necessarily separatist, 'Kabyle' Algerian nationalism was instead put forward as the ideal version of Algerian nationalism.

Feminist Anti-colonial Nationalism

In 1979, an official notification forbade women from leaving the national territory without the authorisation of a male tutor. In 1984, a Family Code, based on a conservative interpretation of Islamic law (*sharia*), was passed which made a matrimonial tutor obligatory for women, legally obliged women to obey their husbands, fixed in law men's right to polygamy and repudiation and restricted women's grounds for divorce. The Family Code did not get through the Algerian National Assembly easily: some of the best-known women from the anti-colonial struggle were amongst the leading figures campaigning against it. These campaigns sparked interest in the role of women in the Revolution, with activists arguing that a lack of knowledge about women's major contribution in part explained women's current marginalisation. The first PhD on the role of women in the war, written by a female veteran, Djamila Danièle Amrane Minne (1939–2017), was defended in France in 1988 (the book of her PhD was published in 1991, Amrane, 1991; in English see Mortimer, 2018). Algeria's leaders since 1962 had used their participation in the war, real or claimed, as the basis of their political legitimacy. In the 1980s, Algerian female veterans campaigning against the Family Code also began to instrumentalise their combatant status, using this symbolic resource to make their voices heard. Rewriting women back into history, recovering both their role in the Algerian Revolution and in resisting the nineteenth-century French invasion (for example, through the figure of Lalla Fatma N'Soumer), became a means to challenge patriarchal legislation in the present. For this to work, relations between men and women during the war had to be idealised to a certain extent, and any sexism, misogyny or male violence which women might have experienced had to be blamed exclusively on false *mujahidin* (Vince 2015, 2014; see also El Korso 1996 and Seferdjeli 2012) (<<Chap. 4, pp. 168–9).

Good Muslim Algerians

In the 1980s, Algerian Islamists sought to critique the party of the FLN, the political system and their version of 'Algerianness' by reappropriating some of the key figures of the early AUMA as their ancestors (Courrèye 2016, 660). Indeed, amongst the founders of the Islamic Salvation Front (Front islamique du salut, al-jabha al-islamiyya lil-inqādh, FIS), which was formally created in 1989, were two former members of the AUMA: Abdelatif Ben Ali al-Soltani (1902–84) and Abbasi Madani (b. 1931–2019). As in other alternative nationalist histories, Algerian Islamists idealised what they claimed was the 'true' FLN of the war (morally upright, united and courageous). Where Islamists differed from 'culturally plural' and 'feminist' versions, however, was that they declared that they were picking up from where the party of the FLN had failed in 1962, by continuing the revolution against Algeria's interior enemies. For the Islamists, these were Algerians whom they considered to be bad Muslims, who they claimed promoted the neo-colonial interests of France and the West. Appropriating the term which Algeria's rulers had used against its critics since independence, Islamists denounced those in power as *hizb fransa*, the party of France. Unsurprisingly, this characterisation was firmly resisted by the Algerian state, determined to maintain its monopoly on the language of nationalism and religion, and still counting a number of former *'ulama* in its ranks. In order for Islamist version to work, the role of the *'ulama* in the nationalist struggle and in the creation of the FLN had to be exaggerated (<<Chap. 2, pp. 34–5; >> Chap. 4, p. 186).

(Still) debating the nature of Algerian nationalism: alternative versions of the past as a way to criticise the politico-military system
What is noteworthy is the common core shared across Algerian official history (which is used to legitimise those in power) and these alternative versions of the past (which are used to delegitimise those in power) (Temlali 2015). They all emphasise the same core values—unity, shared purpose, sacrifice, one sole hero the people, by the people, for the people, anti-colonialism and freedom from foreign interference. In all of these versions of the past, the Algerian Revolution is fundamentally just—this is not up for debate. What these different versions disagree on is who gave the most, who benefited the most, and what it should all mean in the post-independence period—and this is where the political debate takes place, using the language of 'true' and 'false' patriots.

The Response of the Algerian Politico-military System: Towards Saturation and Victimhood

The Algerian politico-military system did not let these alternative versions of past, present and future be told without revisiting and refreshing its own narrative. By the 1980s, the big industrial and infrastructure projects which were meant to define a modern and forward-looking Algeria were faltering. Unemployment and price rises multiplied, aggravated by attempts to move Algeria from a socialist to a capitalist economy. As it became harder to 'sell' the version of the war in which independence had resolved, or would soon resolve, all of Algeria's economic, social and cultural issues, the official version of Algerian history shifted, as did the manner in which it was commemorated. Firstly, the loss of confidence in the ability of the official story of the war to function as a unifying narrative providing political legitimacy to those in power prompted an urge to make it all the more visible. Inaugurated in 1982, the 92-metre-high *maqam al-shahid* (Monument to the martyr) has dominated the Algiers skyline ever since, one of a range of highly visible commemorative projects. Secondly, whilst a glorified version of the war was never abandoned, it became less focused on the heroic exploits of the *mujahidin* which might open up awkward conversations about 'true' and 'false' *mujahidin* and their relationship to political power. Instead, the official narrative began to focus more on the horrific violence inflicted on Algerian fighters and civilians by the French army and settlers. This was a shared experience which could be unanimously denounced (Vince 2015, 216–218). This shift in emphasis from heroes to victims in 1980s Algeria was mirrored in Europe in the 1980s. By the 1990s, the language of trauma and victimhood had become the most effective means for individuals and groups in France to publicly discuss the legacy of the Algerian War and articulate demands for apologies and/or compensation from the state.

1990s: The Transnational Memory Turn—Crimes Against Humanity, Genocide, Reparation, Apologies and Law-making

France: Courts, Laws and Victimhood

Connecting the local, national, transnational and global: transnational memory frames

By the 1990s, the Algerian War was being revisited in France through a new transnational language and legal framework. This was borrowed from scholars studying the memory of the Holocaust and from courtrooms which, decades later, were prosecuting perpetrators of genocide during the Second World War. This was a language of crimes against humanity, reparation and the duty to remember. The legal system was increasingly being used to try and secure official recognition for historical victims.

The Algerian War would be firmly connected to these developments through the lengthy trial of Maurice Papon. In 1998, following a legal process which had dragged on since 1981, Papon was found guilty of committing war crimes for his role in organising the deportation of 1690 Jews, including 200 children, whilst a civil servant in Bordeaux, under the Vichy regime. The trial brought the rest of Papon's long career under public scrutiny. Although Papon was on trial for crimes committed during the Second World War, the journalist and researcher Jean-Luc Einaudi seized the opportunity when giving evidence to also expose Papon's responsibility in the deadly violence committed against Algerian demonstrators on 17 October 1961 (Einaudi, 1991). This in turn entailed its own legal battle when, in 1998–9, Papon unsuccessfully sued Einaudi for defamation.

Pied-noir, *harki* and 17 October memory activists were all paying attention to this new language and legal mechanisms for securing public recognition. More than ever, they presented themselves as victims, and called upon the French state to recognise its 'state crimes' and represent their version of history in the commemorative landscape, school textbooks and national days. For *pied-noir* memory activists, this might be considered an audacious move—they were the former colonisers in a period where the days of publicly glorifying empire seemed long gone. *Pied-noir* associations nevertheless argued that they were doubly victims. Firstly, they positioned themselves as collateral damage of the Gaullist steamroller towards decolonisation. Secondly, they claimed that they were victims of a 'politically correct' left-wing mainstream media which sympathised with the FLN and only represented *pieds noirs* in pejorative, stereotypical ways.

Websites and social media have been a particularly useful platform for these groups to challenge this perceived marginalisation. As use of the internet generalised from the 1990s onwards, individual *pieds noirs* as well as *pied-noir* associations have been very active online, gathering and publishing old photographs (from smiling classrooms of children to gory images of violence committed against European civilians by the FLN), personal recollections, closely monitoring developments in the law which affect them and producing rebuttals to historians, documentary-makers and film directors who are seen as unsympathetic to 'their' side of the story, which they present as 'the truth'. Again, these associations are not monolithic—some focus on recipe collections and colonial postcards, others have direct links to far-right websites (Scioldo-Zürcher 2012). *Harki* and 17 October campaigners are also very active online.

From the turn of the century onwards, multiple unsuccessful attempts were made to bring cases to French courts for 'state crimes'. In 2001, some *harki* groups attempted to bring a case against the French state for disarming them and abandoning them in 1962. In 2014, some *pied-noir* associations sought to bring a case against the French state for abandoning them and forcing them into exile in 1962. Although these legal cases floundered faced with the letter of the law, such demands were successful in pushing politicians to make public statements which acknowledged state responsibility in past human suffering.

Algeria: A Post-colonial Haunting?

On the other side of the Mediterranean in the 1990s, Algeria was experiencing the gravest political crisis in its post-independence history so far. In October 1988, angry at high unemployment, corruption and the lack of opportunities for their generation, youths took to the streets in protest. President Chadli Bendjedid (1929–2012, most commonly referred to by his first name, Chadli) fell from power and in February 1989 a new constitution established multipartyism. The FLN was no longer the only permitted political party in Algeria. In the context of the global rise in the popularity of political Islam and the rejection of the FLN in Algeria, the Islamic Salvation Front (FIS) rapidly emerged as the biggest political party. To prevent the FIS gaining a parliamentary major-ity, in January 1992, the Algerian army cancelled the second round of legisla-tive elections. A decade of civil violence ensued, pitting the Algerian state against Islamists who took to the mountains and carried out urban assassina-tions and bomb attacks. The Algerian army responded using many of the tac-tics which had been used 1954–62, including internment, torture and 'disappearances'. In February 1992, in a bid to end the crisis, the army brought back a war veteran who had been on the losing side of the 1962 infighting, Mohamed Boudiaf. One of the historic leaders of the FLN in 1954, for the previous 27 years Boudiaf had been living in exile in Morocco. He headed up a High Council of State (Haut conseil d'Etat, HCE) but was assassinated by his bodyguard in June 1992. It is popularly suspected that, having brought him back as a fresh face with historical legitimacy, the politico-military system rap-idly decided to eliminate Boudiaf before he started undermining their vested interests. The election in 1999 of Abdelaziz Bouteflika marked the beginning of the end of the violence, although his 2005 Charter for Peace and National Reconciliation, which was meant to draw a line under the civil violence, failed to silence ongoing recriminations about the period referred to as the 'black decade' in Algeria.

Presenting the 1990s civil violence as a 'Second Algerian War' or depicting the conflict as the result of Algerians being collectively 'traumatised' or 'haunted' by the unfinished business of its anti-colonial struggle were popular tropes in media reporting in both France and Algeria at the time. This parallel is fundamentally ahistorical, making too much of the similarities and ignoring the obvious differences. Moreover, the idea that nations can be 'haunted' by their pasts in a similar way to how individuals can experience Post-Traumatic Stress Disorder (PTSD) is highly questionable. Nevertheless, this parallel was made tempting by the fact that a range of different actors borrowed language from the anti-colonial struggle to try and reinforce their legitimacy at home and abroad. Much mileage was gained from the veteran status of all the men who were head of state in this decade: all of Boudiaf's successors were also veterans of the revolution: Ali Kafi (1928–2013; chairman of the HCE 1992–4); Liamine Zeroual (b.1941, president 1995–9) and Bouteflika. In 1995, Zeroual would describe the Islamists as *harkis* or sons of *harkis* trying to continue the war that they could not win in 1962. As women became particular targets of Islamist violence, the state co-opted aspects of the feminist national-ist narrative of the war (<<Chap. 4, p. 177), drawing a straight line from Lalla Fatma N'Soumer (who was also a 'Berber' figure) (<<Chap. 4, pp. 176–7) to the women who participated in the War of Liberation, to Hassiba Boulmerka (b. 1968), the Algerian middle distance athlete who defied Islamist death threats to win a Gold medal at the 1992 Olympics (Vince 2015, 206). This was presented as evidence, notably to the international community, that Algerian women had always courageously resisted in the face of threats to the nation and that the Algerian state and army were their best defenders. Previously banished figures were also brought into official history in order to suggest that the

politico-military system was plural, without enacting any root-and-branch reforms. Both Messali Hadj (ostracised since 1954) and Ben Bella (who had been banished from official history since 1965) had airports named after them. In 2016, Tamazight (Berber) was adopted as a national language.

At the same time, the violence of the 1990s exposed the post-1962 political elite issued from the war to virulent critique which was also expressed through the language of the war. They were blamed for sacralising violence and denigrating politics by privileging the military over the political (<<Chap. 3, pp. 86, 107, 143–4). Those in power were regularly accused of being 'false *mujahidin*'. All of these claims about legitimate and illegitimate heirs of the revolution were historically dubious, simply because history is much messier than the neat categories of 'hero' and 'traitor', 'right' and 'wrong'. The language of true and false veterans, of right and wrong paths, was nevertheless politically powerful.

Once again, crucially, the justness of the war and the heroism and legitimacy of its true veterans were never called into question, whatever side you found yourself on in this debate. Indeed, the strength of this core message is reflected in the fact that it can be found in some unexpected places—for example, in Pierre Daum's interviews with *harkis* who stayed in Algeria after 1962. Unlike the memory of *harkis* and their families who went to France (<<Chap. 4, pp. 161–5, 172–4), the memory of those who stayed in Algeria is not institutionalised and has no collective expression: it has no place in the official narrative (apart from the oft-repeated trope of *harkis* as colonial and neo-colonial bogeymen), it has no presence through associations and it has no media visibility. And yet, one of the themes which emerges from Daum's oral history interviews conducted many years later is that the worst acts of violence against former *harkis* in 1962 were not committed by real *mujahidin* but rather by last minute resisters trying to prove their worth, or indeed former informants for the French army. In the words of former *harki* Hassen Derouiche 'these people wanted to erase their past by killing us' (Daum 2015, 363). Far from existing awkwardly on the margins, such stories can be woven into a dominant oppositional narrative in Algeria today—that independence was stolen by fakes, and that like all ordinary Algerians, *harkis* who stayed in Algeria found themselves marginalised victims of an illegitimate order. Algeria was not being 'haunted', rather the past was being deliberately excavated and repackaged for the purposes of conducting political debate in the present.

Franco-Algerian 'Memory Wars': A Misnomer?

In France and Algeria, the conflicts about memory were about different aspects of the Algerian War/Algerian Revolution. In Algeria, arguments raged about who were the true *mujahidin*, what was the 'authentic' nature of the nationalist movement, and whether or not independence was 'stolen'. In France, impassioned debates surrounded recognising French responsibility in 'abandoning' the *harkis* and the *pieds noirs* and 'massacring' Algerian nationalists in France. When, in June 2000, President Bouteflika made a state visit to France, he compared the *harkis* to France's Second World War collaborators, borrowing from a register instantly recognisable (and pejorative) in a French context. This created lively protests in France from *harki* associations, but barely made waves in Algeria where all Bouteflika was repeating was a widely held consensus. In reaction to Bouteflika's statement, some *harki* associations decided to bring an action against 'X' for 'crimes against humanity and complicity'—but in a French court and with their main target being the French state. In France and Algeria, different groups are fighting to obtain or maintain political legitimacy, access to power and resources and secure a place within the respective French and Algerian national narratives. In both cases, they have tapped into and seek to strategically use a transnational language of war crimes and remembrance to do this. But the sites of the struggles and the groups involved are different. Even when arguments do have a Franco-Algerian dimension, they resonate differently on each side of the Mediterranean.

This is demonstrated by the case of Louisette Ighilahriz (b. 1936) and the reopening of the torture debate. On 20 June 2000, just after Bouteflika's state visit to France, *Le Monde* featured on its front page an interview with Ighilahriz, a former FLN militant who was brutally tortured—and later, it emerged, raped—after her capture by the French army in September 1957 during 'the Battle of Algiers'. The article provoked a media storm in France. Other former FLN militants were interviewed and gave their accounts of being tortured. Retired army generals Jacques Massu and Paul Aussaresses (1918–2003) both gave interviews—Massu admitted and regretted the use of torture whilst Aussaresses admitted and justified the use of torture. General Marcel Bigeard (1916–2010) and General Maurice Schmitt (b. 1930) both vigorously denied the use of torture and specific allegations made against them (Beaugé 2005).

That torture was used during the war was not a new revelation. It was known at the time, and had been the basis of much anti-war campaigning in France and internationally (<<Chap. 3, pp. 94–5, 121). The debate in 2000 was framed in different terms, and served a different purpose. On 31 October 2000, communist newspaper *L'Humanité* published a 'Call of the twelve' ('Appel des douze') signed by 12 Frenchmen and women, including Henri Alleg, Germaine Tillion, Pierre Vidal-Naquet, Josette Audin (1931–2019) and Gisèle Halimi, all of whom had sympathised with or been active in the Algerian struggle for independence. They called for the memory of the war to be confronted so that healing could take place. The *pied-noir* Cercle algérianiste, in contrast, denounced a news programme which screened an interview with Ighilahriz as a 'pseudo-documentary'. The Association to Support the French Army (Association soutien à l'armee française, ASAF) created in 1983 with the goal of defending 'the honour of the army and its soldiers', unsuccessfully sought to lodge a complaint against Ighilahriz for defamation (Vince 2012, 320). In 2002, Ighilahriz took General Schmitt—the latter supported by various army associations—to court after he denounced her autobiography as a 'web of fabrications and untruths' on television (Vince 2015, 242). She was

awarded a symbolic one euro in October 2003, which she lost on appeal as Schmitt benefitted from earlier amnesty laws.

In Algeria, the Algerian state did not get involved to support Ighilahriz, even though she had been a member of the FLN's Algiers bomb network. Nor was she supported by all of her fellow veterans. Some women found the fact that she broke social and cultural taboos—notably surrounding rape—difficult to deal with. A few were resentful of the international media attention she attracted in an Algerian context where there was 'one sole hero, the people'.

Although Ighilahriz's story was about the role of the French army during the 'Battle of Algiers' in 1956–7, it meant different things on opposite sides of the Mediterranean. But this was not a Franco-Algerian dispute about how to interpret the past. In France, the story of Louisette Ighilahriz was understood either as a story which could help improve social relations between groups of different national origins living in France today through collectively confronting the past, or it was considered a threat to the honour of the French army and national pride. In Algeria, Ighilahriz's story raised questions about who has the right to speak for veterans, and what they have the right to say. The violence which Ighilahriz had endured more than 40 years previously took second stage to discussions about much more contemporary Algero-Algerian and Franco-French issues.

Five years after Ighilahriz's story was first published in *Le Monde*, the 23 February 2005 law (2005–158) would be passed. This law was pushed for by a group of *pied-noir* and *harki* associations. It was prepared by deputies in the right-wing Union for a Popular Movement (Union pour un mouvement populaire, UMP, now called Les Républicains [the Republicans]), and also had support from left-wing deputies from areas in the south of France which have a high concentration of *pieds noirs* and *harkis*. Like much previous legislation, it provided further financial support for *pieds noirs* and *harkis* and recognised their suffering. It forbade insulting someone for their real or supposed status as a *harki*, and banned justifying crimes against *harkis*. These latter provisions were similar to other memory laws, such as the 1990 Gayssot law against Holocaust denial or the 2001 Taubira law which recognises slavery as a crime against humanity. What provoked controversy about the 23 February 2005 law was its article 4. This demanded that 'school programmes recognise in particular the positive role of the French presence overseas, notably in North Africa, and give to the history and to the sacrifices of combatants of the French army with origins in these territories the eminent place to which they are entitled'. Initially, the law only attracted attention from a small group of historians, horrified at the idea of being forced to teach an official history which glorified colonialism. Their opposition would develop into a national campaign (Liauzu and Manceron 2006; in English see Jansen 2010). The law was also criticised by some *harki* associations such as *Harkis* and Human Rights (Harkis et droits de l'homme) who, whilst welcoming financial aid and protection from insults, rejected article 4 which glorified colonial Algeria.

The Algerian press then picked up on the story. The non-governmental association 8 May 1945 Foundation (Fondation du 8 mai 1945), created in 1990 to raise public awareness of the massacres committed by the French army and settler militias against Algerians in the Constantinois region at the end of the Second World War (<<Chap. 2, pp. 47–9), criticised the law for celebrating *harkis* whilst ignoring colonial crimes committed against Algerians. The response of the Algerian state, however, was muted. In February 2010, a group of Algerian deputies of various parties including the FLN, with the support of associations such as the 8 May 1945 Foundation, signed a proposition for a law criminalising colonialism and envisaging the creation of a special tribunal to try those accused of colonial crimes. This proposal provoked the ire of the Cercle algérianiste in France but never made it into the Algerian parliament. In the end, it was President Jacques Chirac (1932–2019, president 1995–2007) who would repeal article 4, declaring in his 2006 New Year's address to the press 'The current text divides the French people' (Vince 2012, 322–334). The conflicts around 23 February 2005 were much more about contemporary French politics and society than they were about Franco-Algerian relations.

Since the 1970s in France, *pied-noir* and, later, *harki* associations and those campaigning around 17 October 1961, had been seeking to bring their divergent interpretations of France's colonial history to public attention. By 2005, they had made significant progress in doing so. Indeed, by this point, the theme of colonial history generated sufficient media interest and political attention that, rather than being an object to be recovered, it could be used as a location for proxy debates about other issues and as a tool to gather political support.

MID-2000s ONWARDS: THE COLONIAL/ANTI-COLONIAL PAST AS POLITICAL CODE AND STRATEGIC WEAPON

In Algeria and France today, having a view on the Algerian Revolution/Algerian War is a useful—and much used—way for politicians and activists to position themselves politically by employing a few key terms or references.

In Algeria, we have seen that since the 1980s 'feminist', 'Islamist' and 'culturally plural' versions of the war have all been used to articulate different visions of what Algerian politics, culture and society should be. All of these versions—like the official version of Algerian history—demand a very selective reading of Algerian history, picking specific figures and events and ignoring others. Because of the way that they go back into the past to search for a 'better' version of Algerian nationalism, they also all have the tendency to search for the 'original sin', the moment when the path to a glorious future was not taken. In addition, there is a strong belief that the 'truth' about the past can 'fix' the present (Benkhaled and Vince 2017).

(Still) debating the nature of Algerian nationalism: or rather, weaponising the language of the national past in the 2019 protests in Algeria

In 2019, large-scale popular protests against President Bouteflika standing for a fifth term in office, and against the politico-military system in general, took place every Friday in Algeria. Demonstrators drew extensively on the language and symbols of the anti-colonial struggle through banners, slogans and chants. Protesters proudly carried pictures of well-known heroes and heroines who died during the war, holding up these 'true *mujahidin*' as an example to use against those in power, who they accused of being 'false *mujahidin*' who 'stole' independence in 1962 (<<Chap. 4, pp. 168–9) The presence in demonstrations of former female combatants—Djamila Bouhired, Louisette Ighilahriz as well as the sister of Larbi Ben M'Hidi, Drifa Ben M'Hidi—has been widely celebrated by protesters, as women who participated in the war are generally seen as less tarnished by behind-the-scenes machinations than their male counterparts. The protestors are ideologically diverse. Those in favour of ending army interference in political life have called for a return to the principles of the 1956 Soummam Congress (and notably the principal that the political should have primacy over the military) (<<Chap. 3, pp. 85–7). Protestors who—on the contrary—believe that the army has a role to play in 'purifying' political life have called for a return to 'novembaria Badissia'—which literally translates as 'a return to the principles of 1 November 1954 inspired by Ben Badis'. This is completely ahistorical— Ben Badis's *'ulama* did not play a role founding the FLN (<<Chap. 2, pp. 34–5; Chap. 3, p. 81). By suggesting that they did, this expression calls for a 'return' to an Arabo-Islamic form of nationalism which did not exist in 1954. The concept of 'novembria Badisiyya' is actually quite close to the Islamist version of Algerian history (<<Chap. 4, pp. 177–8), but without the politically toxic connotations of the party of the FIS after the civil violence of the 1990s. Finally, some of those who are in favour of maintaining the status quo have attacked the protestors as 'Zouaves'. During the Algerian War, the 'Zouaves' were a French army unit mainly composed of Europeans from Algeria (<<Chap. 3, p. 120), but further back in time, when the French invaded Algeria in 1830, they had initially built their Zouave units from volunteers drawn from the Zwāwa group of tribes in Tamazight (Berber)-speaking Kabylia. In 2019, insulting those who are demonstrating against the politico-military system as 'zouaves'— however inaccurate and ahistorical—seeks to stigmatise them as separatist 'Berberists' (<<Chap. 2, pp. 54–55) acting to advance the interests of the former colonial power ('*hizb fransa*').

In France, the position taken on the colonial past/the Algerian War since the 1990s by different political parties often involves obscuring the position that same party (or its political ancestor) actually held at that point in history. Indeed, denunciations of colonialism by any French political party are relatively recent. Parliamentary debates in the 1980s on issues surrounding the repatriates or OAS amnesties reveal that politicians from all parties spun similar lines glorifying colonialism and the 'civilising mission', even if communist and some socialist deputies did not participate in the colonial apologia and voted against amnesties (Scioldo-Zürcher 2010, 372–373). Today, the PCF positions itself as a firm critic of colonialism, and notably commemorates those who were killed at the anti-OAS Charonne demonstration in February 1962 (<<Chap. 3, pp. 137–8). The ambiguous position of the PCF on the question of independence for much of the period of colonial rule, and notably the fact that PCF deputies in the National Assembly voted for Special Powers in 1956 (<<Chap. 3, p. 83), is quietly forgotten.

The Socialist Party and successive right-wing Gaullist parties have undergone even more striking transformations of their wartime position on Algeria. In 1956, it had been socialists in government (supported by communist votes) who had intensified the war in Algeria (<<Chap. 3, pp. 82–3). As Minister for Justice, François Mitterrand had sent many Algerian activists to their death through the use of the death penalty. In the 1980s, as France's first Socialist president, he had sought to complete de Gaulle's cycle of amnesties to the OAS, although this encountered the resistance of younger members of the party. Yet by the 2000s, the Socialist mayor of Paris, Bertrand Delanoë, was unveiling a plaque on the Saint Michel bridge in memory of Algerians killed on 17 October (<<Chap. 3, pp. 134–7), and François Hollande's (b. 1954) first official engagement as the Socialist Party's presidential candidate on 17 October 2011 was to throw a rose—the symbol of the Socialist Party—into the Seine, in memory of the Algerians who died there (it should be noted that local politics do not always follow the national line, see, e.g., Chabal 2014). For both the socialist and communist parties, the underlying assumption—and policy driver—is that bringing together a multiplicity of memories will enable the nation to 'come to terms' with the past, heal wounds across different groups and thus fix problems such as social exclusion, racism and political and religious radicalisation in the present. There is little evidence to back this up.

On the right, it was under a right-wing politician, de Gaulle, that Algeria became independent. He was—and still is—a hated figure for many *pieds noirs*, he did not see the *harkis* as belonging to the French nation (<<Chap. 3, p. 114) and the OAS tried to assassinate him. After 1962, he sought to forget Algeria, reducing it to one chapter amongst others in his 'successful decolonisation' of Africa. Since the mid-1990s, leading politicians who lay claim to the Gaullist heritage have adopted distinctly different positions to those of de Gaulle himself. President Chirac sought to respond to demands for recognition from different groups, notably those close to army. In 1999, the 'Algerian War' was officially recognised as such in legislation. In 2001, 25 September was

designated a day of recognition for the *harkis* and in 2003, 5 December was chosen as the official day for those who 'died for France' during the Algerian War and in Morocco and Tunisia. Neither date marks any particular event and they are thus less controversial than the 19 March (<<Chap. 4, p. 172). The designation of 5 December was accompanied by the inauguration of national memorial to the Algerian War on the Quai Branly in Paris. Chirac's successor, Nicolas Sarkozy (b. 1955, president 2007–12), although of the same party as Chirac, was often closer to the far-right position on the Algerian War and colonialism. He denounced apologising for (or even recognising the existence of) colonial crimes as form of self-flagellating repentance which, he claimed, was damaging to the nation. There is no evidence to back this claim up.

The position of the French far-right today on the colonial past contains a number of unacknowledged contradictions. Parties such as the National Front (FN, since 2018 known as the National Rally [Rassemblement national]) promote a nostalgia for empire, colonialism and the 'civilising mission', without acknowledging that empires were multi-ethnic and the 'civilising mission' was a centre-left, Republican project (<<Chap. 1, pp. 4–6). This imperial nostalgia is in tension with both far-right claims that Blacks, Arabs and Muslims in France are a threat to national identity, and their virulent opposition to immigration, which they pejoratively depict as 'reverse colonialism' (Flood and Frey 2003; Stoler 2002). For the far-right, and indeed many of those on the right such as Sarkozy, 'empire' is a vague metaphor for France being unashamedly powerful and any criticism of France's actions as a colonial power is presented as a French loss of pride and direction under the yoke of 'political correctness gone mad'.

Current French President Emmanuel Macron (b. 1977, president since 2017), who founded his own centrist political party, The Republic on the Move (La République en marche) in 2016, has sought to secure a middle ground amongst voters by presenting himself as both 'progressive' (ready to acknowledge the past) and 'unashamed' (refusing to be 'too repentant'). In September 2018, Macron formally admitted French responsibility in the killing of Maurice Audin, a pro-independence communist mathematician at the University of Algiers who was arrested and then 'disappeared' from French custody in 1957 (<<Chap. 3, p. 95). This was part of a broader acknowledgement—for the first time—of the systematic use of torture during the war. Macron was the eighth French president to whom Maurice Audin's wife, Josette Audin, had appealed for the truth about her husband's disappearance. This official recognition was welcomed by historians and activists in favour of 'coming to terms' with the past as a step towards community reconciliation. Less than two months later, Macron angered this same group, and pleased those who see critical re-evaluation of France's history as a damaging form of self-flagellation, by honouring the role of Marshall Phillippe Pétain as a distinguished figure of the First World War. Pétain also collaborated with the Nazis in the deportation and murder of Jews in France and led a brutal military campaign against Moroccan nationalists in the 1920s (<<Chap. 2, p. 41). As in Algeria, all these positions on the past provide a code for French politicians to situate *in the present* their vision of what France should be politically, socially and culturally.

The colonial past can also be a starting point to publicly engage with a range of contemporary, difficult-to-talk-about issues. In Algeria today, the place which religion should occupy in politics and society can be difficult to debate in a context where there is a significant degree of religious conformism. Talking about the *'ulama* provides point of access for more secular political activists to open up debate, as they present the *'ulama*, and Ben Badis in particular, as the embodiment of a 'good Islam', rooted in enlightenment, reform and a desire to improve Algerians. This use of Ben Badis is not the same as that made by the 2019 protestors calling for 'novembaria Badissia', rather, secular-leaning activists use 'their' Ben Badis to delegitimise the 'bad Islam' of the FIS and the Islamists, which they depict as regressive, oppressive and a foreign import from Saudi Arabia (Lazreg 2000). In France, one of the great challenges of anti-racist campaigners since the 1980s has been talking about 'race'. The Republic is, supposedly, 'colour blind' and all citizens are 'neutral'. Collecting statistics on race or ethnicity is illegal and ethnic minorities who group together to address shared problems of discrimination are often delegitimised by their opponents as engaging in 'communitarianism'— i.e. rejecting the universal principals of the Republic in favour of the narrow interests of their group. Resurrecting certain aspects of colonial history— when statistics on ethnicity were most certainly collected and colonised people were racialised subjects (<<Chap. 1, pp. 7–10) and most definitely not neutral citizens—can be a weapon to challenge the Republic's claim to be 'colour blind'. It provides a language to talk about the failings of the contemporary Republic, particularly in relation to the subject of race. It is for this reason that Itay Lotem (2016, 294) describes the language of colonial memory as 'a new tool in the arsenal of French anti-racism', although he is sceptical about whether or not it actually works: 'focusing the public conversation on the role of colonial continuities did not change power relations between the postcolonial state and its subjects'.

Conclusion: Towards New Frameworks and Timeframes

The notion of colonial continuities or 'aftershocks' has been much used in the past 30 years, by liberal- and left-leaning academics, politicians and journalists. It has been used to explain linguistic and ethnic divisions, socio-economic inequality and crises of political legitimacy in former colonies. In those countries which were formerly colonial powers, the idea of colonial 'aftershocks' has been employed as a way to understand racism, Islamophobia, socio-economic inequality and even, for a tiny minority of Black, Arab or Asian citizens, the appeal of Isis and al-Qaeda. As an interpretative lens, the idea that history repeats itself, or that colonialism has never ended, is problematic. In a leading work on the 'colonial fracture' in France, Pascal Blanchard, Nicolas Bancel and Sandrine Lemaire warn that contemporary discrimination and divisions in France today are not the straightforward reproduction of colonial forms of oppression. Instead, they argue that close attention needs to be paid to how attitudes and practices from the colonial period intersect with new, contemporary issues to shape debates on

Islam, race, immigration and history (Bancel et al. 2005; and for an updated work translated into English see Bancel et al. 2017).

In short, colonial 'continuities' need to be treated with significant caution, to avoid what Frederick Cooper (2005, 19–20) has described as the fallacy of 'leapfrogging legacies', whereby the past and present are juxtaposed with each other with little attention paid to the history of the intervening period. That is not to say that we adopt the reactionary position of demanding that formerly colonised peoples 'get over it' and 'stop complaining', of claiming that the colonial past has no impact on the present or of reproducing a distorted and racist vision of empires bringing railways and doctors to 'backwards' peoples. Rather, avoiding leapfrogging legacies means, firstly, treating 'memory' not as something which erupts uncontrollably into the nation's consciousness, but rather as something which is consciously activated for political, economic and/ or social reasons. The conditions in which this activation takes place, and the purposes it serves, require close analysis. The 'memories' themselves need to be treated not as straightforward recollections of past events, but instead studied as highly selective recalls, in which symbolic meanings are often more important than the substance of what happened. Moreover, these symbolic meanings can shift over time, as names, dates, events and terminology are repurposed for new needs in the present. Factual accuracy is often a secondary consideration.

Secondly, to avoid leapfrogging legacies we need to pay much closer attention to the understudied period between the end of empire in the early 1960s and the early 1990s, when the boom in 'remembering' the colonial past began. How were practices and attitudes—ways of doing things—which had developed in the colonies 'transferred' back to the metropole through people and organisations, and what mutations took place in the course of these transfers (Dimier 2014; Naylor 2013)? How were the kinds of economic planning which developed in the late colonial period adapted by newly independent states in the 1960s and 1970s (Davis 2010, 2018; Byrne 2016)? How were political cultures—ways of doing politics—which had developed within the confines of the highly repressive colonial context reproduced but also reimagined in the post-independence period when political parties not sanctioned by the state were banned (Rahal 2018)? It is around such questions that much of the new and emerging historical work is focused.

References

Amrane, Djamila. 1991. *Les Femmes algériennes dans la guerre* [Algerian Women in the War]. Paris: Plon.

Bamia, Aida. 2001. *The Graying of the Raven: Cultural and Sociopolitical Significance of Algerian Folk Poetry*. Cairo and New York: American University in Cairo Press.

Bancel, Nicolas, Pascal Blanchard, and Sandrine Lemaire, eds. 2005. *La Fracture coloniale: la société française au prisme de l'héritage colonial* [The Colonial Fracture: French Society in the Prism of Its Colonial Heritage]. Paris: La Découverte.

Bancel, Nicolas, Pascal Blanchard, and Dominic Thomas, eds. 2017. *The Colonial Legacy in France: Fracture, Rupture, and Apartheid*. Trans. Alexis Pernsteiner. Bloomington: Indiana University Press.

Beaugé, Florence. 2005. *Algérie: Une Guerre sans gloire. Histoire d'une enquête* [Algeria: A War Without Glory. Story of an Investigation]. Paris: Calmann-Lévy.

Benkhaled, Walid, and Natalya Vince. 2017. Performing Algerianness: The National and Transnational Construction of Algeria's 'Culture Wars'. In *Algeria: Nation, Culture and Transnationalism, 1988–2015*, ed. Patrick Crowley, 243–269. Liverpool: Liverpool University Press.

Branche, Raphaëlle. 2005. *La Guerre d'Algérie: une histoire apaisée?* [The Algerian War, a Calmed History?]. Paris: Seuil.

Byrne, Jeffrey James. 2016. *Mecca of Revolution: Algeria, Decolonization and the Third World Order*. Oxford: Oxford University Press.

Chabal, Emile. 2014. Managing the Postcolony: Minority Politics in Montpellier, c. 1960–c.2010. *Contemporary European History* 23 (2): 237–258. https://doi.org/10.1017/S096077731400006X.

Choi, Sung-Eun. 2016. *Decolonization and the French of Algeria: Bringing the Settler Colony Home*. Basingstoke: Palgrave Macmillan.

Cohen, William B. 2006. The *harkis*: History and Memory. In *Algeria and France 1800–2000: Identity, Memory, Nostalgia*, ed. Patricia Lorcin. Syracuse, NY: Syracuse University Press.

Cole, Joshua. 2003. Remembering the Battle of Paris: 17 October 1961 in French and Algerian Memory. *French Politics, Culture and Society* 21 (3): 21–50. https://doi.org/10.3167/153763703782370251.

Comtat, Emmanuelle. 2009. *Les pieds noirs et la politique: quarante ans après le retour* [Pieds Noirs and Politics: Forty Years After the Return]. Paris: Presses de Sciences Po.

Cooper, Frederick. 2005. *Colonialism in Question: Theory, Knowledge, History*. Berkeley: University of California Press.

Courrèye, Charlotte. 2016. L'association des Oulémas Musulmans Algériens et la construction de l'Etat algérien indépendant: foundation, héritages, appropriations et antagonisms. [The Association of the Algerian Muslim 'Ulama and the Construction of the Independent Algerian State]. PhD Thesis, INALCO, Paris.

Daum, Pierre. 2015. *Le dernier tabou: les "harkis" restés en Algérie après l'indépendance* [The Last Taboo: 'Harkis' Who Stayed in Algeria After Independence]. Arles and Paris: Solin, Actes Sud.

Davis, Muriam Haleh. 2010. Restaging Mise en Valeur: 'Postwar Imperialism' and the Plan de Constantine. *Review of Middle East Studies* 44 (2): 176–186. https://doi.org/10.1017/S215134810000149X.

———. 2018. North Africa and the Common Agricultural Policy: From Colonial Pact to European Integration. In *North Africa and the Making of Europe: Governance, Institutions and Culture*, ed. Muriam Haleh Davis and Thomas Serres, 43–66. London: Bloomsbury.

Dimier, Véronique. 2014. *The Development of a European Development Aid Bureaucracy: Recycling Empire*. Basingstoke: Palgrave Macmillan.

Einaudi, Jean-Luc. 1991. *La Ferme Améziane: Enquête sur un centre de torture pendant la Guerre d'Algérie* [The Améziane Farm: Investigation into a Torture Centre During the Algerian War]. Paris: L'Harmattan.

El Korso, Malika. 1996. Une double realité pour un même vécu. [A dual Reality for the Same Experience]. *Confluences Méditerranée* 17: 99–108.

Eldridge, Claire. 2009. 'We've never had a voice': Memory Construction and the Children of the Harkis (1962–1991). *French History* 23 (1): 88–107. https://doi.org/10.1093/fh/crn062.

———. 2012. Remembering the Other: Postcolonial Perspectives on Relationships Between Jews and Muslims in French Algeria. *Journal of Modern Jewish Studies* 11 (3): 299–317. https://doi.org/10.1080/14725886.2012.720510.

———. 2016. *From Empire to Exile: History and Memory Within the Pied-noir and Harki Communities, 1962–2012.* Manchester: Manchester University Press.

Evans, Martin. 2012. *Algeria: France's Undeclared War.* Oxford: Oxford University Press.

Fabbiano, Giulia. 2008. Devenir harki: les modes d'énonciation identitaire des descendants des anciens supplétifs de la guerre d'Algérie [Becoming a Harki: Ways of Expressing Identity Amongst Descendants of Former Auxiliaries in the Algerian War]. *Migrations Société* 120: 155–171. https://doi.org/10.3917/migra.120.0155.

Flood, Christopher, and Hugo Frey. 2003. Questions of Decolonisation and Post-Colonialism in the Ideology of the French Extreme Right. In *The Decolonisation Reader*, ed. James Le Sueur, 388–413. London: Routledge.

Fontaine, Darcie. 2016. *Decolonizing Christianity: Religion and the End of Empire in France and Algeria.* New York: Cambridge University Press.

Gacon, Stéphane. 2005. Les amnisties de la guerre d'Algérie (1962–1982) [The Amnesties of the Algerian War (1962–1982)]. *Histoire de la justice* 16: 271–279. https://doi.org/10.3917/rhj.016.0271.

Hammerman, Jessica. 2018. By Sentiment and by Status: Remembering and Forgetting Crémieux during the Franco-Algerian War. *French Politics, Culture and Society* 36 (1): 76–102. https://doi.org/10.3167/fpcs.2018.360104.

House, James. 2001. Antiracist Memories: The Case of 17 October 1961 in Historical Perspective. *Modern and Contemporary France 2001* 9 (3): 355–368. https://doi.org/10.1080/09639480120065999.

House, James, and Neil Macmaster. 2006. *Paris 1961: Algerians, State Terror, and Memory.* Oxford: Oxford University Press.

Jansen, Jan C. 2010. Politics of Remembrance, Colonialism and the Algerian War of Independence in France. In *A European Memory? Contested Histories and Politics of Remembrance*, ed. Małgorzata Pakier and Bo Stråth, 275–293. New York and Oxford: Berghahn Books.

Lazreg, Marnia. 2000. Islamism and the Recolonization of Algeria. In *Beyond Colonalism and Nationalism in the Maghrib*, ed. Ali Abdullatif Ahmida, 147–164. Basingstoke: Palgrave Macmillan.

Le Foll Luciani, Pierre-Jean. 2015. Les juifs d'Algérie face aux nationalités française et algérienne (1940–1963) [The Jews of Algeria Faced with French and Algerian Nationalities]. *Revue des mondes musulmans et de la Méditerranée* 137: 115–132. https://doi.org/10.4000/remmm.9057.

Liauzu, Claude, and Gilles Manceron, eds. 2006. *La Colonisation, la loi et l'histoire* [Colonisation, Law and History]. Paris: Editions Syllepse.

Lotem, Itay. 2016. Anti-racist Activism and the Memory of Colonialism: Race as Republican Critique After 2005. *Modern and Contemporary France* 24 (3): 283–298. https://doi.org/10.1080/09639489.2016.1159188.

Mann, Gregory. 2006. *Native Sons: West African Veterans and France in the Twentieth Century.* Durham, NC: Duke University.

Miller, Jeannette E. 2013. A Camp for Foreigners and 'Aliens': The Harkis' Exile at the Rivesaltes Camp (1962–1964). *French Politics, Culture & Society* 31 (3): 21–44.

Mortimer, Mildred. 2018. *Women Fight, Women Write: Texts on the Algerian War*. Charlottesville, VA: University of Virginia Press.

Moumen, Abderahmen. 2010. La notion d'abandon des harkis par les autorités françaises [The Notion of the Abandon of Harkis by the French Authorities]. In *Les Harkis: histoire, mémoire et transmission* [The Harkis: History, Memory and Transmission], ed. Fatima Besnaci-Lancou, Benoit Falaize, and Gilles Manceron, 47–62. Ivry-sur-Seine: Editions de l'atelier.

———. 2011. Violences de fin de guerre. Les massacres des harkis après l'indépendance algérienne (1962–1965) [Violences at the End of War. The Massacres of Harkis After Algerian Independence (1962–1965)]. In *Violence(s) de la préhistoire à nos jours* [Violences from Prehistory to the Present], ed. Marie-Claude Marandet, 331–346. Perpignan: Presses Universitaires de Perpignan. https://books.openedition.org/pupvd/3422. Accessed 1 June 2020.

———. 2012. Housing the 'Harkis': Long Term Segregation. Trans. Oliver Waine. Metropolitics.org. https://www.metropolitiques.eu/Housing-the-harkis-long-term.html. Accessed 1 June 2020.

Narayanan, Anndal. 2014. 'Ready to Fight': Veterans of the Algerian War Take the Battle to France, 1958–1974. *Journal of the Western Society for French History* 42. http://hdl.handle.net/2027/spo.0642292.0042.013. Accessed 1 June 2020.

Naylor, Edward. 2013. 'Un âne dans l'ascenseur': Late Colonial Welfare Services and Social Housing in Marseille. *French History* 27 (3): 422–227. https://doi.org/10.1093/fh/crt052.

Ouerdane, Amar. 1987. La "crise berbériste" de 1949, un conflit à plusieurs faces. [The 'Berberist Crisis' of 1949: A Conflict with Many Faces]. *Revue de l'Occident musulman et de la Méditerranée* 44: 35–47. https://www.persee.fr/doc/remmm_0035-1474_1987_num_44_1_2153. Accessed 1 June 2020.

Rahal, Malika. 2018. *L'UDMA et les UDMISTES: Contribution à l'histoire du nationalisme algérien* [UDMA and Its Members: Contribution to the History of Algerian Nationalism]. Algiers: Barzakh.

Remaoun, Hassan. 1994. Enseignement de l'histoire et conscience nationale. [Teaching History and National Consciousness]. *Confluences Méditerranée* 11: 25–32.

Rousso, Henry. 1991. *The Vichy Syndrome: History and Memory in France Since 1944*. Trans. Arthur Goldhammer. London: Harvard University Press.

Savarese, Eric. 2002. *L'invention des pieds noirs* [The Invention of the Pieds Noirs]. Biarritz: Séguier.

———. 2006. After the Algerian War: Reconstructing Identity Among the Pieds-noirs. *International Social Science Journal* 189: 457–466. https://doi.org/10.1111/j.1468-2451.2007.00644.x.

Scioldo-Zürcher, Yann. 2010. *Devenir Métropolitain. Politique d'intégration et parcours de rapatriés d'Algérie en métropole (1954–2005)* [Becoming Metropolitan. Integration Policy and Trajectories of Repatriates from Algeria in the Metropole]. Paris: EHESS.

———. 2012. Memory and Influence on the Web: French Colonial Repatriates from 1950 to the Present. *Social Science Information* 51 (4): 475–501. https://doi.org/10.1177/0539018412456917.

———. 2016. The Postcolonial Repatriations of the French of Algeria in 1962: An Emblematic Case of a Public Integration Policy. In *Vertriebene and Pieds-Noirs in*

Postwar Germany and France: Comparative Perspectives, ed. Manuel Borutta and Jan Jansen, 95–112. London: Palgrave Macmillan.

Seferdjeli, Ryme. 2012. Rethinking the History of the Mudjahidat During the Algerian War: Competing Voices, Reconstructed Memories and Contrasting Historiographies. *Interventions: International Journal of Postcolonial Studies* 14 (2): 238–255. https://doi.org/10.1080/1369801X.2012.687902.

Shepard, Todd. 2006. *The Invention of Decolonization. The Algerian War and the Remaking of France.* Ithaca and London: Cornell University Press.

Sidi Moussa, Nedjib. 2014. La révolution au pluriel. Pour une historiographie de la question messaliste. [The Revolution in the Plural. For a Historiography of the Messalist Question]. *L'Année du Maghreb* 10: 99–114. https://doi.org/10.4000/anneemaghreb.2048.

Simon, Catherine. 2011 [2009]. *Algérie, les années pieds-rouges. Des rêves de l'indépendance au désenchantement* [Algeria, the Pied-Rouge Years. From Dreams of Independence to Disillusion]. Paris: La Découverte.

Sims, Laura Jeanne. 2016. Rethinking France's 'Memory Wars': Harki Collective Memories, 2003–2010. *French Politics, Culture and Society* 34 (3): 83–104. https://doi.org/10.3167/fpcs.2016.340305.

Slyomovics, Susan. 2014. Algerian Women's Būqālah Poetry: Oral Literature, Cultural Politics, and Anti-Colonial Resistance. *Journal of Arabic Literature* 45: 145–186. https://doi.org/10.1163/1570064x-12341283.

Slyomovics, Susan, and Sarah Abrevaya Stein. 2012. Jews and French colonialism in Algeria: An Introduction. *Journal of North African Studies* 17 (5): 749–755. https://doi.org/10.1080/13629387.2012.723427.

Stein, Sarah Abrevaya. 2012. Dividing South from North: French Colonialism, Jews, and the Algerian Sahara. *Journal of North African Studies* 17 (5): 773–792. https://doi.org/10.1080/13629387.2012.723429.

Stoler, Ann Laura. 2002. Racist Visions for the Twentieth Century: On the Cultural Politics of the French Radical Right. In *Relocating Postcolonialism*, ed. David Theo Goldberg and Ato Quayson, 103–121. Oxford: Blackwell.

Stora, Benjamin. 1991. *La Gangrène et l'oubli: la mémoire de la guerre d'Algérie.* [Gangrene et Forgetting: the Memory of the Algerian War]. Paris: La Découverte.

———. 2005. *Les mots de la guerre d'Algérie* [The Words of the Algerian War]. Toulouse: Presse universitaires du Mirail.

Temlali, Yassine. 2015. *La Genèse de la Kabylie: aux origines de l'affirmation berbère en Algérie (1830–1962)* [The Genesis of Kabylia: The Origins of the Berber Affirmation in Algeria (1830–1962)]. Algiers: Barzakh.

Vince, Natalya. 2012. Questioning the Colonial Fracture: The Algerian War as a 'Useful Past' in Contemporary France and Algeria. In *France and the Mediterranean: International Relations, Culture and Politics*, ed. Emmanuel Godin and Natalya Vince, 305–343. Oxford: Peter Lang.

———. 2014. 1962 as Event and Metaphor in Women's Oral Histories in Algeria. Roundtable: The Afterlives of the Algerian Revolution. *JADMAG* 2 (1): 16–18. http://www.jadaliyya.com/Details/29731/1962-As-Event-and-Metaphor-in-Women%E2%80%99s-Oral-Histories-in-Algeria. Accessed 1 June 2020.

———. 2015. *Our Fighting Sisters: Nation, Memory and Gender in Algeria, 1954–2012.* Manchester: Manchester University Press.

GLOSSARY

Assimilation becoming legally and/or culturally French. In fact, 'assimilation' had multiple and shifting meanings. See Index entries integration and assimilation.

Autochthonous a more neutral term than 'indigenous' or 'native'—both of which have pejorative connotations as a result of their use in the colonial context.

Blood tax/blood debt in the nineteenth century, the idea of the citizen-soldier emerged: men would be conscripted to fight for states (and were willing to risk their lives—i.e., shed blood), but in return they would have political rights and a say in the running of the state (i.e. the debt would be repaid). This differed from earlier methods to recruit soldiers (coercion via local enforcers or paying mercenaries) and later professional armies (where joining the army is a career). The idea of the blood debt was used by early Algerian anti-colonial activists to campaign for greater political rights and is also a narrative used by women and men to make claims in post-independence Algeria and post-colonial France. See Index entry.

Casbah the historic citadel of Algiers where much of the Algerian population lived.

'Civilising mission' a justification for colonial rule based on the claim that 'more developed' peoples have a duty to bring the 'benefits of civilisation' to 'less developed' peoples. See Index entry.

'Europeans' the term used to describe the population of Algeria with full French citizenship. In 1954, there were around one million 'Europeans' for 8.5 million 'French Muslims'. Most of these people were settlers or the descendants of settlers. The Jewish population of Algeria, even though it predates French colonialism, is generally included in the category of 'Europeans', because from 1870 onwards the majority of Jews in Algeria were granted full French citizenship. See *pieds noirs* and repatriates (below), and Index entries Crémieux decree, Jewish population of Algeria and settlers.

© The Author(s) 2020
N. Vince, *The Algerian War, The Algerian Revolution*,
https://doi.org/10.1007/978-3-030-54264-1

Harki term used to describe Algerians who served as either soldiers or auxiliaries in the French army during the Algerian War/Algerian Revolution. For its shifting meanings, see Index entry.

Indigénat (indigenous code) a series of repressive measures in place between 1881 and 1944 which only applied to French subjects (i.e., in the Algerian case, 'Muslims', see below) and not citizens. Activities prohibited by the *indigénat* included meeting without authorisation, disrespect to an agent of authority even when he was off duty and leaving the local area without authorisation. Infractions were punishable by fine or imprisonment, or indeed collective punishments such as burning down a local forest. See Index entry.

Laïcité loosely translatable as state secularism, *laïcité* is the idea that the state should not interfere in the affairs of religious institutions, and that religious institutions should not have a say in the affairs of the state. Considered a founding principle of French Republicanism, a law passed in 1905 formally separated Church and State in metropolitan France. The law was never applied in Algeria, as the colonial authorities wanted to keep control over what was going on in mosques. See Index entry.

Maquis rural guerrilla groups. The term was used to describe the French rural resistance against the Nazis/collaboration during the Second World War in France, and then also used by the Algerian FLN/ALN and indeed Messali Hadj's MNA. A member of the *maquis* is a *maquisard* (for a man)/*maquisarde* (for a woman).

Metropole (noun)/metropolitan (adj.) the imperial centre, as opposed to colonial or overseas territories. For example, mainland France (on the European continent) was the metropole of the French empire.

Mujahidin a term employed by the FLN/ALN to describe rural and urban combatants. The singular is *mujahid* for a man, and *mujahida* for a woman. The plural is sometime transliterated, especially in French-language works, as *moudjahidine*. The term means holy warrior, but this does not mean that the Algerian Revolution was a religious conflict. Rather, religious terminology was employed as an instantly recognisable, unifying language to bring people together in nationalist struggle. See Chap. 3, p. 127; Chap. 4, pp. 168–9, 186.

Muslim personal status aspects of Muslim family law which the French state considered to be distinctive from the French civil code, notably polygamy, the right of husbands to unilaterally end their marriage (repudiation) and the privileging of male children over female children in inheritance. For most of the colonial period, 'Muslims' (see 'Muslims', below) had to individually renounce their 'Muslim personal status' in order to be naturalised as full French citizens. Most refused to do so, and in any case the process was complicated. 'Muslim personal status' was seen by many Algerian anti-colonialists as central to the construction of a separate identity of the colonised. See Chap. 1, p. 7 and Index entry.

'**Muslims**' in colonial Algeria, 'Muslim' was not just a religious identity, it was an ethnic–legal category created by the French state to determine political rights. It was judged that the majority of the autochthonous population in Algeria could not benefit from full French citizenship because they followed Muslim family law (see Muslim personal status, above). After 1958, full French citizenship was granted to all 'French Muslims' in Algeria. See Index entries Muslim personal status and citizenship.

Pacification a euphemistic term used by the French state in the course of the Algerian War to describe the actions used to bring civilian populations under their control, including mass round-ups, propaganda, 'winning hearts and minds', collective punishment, extra-judicial killings as well as regular warfare.

Pieds noirs literally 'black feet'. A term used, notably after 1962, to describe the Europeans of Algeria (see 'Europeans', above). The origin of the name 'pied noir' is uncertain—for some it is a reference to being born on African soil, others claim that this is what the autochthonous population called the French soldiers landing in Algiers in 1830 when they saw their black boots. See Index entries *Pieds noirs* (memory politics), settlers and repatriates.

Protectorate a country which is under the control of a foreign power whilst maintaining some autochthonous structures of decision-making in domestic matters. Tunisia and Morocco were French protectorates.

Repatriate the term used to describe Europeans of Algeria (see 'Europeans', above) who were 'repatriated' to France in 1962. France was not the country of origin of many of these European 'repatriates', whose ancestors came from across the Mediterranean basin or were part of the autochthonous Jewish population of Algeria. A distinction was made between 'repatriates' who were considered 'European' and automatically French, and 'Muslim' repatriates (see 'Muslims', above), who were often referred to as 'repatriates of North African origin' or 'refugees'. See Index entry.

Revolutionary warfare a form of asymmetric warfare in which smaller powers wear down larger powers' will and ability to continue an armed conflict, through rural and urban guerrilla warfare. The survival of guerrilla groups necessitates ideologically winning over the wider population to secure material and logistical support. The line between combatant and civilian is thus blurred. See Index entry.

Self-determination a term which emerged after the First World War, expressing the idea that nations (i.e. a group of people who through language, history, ethnicity, shared values, etc.) living within a given geographical space have the right to choose ('to determine') the political system which rules over them. See Index entry.

Third Worldism a political movement which emerged in the early 1950s, in the context of the Cold War, in which newly independent countries in Africa, Asia and the Middle East sought to avoid becoming either part of the capitalist bloc under the domination of the United States or part of the communist bloc under the domination of the USSR. Although the term 'Third

World' came to be seen as a pejorative term used to describe economically poorer 'developing countries' (for which the term 'Global South' would today be used), Third Worldism needs to be understood in the context of the 1950s and 1960s as a fiercely anti-imperialist political movement. Third Worldists sought to avoid both the exploitation and inequalities of capitalist countries and the totalitarianism of communist countries. Third Worldism is often seen as synonymous with the Non-Aligned Movement. See Index entries Afro-Asian conference and Third Worldism.

Transnational transnational history seeks to avoid what is termed 'methodological nationalism'—that is to say, assuming that the starting point for writing any history is the national framework. For example, an Algerian national history of the Algerian Revolution would look at the emergence of the FLN, the combat in Algeria and the FLN's political struggle internationally. A French national history would look at how successive governments in Paris tried to deal with 'the Algerian problem', the actions of the French military and interactions with the 'European' and 'Muslim' populations in Algeria. A transnational history looks at connections across national borders, and indeed across empires. It is particularly focused on people and ideas and how they travel. See, for example, the Index entry for the League Against Imperialism. Transnational history is different from international history, which tends to refer to state-to-state diplomacy. It is, however, connected to global history in that it seeks out connections and parallels in different places across the world.

Wilaya a military zone of the ALN during the war. The plural is *wilayat*. See Index entries for *wilaya* 1, 2, 3, 4, 5 and 6.

BIBLIOGRAPHY

Abbink, Jon, Klaas van Walraven, and Mirjam de Bruijn. 2002. *Rethinking Resistance: Revolt and Violence in African History*. Leiden: Brill.

Abitbol, Michel. 1989. *The Jews of North Africa during the Second World War*. Trans. Catherine Tihanyi Zentelis. Detroit: Wayne State University Press.

Adel, Khedidja. 2019. La prison des femmes de Tifelfel. Enfermement et corps en souffrance [The Women's Prison of Tifelfel. Imprisonment and Suffering Bodies]. *L'Année du Maghreb* 20 (1): 123–158. https://doi.org/10.4000/anneemaghreb.4674.

Ageron, Charles-Robert. 1966. Enquête sur les origines du nationalisme algérien. L'emir Khaled, petit-fils d'Abdelkader, fut-il le premier nationaliste algérien? [Investigation into the Origins of Algerian Nationalism. Was the Emir Khaled, the Son of Abdelkader, the First Algerian Nationalist?]. *Revue des mondes musulmans et de la Méditerranée* 2: 9–49. https://doi.org/10.3406/remmm.1966.929.

———. 1982. La perception de la puissance française en 1938–9: le mythe imperial [The Perception of French Power in 1938–9: The Imperial Myth]. *Revue française d'Histoire Outre-Mer* 69 (254): 7–22. https://doi.org/10.3406/outre.1982.2331.

———. 1997. L'insurrection du 20 août 1955 dans le Nord-Constantinois: de la résistance armée à la guerre du peuple [The 20 August 1955 Insurrection in the North-Constantine Region: From Armed Resistance to People's War]. In *La Guerre d'Algérie et les Algériens, 1954–1962* [The Algerian War and the Algerians, 1954–1962], ed. Charles-Robert Ageron, 27–50. Paris: Armand Colin/Masson.

Ainad Tabet, Redouane. 2002 [1985]. *8 Mai 1945, le génocide* [8 May 1945, the Genocide]. Algiers: ANEP.

Aissaoui, Rabah. 2009. *Immigration and National Identity: North African Political Movements in Colonial and Postcolonial France*. London and New York: Tauris Academic Studies.

———. 2012. Fratricidal War: The Conflict Between the Mouvement national algérien (MNA) and the Front de libération nationale (FLN) in France During the Algerian War (1954–1962). *British Journal of Middle Eastern Studies* 39 (2): 227–240. https://doi.org/10.1080/13530194.2012.709701.

© The Author(s) 2020

N. Vince, *The Algerian War, The Algerian Revolution*,
https://doi.org/10.1007/978-3-030-54264-1

———. 2017. 'Between two worlds': Emir Khaled and the Young Algerians at the Beginning of the Twentieth Century in Algeria. In *Algeria Revisited: History, Culture and Identity*, ed. Rabah Aissaoui and Claire Eldridge, 56–78. London and New York: Bloomsbury.

Aït-el-Djoudi, Dalila. 2007. *La guerre d'Algérie vue par l'ALN 1954–1962: l'armée française sous le regard des combattants algériens* [The Algerian War Seen by the ALN 1954–1962: The French Army as Seen by Algerian Combatants]. Paris: Autrement.

Alexander, Martin S., and John F. V. Keiger, eds. 2002. *France and the Algerian War 1954–62: Strategy, Operations and Diplomacy*. London: Frank Cass.

Alleg, Henri. 2006 [1958]. *The Question*. Trans. John Calder. Lincoln: University of Nebraska Press.

Amara, Mahfoud. 2005. Global Sport and Local Identity in Algeria: The Changing Role of Football as a Cultural, Political and Economic Vehicle. In *Transition and Development in Algeria: Economic, Social and Structural Challenges*, ed. Margaret Majumdar and Mohammed Saad, 145–158. Bristol: Intellect.

Amiri, Linda. 2004. *La bataille de France. La guerre d'Algérie en metropole* [The Battle of France. The Algerian War in the Metropole]. Paris: Robert Laffont.

———. 2014 [2012]. La Fédération de France du FLN, acteur majeur de la guerre d'indépendance [The Federation of France of the FLN, Major Actor in the War of Independence]. In *Histoire de l'Algérie à la période coloniale* [History of Algeria During the Colonial Period], ed. Abderrahmane Bouchène, Jean-Pierre Peyroulou, Ouanassa Siari Tengour, and Sylvie Thénault, 576–582. Paris: La Découverte.

Amrane, Djamila. 1991. *Les Femmes algériennes dans la guerre* [Algerian Women in the War]. Paris: Plon.

André, Marc. 2016. *Femmes dévoilées: Des Algériennes en France à l'heure de la décolonisation* [Unveiled Women: Algerian Women in France at the Hour of Decolonisation]. Lyon: ENS Editions.

Arezki, Saphia. 2015. La formation militaire des combattants de l'ALN aux frontières de l'Algérie et à l'étranger [The Military Training of ALN Combatants on the Borders of Algeria and Abroad]. In *La guerre d'Algérie revisitée: nouvelles générations, nouveaux regards* [The Algerian War Revisited: New Generations, New Perspectives], ed. Aissa Kadri, Moula Bouaziz, and Tramor Quemeneur, 231–242. Paris: Karthala.

———. 2018. *De l'ALN à l'ANP. La construction de l'armée algérienne 1954–1991* [From the ALN to the ANP: The Construction of the Algerian Army 1954–1991]. Algiers: Barzakh.

Arnaud, Georges, and Jacques Vergès. 1957. *Pour Djamila Bouhired* [For Djamila Bouhired]. Paris: Editions de minuit.

Asseraf, Arthur. 2018. 'A New Israel': Colonial Comparisons and the Algerian Partition That Never Happened. *French Historical Studies* 41 (1): 95–120. https://doi.org/10.1215/00161071-4254631.

Bamia, Aida. 2001. *The Graying of the Raven: Cultural and Sociopolitical Significance of Algerian Folk Poetry*. Cairo and New York: American University in Cairo Press.

Bancel, Nicolas, Pascal Blanchard, and Sandrine Lemaire, eds. 2005. *La Fracture coloniale: la société française au prisme de l'héritage colonial* [The Colonial Fracture: French Society in the Prism of Its Colonial Heritage]. Paris: La Découverte.

Bancel, Nicolas, Pascal Blanchard, and Dominic Thomas, eds. 2017. *The Colonial Legacy in France: Fracture, Rupture, and Apartheid*. Trans. Alexis Pernsteiner. Bloomington: Indiana University Press.

Bantigny, Ludivine. 2007. Temps, âge et generation à l'épreuve de la guerre: la mémoire, l'histoire et l'oubli des appelés en Algérie [Time, Age and Generation Under the Strain of War: Memory, History and Forgetting Amongst Conscripts in Algeria]. *Revue historique* 641: 165–179. https://doi.org/10.3917/rhis.071.0165.

Barkaoui, Miloud. 1999. Kennedy and the Cold War Imbroglio: The Case of Algeria's Independence. *Arab Studies Quarterly* 21 (2): 31–45.

Beaugé, Florence. 2005. *Algérie: Une Guerre sans gloire. Histoire d'une enquête* [Algeria: A War Without Glory. Story of an Investigation]. Paris: Calmann-Lévy.

Bedjaoui, Ahmed. 2015. Sixty Years of Algerian Cinema. *Black Renaissance/Renaissance Noire* 15 (1): 126–139.

Belmessous, Saliha. 2013. *Assimilation and Empire: Uniformity in the French and British Colonies, 1541–1954*. Oxford: Oxford University Press.

Benkada, Saddek. 2004. La revendication des libertés publiques dans le discours politique du nationalisme algérien et de l'anticolonialisme français (1919–1954) [The Demand for Public Freedoms in the Political Discourse of Algerian Nationalism and French Anti-colonialism (1919–1954)]. *Insaniyat* 25–26: 179–199. https://doi.org/10.4000/insaniyat.6387.

Benkhaled, Walid, and Natalya Vince. 2017. Performing Algerianness: The National and Transnational Construction of Algeria's 'Culture Wars'. In *Algeria: Nation, Culture and Transnationalism, 1988–2015*, ed. Patrick Crowley, 243–269. Liverpool: Liverpool University Press.

Benrabah, Mohamed. 2013. *Language Conflict in Algeria: From Colonialism to Post-independence*. Bristol: Multilingual Matters.

Blanchard, Emmanuel. 2011. *La police parisienne et les algériens (1944–1962)* [The Parisian Police and Algerians (1944–1962)]. Paris: Nouveau Monde.

———. 2012a. La Goutte d'Or, 30 juillet 1955: une émeute au coeur de la métropole coloniale [The Goutte d'Or, 30 July 1955: A Riot in the Heart of the Colonial Metropole]. *Actes de recherche en sciences sociales* 195: 98–111. https://doi.org/10.3917/arss.195.0098.

———. 2012b. 14 juillet 1953: repression coloniale, place de la Nation. *Histoire coloniale et postcoloniale* [14 July 1953: Colonial Repression, Place de la Nation, Extracts from Blanchard 2011]. https://histoirecoloniale.net/14-juillet-1953-repression.html. Accessed 1 June 2020.

Boulebier, Djamel. 2007. Constantine, fait colonial et pionniers musulmans du sport. [Constantine, Colonialism and the Muslim Sporting Pioneers]. *Insaniyat* 35-36: 21–61. https://doi.org/10.4000/insaniyat.3702.

Branche, Raphaëlle. 2001. *La Torture et l'armée pendant la Guerre d'Algérie, 1954–62* [Torture and the Army During the Algerian War]. Paris: Gallimard.

———. 2002. Des viols pendant la Guerre d'Algérie [Rape During the Algerian War]. *Vingtième siècle* 75: 123–132. https://doi.org/10.3917/ving.075.0123.

———. 2005. *La Guerre d'Algérie: une histoire apaisée?* [The Algerian War, a Calmed History?]. Paris: Seuil.

———. 2007. FLN et OAS: deux terrorismes en guerre d'Algérie [FLN and OAS: Two Terrorisms in the Algerian War]. *European Review of History/Revue européenne d'histoire* 14 (3): 325–342. https://doi.org/10.1080/13507480701611597.

———. 2014. The French Military in Its Last Colonial War: Algeria, 1954–1962, the Reign of Torture. In *Interrogation in War and Conflict: A Comparative and Interdisciplinary Analysis*, ed. Simona Tobia and Christopher Andrew, 169–184. London and New York: Routledge.

————. 2017. 'The best Fellagha Hunter is the French of North African Descent': Harkis in French Algeria. In *Unconventional Warfare from Antiquity to the Present Day*, ed. Brian Hughes and Fergus Robson, 47–66. Cham, Switzerland: Palgrave Macmillan.

————. 2018. Parallel Ambiguities: Prisoners During the Algerian War of Independence. In *The Civilianization of War*, ed. Andrew Barros and Martin Thomas, 100–115. Cambridge: Cambridge University Press.

————. 2019. Combattants indépendantistes et société rurale dans l'Algérie colonisée [Combatants for Independence and Rural Society in Colonial Algeria]. *Revue d'histoire* 141: 113–127. https://doi.org/10.3917/vin.141.0113.

Brazzoduro, Andrea. 2012. Postcolonial Memories of the Algerian War of Independence, 1955–2010: French Veterans and Contemporary France. In *France and the Mediterranean: International Relations, Culture and Politics*, ed. Emmanuel Godin and Natalya Vince, 275–303. Oxford: Peter Lang.

Brown, Megan. 2017. Drawing Algeria into Europe: Shifting French Policy and the Treaty of Rome (1951–1964). *Modern and Contemporary France* 25 (2): 191–208. https://doi.org/10.1080/09639489.2017.1281899.

Byrne, Jeffrey James. 2009. Our Own Special Brand of Socialism: Algeria and the Contest of Modernities in the 1960s. *Diplomatic History* 33 (3): 427–447. https://doi.org/10.1111/j.1467-7709.2009.00779.x.

————. 2010. 'Je ne vous ai pas compris': de Gaulle's decade of negotiation with the Algerian FLN, 1958-1969. In *Globalising de Gaulle: International Perspectives on French Foreign Policies, 1958–1969*, ed. Christian Nuenlist, Anna Locher, and Garret Martin, 225–250. Lanham, MD: Rowman and Littlefield.

————. 2016. *Mecca of Revolution: Algeria, Decolonization and the Third World Order*. Oxford: Oxford University Press.

Carlier, Omar. 1995. *Entre nation et jihad: histoire sociale des radicalismes algériens* [Between Nation and Jihad: A Social History of Algerian Radicalisms]. Paris: Presses de Sciences Po.

————. 1997. Scholars and Politicians: An Examination of the Algerian View of Algerian Nationalism. In *The Maghrib in Question: Essays in History and Historiography*, ed. Michel Le Gall and Kenneth Perkins, 136–169. Austin: University of Texas Press.

Chaalal, Omar Mokhtar, and Djelloul Haya. 2013. *Aux sources de novembre* [The Sources of November]. Algiers: APIC éditions.

Chabal, Emile. 2014. Managing the Postcolony: Minority Politics in Montpellier, c. 1960–c.2010. *Contemporary European History* 23 (2): 237–258. https://doi.org/10.1017/S096077731400006X.

Chafer, Tony. 2002. *The End of Empire in French West Africa: France's Successful Decolonisation?* Oxford and New York: Berg.

Chafer, Tony, and Amanda Sackur, eds. 1999. *French Colonial Empire and the Popular Front: Hope and Disillusion*. Basingstoke: Palgrave Macmillan.

Chakrabarty, Dipesh. 2010. The Legacies of Bandung: Decolonisation and the Politics of Culture. In *Making a World After Empire: The Bandung Moment and Its Political Afterlives*, ed. Christopher J. Lee, 45–68. Athens, OH: Ohio University Press.

Choi, Sung-Eun. 2016. *Decolonization and the French of Algeria: Bringing the Settler Colony Home*. Basingstoke: Palgrave Macmillan.

Cohen, William B. 2006. The *harkis*: History and Memory. In *Algeria and France 1800–2000: Identity, Memory, Nostalgia*, ed. Patricia Lorcin. Syracuse, NY: Syracuse University Press.

Cole, Joshua. 2003. Remembering the Battle of Paris: 17 October 1961 in French and Algerian Memory. *French Politics, Culture and Society* 21 (3): 21–50. https://doi.org/10.3167/153763703782370251.

———. 2019. *Lethal Provocation: The Constantine Murders and the Politics of French Algeria.* Ithaca, NY: Cornell University Press.

Comtat, Emmanuelle. 2009. *Les pieds noirs et la politique: quarante ans après le retour* [Pieds Noirs and Politics: Forty Years After the Return]. Paris: Presses de Sciences Po.

Conklin, Alice L. 1997. *A Mission to Civilize: The Republican Idea of Empire in France and West Africa, 1895–1930.* Stanford, CA: Stanford University Press.

Connelly, Matthew. 2001. Rethinking the Cold War and Decolonization: The Grand Strategy for the Algerian War for Independence. *International Journal of Middle East Studies* 33 (2): 221–245. https://doi.org/10.1017/S0020743801002033.

———. 2002. *A Diplomatic Revolution: Algeria's Fight for Independence and the Origins of the Post-Cold War Era.* Oxford and New York: Oxford University Press.

Cooper, Frederick. 2005. *Colonialism in Question: Theory, Knowledge, History.* Berkeley: University of California Press.

———. 2014. *Citizenship Between Empire and Nation: Remaking France and French Africa 1945–1960.* Princeton and Oxford: Princeton University Press.

Cooper, Frederick, and Randall M. Packard, eds. 1997. *International Development and the Social Sciences: Essays on the History and Politics of Knowledge.* Berkeley, CA: University of California Press.

Cornaton, Michel. 1998. *Les camps de regroupement de la guerre d'Algérie* [Regrouping Camps and the Algerian War]. Paris: L'Harmattan.

Courrèye, Charlotte. 2014. L'école musulmane algérienne de Ibn Bâdîs dans les années 1930, de l'alphabétisation de tous comme enjeu politique [The Algerian Muslim School of Ibn Bâdîs [Ben Badis] in the 1930s, Literacy for All as a Political Tool]. *Revue des mondes musulmans de la Méditerranée* 136. https://doi.org/10.4000/remmm.8500.

———. 2016. L'association des Oulémas Musulmans Algériens et la construction de l'Etat algérien indépendant: foundation, héritages, appropriations et antagonisms. [The Association of the Algerian Muslim 'Ulama and the Construction of the Independent Algerian State]. PhD Thesis, INALCO, Paris.

Dard, Olivier. 2014 [2012]. Qui ont été les membres de l'OAS? [Who Were the Members of the OAS?]. In *Histoire de l'Algérie à la période coloniale* [History of Algeria During the Colonial Period], ed. Abderrahmane Bouchène, Jean-Pierre Peyroulou, Ouanassa Siari Tengour, and Sylvie Thénault, 640–643. Paris: La Découverte.

Daum, Pierre. 2015. *Le dernier tabou: les "harkis" restés en Algérie après l'indépendance* [The Last Taboo: 'Harkis' Who Stayed in Algeria After Independence]. Arles and Paris: Solin, Actes Sud.

Davis, Muriam Haleh. 2010. Restaging Mise en Valeur: 'Postwar Imperialism' and the Plan de Constantine. *Review of Middle East Studies* 44 (2): 176–186. https://doi.org/10.1017/S215134810000149X.

———. 2017. 'The Transformation of Man' in French Algeria: Economic Planning and the Postwar Social Sciences, 195–1962. *Journal of Contemporary History* 52 (1): 73–94. https://doi.org/10.1177/0022009416647117.

———. 2018. North Africa and the Common Agricultural Policy: From Colonial Pact to European Integration. In *North Africa and the Making of Europe: Governance, Institutions and Culture*, ed. Muriam Haleh Davis and Thomas Serres, 43–66. London: Bloomsbury.

Denis, Sébastien. n.d. Parcours thématique: Les médias audiovisuels dans la guerre d'Algérie [Thematic Pathway: Audiovisual Media in the Algerian War (includes a number of French propaganda films to watch online)]: https://fresques.ina.fr/independances/parcours/0003/les-medias-audiovisuels-dans-la-guerre-d-algerie.html. Accessed 1 June 2020.

Derrick, Jonathan. 2002. The Dissenters: Anti-Colonialism in France. In *Promoting the Colonial Idea: Propaganda and Visions of Empire in France*, ed. Tony Chafer and Amanda Sackur, 53–68. Basingstoke: Palgrave Macmillan.

Dimier, Véronique. 2014. *The Development of a European Development Aid Bureaucracy: Recycling Empire*. Basingstoke: Palgrave Macmillan.

Dine, Philip. 2002. France, Algeria and Sport: From Colonisation to Globalisation. *Modern and Contemporary France* 10 (4): 495–505. https://doi.org/10.108 0/0963948022000029574.

Djerbal, Daho. 2003. Mounadiline et mousebbiline. Les forces auxiliaires de l'ALN dans le Nord-Constantinois [Mounadiline and Mousebbiline. Auxiliary Forces of the ALN in the North-Constantine Region]. In *Des Hommes et des femmes en guerre d'Algérie* [Men and Women in the Algerian War], ed. Jean-Charles Jauffret, 282–296. Paris: Autrement.

———. 2010. Les effets des manifestations de décembre 1960 sur les maquis algériens. [The Effects of the December 1960 Demonstrations on the Algerian Maquis]. *NAQD*(supplement 2): 63–92. https://doi.org/10.3917/naqd.hs2.0063.

Drew, Alison. 2014. *We Are No Longer in France. Communists in Colonial Algeria*. Manchester: Manchester University Press.

Drif, Zohra. 2017. *Inside the Battle of Algiers: Memoir of a Woman Freedom Fighter*. [French Title: *Mémoires d'une combattante de l'ALN*]. Trans. Andrew Farrand. Charlottesville, Virginia, VA: Just World Books.

Einaudi, Jean-Luc. 1991. *La Ferme Améziane: Enquête sur un centre de torture pendant la Guerre d'Algérie* [The Améziane Farm: Investigation into a Torture Centre During the Algerian War]. Paris: L'Harmattan.

Eldridge, Claire. 2009. 'We've never had a voice': Memory Construction and the Children of the Harkis (1962–1991). *French History* 23 (1): 88–107. https://doi.org/10.1093/fh/crn062.

———. 2012. Remembering the Other: Postcolonial Perspectives on Relationships Between Jews and Muslims in French Algeria. *Journal of Modern Jewish Studies* 11 (3): 299–317. https://doi.org/10.1080/14725886.2012.720510.

———. 2016. *From Empire to Exile: History and Memory Within the Pied-noir and Harki Communities, 1962–2012*. Manchester: Manchester University Press.

El-Mechat, Samya. 2014 [2012]. Les pays arabes et l'indépendance algérienne, 1945–1962 [The Arab Countries and Algerian Independence, 1945–1962]. In *Histoire de l'Algérie à la période coloniale* [History of Algeria During the Colonial Period], ed. Abderrahmane Bouchène, Jean-Pierre Peyroulou, Ouanassa Siari Tengour, and Sylvie Thénault, 644–651. Paris: La Découverte.

Essemlali, Mounya. 2011. Le Maroc entre la France et l'Algérie (1956–1962) [Morocco Between France and Algeria (1956–1962)]. *Relations Internationales* 146: 77–93. https://doi.org/10.3917/ri.146.0077.

Evans, Martin. 1997. *The Memory of Resistance: French Opposition to the Algerian War (1954–1962)*. Oxford: Berg.

———. 2000. Projecting a Greater France. *History Today* 50 (2): 18–32.

————. 2009. Guy Mollet's Third Way: National Renewal and the French Civilising Mission in Algeria. *French History & Civilization* 2: 169–180. https://h-france. net/rude/wp-content/uploads/2017/08/vol2_Evans_Final_Version_2.pdf. Accessed 1 June 2020.

————. 2010. Patriot Games: Algeria's Football Revolutionaries. *History Today* 60 (7): 42–44.

————. 2012. *Algeria: France's Undeclared War*. Oxford: Oxford University Press.

Eveno, Patrick. 2005. Paroles de soldats en guerre d'Algérie [Words of Soldiers in the Algerian War]. *Les Temps des medias* 4: 127–136. https://doi.org/10.3917/ tdm.004.0127.

Fabbiano, Giulia. 2008. Devenir harki: les modes d'énonciation identitaire des descendants des anciens supplétifs de la guerre d'Algérie [Becoming a Harki: Ways of Expressing Identity Amongst Descendants of Former Auxiliaries in the Algerian War]. *Migrations Société* 120: 155–171. https://doi.org/10.3917/migra.120.0155.

Fanon, Franz. 1965 [1959]. *A Dying Colonialism* [French Title: *L'An V de la Révolution algérienne*]. Trans. Haakon Chevalier. New York: Grove Press.

————. 2001 [1961]. *The Wretched of the Earth* [French Title: *Les Damnés de la terre*]. Trans. Constance Farrington. London: Penguin.

Feichtinger, Moritz. 2017. 'A Great Reformatory': Social Planning and Strategic Resettlement in Late Colonial Kenya and Algeria, 1952–63. *Journal of Contemporary History* 52 (1): 45–72. https://doi.org/10.1177/0022009415616867.

Flood, Christopher, and Hugo Frey. 2003. Questions of Decolonisation and Post-Colonialism in the Ideology of the French Extreme Right. In *The Decolonisation Reader*, ed. James Le Sueur, 388–413. London: Routledge.

Fogarty, Richard S. 2008. *Race and War in France: Colonial Subjects in the French Army, 1914–1918*. Baltimore: Johns Hopkins University Press.

Fontaine, Darcie. 2016. *Decolonizing Christianity: Religion and the End of Empire in France and Algeria*. New York: Cambridge University Press.

Forget, Nelly. 1992. Le Service des Centres Sociaux en Algérie. [The Social Centres service in Algeria]. *Matériaux pour l'histoire de notre temps* 26: 37–47. https://www. persee.fr/doc/mat_0769-3206_1992_num_26_1_404864. Accessed 1 June 2020.

Frémeaux, Jacques. 2002. Les SAS (Sections administratives spécialisées) [The SAS (Special Administrative Sections)]. *Guerres mondiales et conflits contemporains* 208: 55–68. https://doi.org/10.3917/gmcc.208.0055.

————. 2004. Les contingents impérieux au cœur de la guerre [Imperial Contingents in the Heart of the War]. *Histoire, économie et société* 23 (2): 215–233. https://doi. org/10.3917/hes.042.0215.

Fromage, Julien. 2014a [2012]. L'expérience des "Jeunes algériens" et l'émergence du militantisme moderne en Algérie (1880–1919). [The Experience of the 'Young Algerians' and the Emergence of Modern Activism in Algeria (1880–1919)]. In *Histoire de l'Algérie à la période coloniale* [History of Algeria During the Colonial Period], ed. Abderrahmane Bouchène, Jean-Pierre Peyroulou, Ouanassa Siari Tengour, and Sylvie Thénault, 238–244. Paris: La Découverte.

————. 2014b [2012]. Le docteur Bendjelloul et la Fédération des élus musulmans [Dr Benjelloul and the Federation of Muslim Representatives]. In *Histoire de l'Algérie à la période coloniale* [History of Algeria During the Colonial Period], ed. Abderrahmane Bouchène, Jean-Pierre Peyroulou, Ouanassa Siari Tengour, and Sylvie Thénault, 398–401. Paris: La Découverte.

———. 2015. La moblisation des élus musulmans fédérés au cours des années 1930: chaînon manquant entre anticolonialisme et nationalisme? [The Mobilisation of the Federated Muslim Representatives in the 1930s: The Missing Link Between Anticolonialism and Nationalism?]. In *La guerre d'Algérie revisitée: nouvelles générations, nouveaux regards* [The Algerian War Revisited: New Generations, New Perspectives], ed. Aissa Kadri, Moula Bouaziz, and Tramor Quemeneur, 89–99. Paris: Karthala.

Gacon, Stéphane. 2005. Les amnisties de la guerre d'Algérie (1962–1982) [The Amnesties of the Algerian War (1962–1982)]. *Histoire de la justice* 16: 271–279. https://doi.org/10.3917/rhj.016.0271.

Gaulle, Charles de. 1958. Discours du plan de Constantine, le 3 octobre 1958. Charles de Gaulle, paroles publiques. https://fresques.ina.fr/de-gaulle/fiche-media/Gaulle00022/discours-du-plan-de-constantine-le-3-octobre-1958.html. Accessed 1 June 2020.

Ginio, Ruth. 2016. *The French Army and Its African Soldiers: The Years of Decolonization.* Lincoln, NB: University of Nebraska.

Goebel, Michael. 2016. 'The capital of men without a country': Migrants and Anticolonialism in Interwar Paris. *The American Historical Review* 121 (5): 1444–1467. https://doi.org/10.1093/ahr/121.5.1444.

Gordon, Daniel A. 2015. Le 17 octobre et la population française. La collaboration ou la résistance? [17 October and the French Population. Collaboration or Resistance?]. In *La guerre d'Algérie revisitée: nouvelles générations, nouveaux regards* [The Algerian War Revisited: New Generations, New Perspectives], ed. Aissa Kadri, Moula Bouaziz, and Tramor Quemeneur, 339–350. Paris: Karthala.

Haddad-Fonda, Kyle. 2014. An Illusory Alliance: Revolutionary Legitimacy and Sino-Algerian Relations, 1958–1962. *Journal of North African Studies* 19 (3): 338–357. https://doi.org/10.1080/13629387.2013.870039.

Hadjerès, Sadek. 2014. *Quand une nation s'éveille. Mémoires – tome 1 – 1928–1949.* [When a Nation Awakes. Memoirs – Volume 1 – 1928–1949]. Annotated and Postfaced by Malika Rahal. Algiers: Inas Editions.

Halimi, Gisèle, and Simone de Beauvoir. 1962. *Djamila Boupacha.* Paris: Gallimard.

Hammerman, Jessica. 2018. By Sentiment and by Status: Remembering and Forgetting Crémieux During the Franco-Algerian War. *French Politics, Culture and Society* 36 (1): 76–102. https://doi.org/10.3167/fpcs.2018.360104.

Harbi, Mohamed. 1975. *Aux origines du FLN: le populisme revolutionnaire en Algérie* [The Origins of the FLN: Revolutionary Populism in Algeria]. Paris: Bourgois.

———. 1980. *Le FLN, mirage et realité des origines à la prise du pouvoir (1945–1962)* [The FLN, Mirage and Reality from Its Origins to Taking Power (1945–1962)]. Paris: Editions Jeune Afrique.

———. 2005. La guerre d'Algérie a commencé à Sétif. [The Algerian War Started in Sétif]. *Monde diplomatique,* March 1. http://www.monde-diplomatique.fr/2005/05/HARBI/12191#nb4. Accessed 1 June 2020.

Hassett, Dónal. 2019. *Mobilising Memory: The Great War and the Language of Politics in Colonial Algeria, 1918–1939.* Oxford: Oxford University Press.

Hautreux, François-Xavier. 2011. Quelques pistes pour une meilleure compréhension de l'engagement des harkis (1954–1962) [Some Indications for a Better Understanding of Why Harkis Joined Up]. *Les Temps modernes* 666: 44–52. https://doi.org/10.3917/ltm.666.0044.

———. 2013. *La guerre d'Algérie des Harkis, 1954–1962* [The Algerian War of *Harkis,* 1954–1962]. Paris: Perrin.

Hodier, Catherine, and Michel Pierre. 1991. *1931: L'Exposition coloniale* [1931: the Colonial Exhibition]. Brussels: Complexe.

Horne, Alistair. 1977. *A Savage War of Peace: Algeria, 1954–62*. London: Macmillan.

House, James. 2001. Antiracist Memories: The Case of 17 October 1961 in Historical Perspective. *Modern and Contemporary France* 9 (3): 355–368. https://doi.org/10.1080/09639480120065999.

———. 2018. Shantytowns and Rehousing in Late Colonial Algiers and Casablanca. In *France's Modernising Mission: Citizenship, Welfare and the Ends of Empire*, ed. Edward Naylor, 133–163. London: Palgrave Macmillan.

House, James, and Neil Macmaster. 2006. *Paris 1961: Algerians, State Terror, and Memory*. Oxford: Oxford University Press.

Howard, Sarah. 2013. Three Cats and a Watermelon: Summer 1955 and the Arrival of the Algerian War in Paris. *French History* 27 (3): 394–421. https://doi.org/10.1093/fh/crt051.

Izambert, Caroline. 2008. The Example of a Communist Paper Aimed at Algerian Immigrants: *L'Algérien en France* (1950–1960). In *Migration and Activism in Europe Since 1945*, ed. Wendy Pojmann, 99–110. Basingstoke: Palgrave Macmillan.

Jackson, Julian. 2018. *A Certain Idea of France: The Life of Charles de Gaulle*. London: Penguin.

Jansen, Jan C. 2010. Politics of Remembrance, Colonialism and the Algerian War of Independence in France. In *A European Memory? Contested Histories and Politics of Remembrance*, ed. Małgorzata Pakier and Bo Stråth, 275–293. New York and Oxford: Berghahn Books.

Jauffret, Jean-Charles. 2001. Une armée à deux vitesses en Algérie (1954–1962): réserves générales et troupes de secteur [A Two-Speed Army in Algeria (1954–1962)]. In *Militaires et guerrilla dans la guerre d'Algérie* [The Military and the Guerrilla in the Algerian War], ed. Jean-Charles Jauffret and Maurice Vaïsse, 21–37. Brussels: Complexe.

———. 2002. The War Culture of French Combatants in the Algerian Conflict. In *The Algerian War and the French Army: Experiences, Images and Testimonies*, ed. Martin S. Alexander, Martin Evans, and John F.V. Keiger, 101–116. Basingstoke: Palgrave Macmillan.

———. 2011 [2000]. *Soldats en Algérie: expériences contrastées des hommes du contingent* [Soldiers in Algeria: The Contrasting Experiences of Men of the Contingent]. Paris: Autrement.

Johnson, Jennifer. 2012. 'Humanise the conflict': Algerian Health Care Organisations and Propaganda Campaigns, 1954-62. *International Journal of Middle East Studies* 44 (4): 713–731. https://doi.org/10.1017/S0020743812000839.

———. 2016. *The Battle for Algeria: Sovereignty, Health Care, and Humanitarianism*. Philadelphia, PA: University of Pennsylvania Press.

Kaddache, Mahfoud. 2003a. 'Les soldats de l'avenir': les Scouts musulmans algériens (1930–1962) ['The soldiers of the future': Algerian Muslim Scouts (1930-1962)]. In *De l'Indochine à l'Algérie. La jeunesse en mouvements des deux côtés du miroir colonial, 1940–1962* [From Indochina to Algeria. Youth in Movement on Both Sides of the Colonial Mirror, 1940–1962], ed. Nicolas Bancel, Daniel Denis, and Youssef Fates, 68–77. Paris: La Decouverte.

———. 2003b. *Histoire du nationalism algérien. Tome 2, 1939–1951* [History of Algerian Nationalism; Volume 2, 1939–1951]. Paris and Algiers: Paris-Méditerranée, EDIF.

Kalman, Samuel. 2013. *French Colonial Fascism: The Extreme Right in Algeria, 1919–1939.* Basingstoke: Palgrave Macmillan.

Kateb, Kamel. 2005. *Ecole, population et société en Algérie* [School, Population and Society in Algeria]. Paris: L'Harmattan.

Katz, Ethan. 2015. *The Burdens of Brotherhood: Jews and Muslims from North Africa to France.* Cambridge, MA: Harvard University Press.

Khoulé, Cheikh Ahmadou Bamba. 2011. Les tirailleurs sénégalais dans la guerre d'Algérie: la transmission de la mémoire à travers les descendants [*Tirailleurs sénégalais* in the Algerian War: The Transmission of Memory to Descendants]. MA dissertation Université Cheikh Anta Diop de Dakar.

Klose, Fabian. 2013. *Human Rights in the Shadow of Colonial Violence. The Wars of Independence in Kenya and Algeria.* Trans. Dona Geyer. Philadelphia, PA: University of Pennsylvania Press.

Korso, Malika El-. 1996. Une double realité pour un même vécu [A Dual Reality for the Same Experience]. *Confluences Méditerranée* 17: 99–108.

Krais, Jakob. 2017. The Sportive Origin of Revolution: Youth Movements and Generational Conflicts in Late Colonial Algeria. *Middle East – Topics & Arguments* 9: 132–141. https://doi.org/10.17192/meta.2017.9.6965.

Kuby, Emma. 2012. A War of Words Over an Image of War: The Fox Movietone Scandal and the Portrayal of French Violence in Algeria, 1955–1956. *French Politics, Culture and Society* 30 (1): 46–67. https://doi.org/10.3167/fpcs.2012.300103.

———. 2013. From the Torture Chamber to the Bedchamber: French Soldiers, Antiwar Activists, and the Discourse of Sexual Deviancy in the Algerian War (1954–1962). *Contemporary French Civilization* 38 (2): 131–153. https://doi.org/10.3828/cfc.2013.7.

Lane, Jeremy F. 2007. Ferhat Abbas, Vichy's National Revolution, and the Memory of the 'Royaume arabe'. *L'Esprit Créateur* 47 (1): 19–31.

Lazreg, Marnia. 2000. Islamism and the Recolonization of Algeria. In *Beyond Colonalism and Nationalism in the Maghrib*, ed. Ali Abdullatif Ahmida, 147–164. Basingstoke: Palgrave Macmillan.

———. 2008. *Torture and the Twilight of Empire: From Algiers to Baghdad.* Princeton, NJ: Princeton University Press.

Le Foll Luciani, Pierre-Jean. 2015. Les juifs d'Algérie face aux nationalités française et algérienne (1940–1963) [The Jews of Algeria Faced with French and Algerian Nationalities]. *Revue des mondes musulmans et de la Méditerranée* 137: 115–132. https://doi.org/10.4000/remmm.9057.

Liauzu, Claude, and Gilles Manceron, eds. 2006. *La Colonisation, la loi et l'histoire* [Colonisation, Law and History]. Paris: Editions Syllepse.

Lorcin, Patricia. 1995. *Imperial Identities: Stereotyping, Prejudice and Race in Colonial Algeria.* New York, NY: I.B. Tauris.

Lotem, Itay. 2016. Anti-racist Activism and the Memory of Colonialism: Race as Republican Critique After 2005. *Modern and Contemporary France* 24 (3): 283–298. https://doi.org/10.1080/09639489.2016.1159188.

Mack, Andrew. 1975. Why Big Nations Lose Small Wars: The Politics of Asymmetric Conflict. *World Politics* 27 (2): 175–200. https://doi.org/10.2307/2009880.

Macmaster, Neil. 2009. *Burning the Veil: The Algerian War and the 'emancipation' of Muslim Women, 1954–62.* Manchester: Manchester University Press.

————. 2011. The Role of European Women and the Question of Mixed Couples in the Algerian Nationalist Movement in France, Circa 1918–1962. *French Historical Studies* 34 (2): 357–386. https://doi.org/10.1215/00161071-1157376.

————. 2018. From Tent to Village *Regroupement*: The Colonial State and Social Engineering of Rural Space, 1843–1962. In *France's Modernising Mission: Citizenship, Welfare and the Ends of Empire*, ed. Edward Naylor, 109–131. London: Palgrave Macmillan.

Mahieu, Alban. 2001. Les effectifs de l'armée française en Algérie (1954–1962) [Numbers in the French Army (1954–1962)]. In *Militaires et guérillas dans la guerre d'Algérie* [Soldiers and Guerrillas in the Algerian War], ed. Jean-Charles Jauffret and Maurice Vaïsse, 39–47. Brussels: Complexe.

Manela, Erez. 2007. *The Wilsonian Moment: Self-Determination and the International Origins of Anticolonial Nationalism*. New York, NY: Oxford University Press.

Mann, Gregory. 2006. *Native Sons: West African Veterans and France in the Twentieth Century*. Durham, NC: Duke University.

Mann, Michelle. 2017. The Young Algerians and the Question of the Muslim Draft, 1900–1914. In *Algeria Revisited: History, Culture and Identity*, ed. Rabah Aissaoui and Claire Eldridge, 39–55. London and New York: Bloomsbury.

Marangé, Céline. 2016a. De l'influence politique des acteurs coloniaux [The Political Influence of Colonial Actors]. *Vingtième siècle. Revue d'histoire* 131: 3–16. https://doi.org/10.3917/ving.131.0003.

————. 2016b. André Ferrat et la création du Parti communiste algérien (1931–1936) [André Ferrat and the creation of the Algerian Communist Party]. *Histoire@Politique* 29: 190–219. https://doi.org/10.3917/hp.029.0190.

Marynower, Claire. 2011. Réformer l'Algérie? Des militants socialistes en "situation coloniale" dans l'entre-les-deux-guerres [Reform Algeria? Socialist Activists in a 'colonial situation' in the Interwar Period]. *Histoire@politique* 13: 112–124. https://doi.org/10.3917/hp.013.0010.

————. 2014 [2012]. 1936. Le Front Populaire en Algérie et le Congrès musulman algérien [1936. The Popular Front in Algeria and the Algerian Muslim Congress]. In *Histoire de l'Algérie à la période coloniale* [History of Algeria During the Colonial Period], eds. Abderrahmane Bouchène, Jean-Pierre Peyroulou, Ouanassa Siari Tengour, and Sylvie Thénault, 401–404. Paris: La Découverte.

Mauss-Copeaux, Claire. 1998. *Appelés en Algérie. La Parole confisquée* [Conscripts in Algeria. The Confiscated Word]. Paris: Hachette.

————. 2011. *Algérie, 20 août 1955. Insurrection, repression, massacres* [Algeria, 20 August 1955. Insurrection, Repression, Massacres]. Paris: Payot.

————. 2017. *Hadjira. La ferme Ameziane et au delà* [Hadjira. The Ameziane Farm and Beyond]. Paris: Les Chemins du présent.

Mbaye, Cheikh Anta. 2011. Les tirailleurs sénégalais dans la guerre d'Algérie (1954–1962) [*Tirailleurs sénégalais* in the Algerian War (1954–1962)]. MA Dissertation, Université Cheikh Anta Diop, Dakar.

McDonnell, Hugh. 2018. Complicity and Memory in Soldiers' Testimonies of Decolonisation in *Esprit* and *Les Temps modernes*. *Memory Studies*. https://doi.org/10.1177/1750698018784130.

McDougall, James. 2005. Savage Wars? Codes of Violence in Algeria, 1830s–1990s. *Third World Quarterly* 26 (1): 117–131. https://doi.org/10.1080/0143659042000322946.

————. 2006. *History and the Culture of Nationalism in Algeria*. Cambridge: Cambridge University Press.

————. 2017a. *A History of Algeria*. Cambridge: Cambridge University Press.

————. 2017b. The Impossible Republic: The Reconquest and the Decolonization of France, 1945–1962. *Journal of Modern History* 89 (4): 772–811. https://doi.org/10.1086/694427.

Merom, Gil. 1999. A 'Grand Design?' Charles de Gaulle and the End of the Algerian War. *Armed Forces and Society* 25 (2): 267–288. https://doi.org/10.1177/0095327X9902500205.

Meynier, Gilbert. 2002. *Histoire intérieure du FLN 1954–1962* [The Internal History of the FLN]. Paris: Fayard.

————. 2007. *L'Algérie des origines. De la préhistoire à l'avènement de l'islam* [Algeria from Its Origins. From Prehistory to the Coming of Islam]. Paris: La Découverte.

————. 2015 [1981]. *L'Algérie révélée: la guerre de 1914–1918 et le premier quart du XXe siècle* [Algeria Revealed: The 1914–18 War and the First Quarter of the Twentieth Century]. Saint Denis: Editions Bouchène.

————. 2016. Algerians and the First World War. *Orient XXI*. https://orientxxi.info/l-orient-dans-la-guerre-1914-1918/algerians-and-the-first-world-war,0645,0645. Accessed 1 June 2020.

Miller, Jeannette E. 2013. A Camp for Foreigners and 'Aliens': The Harkis' Exile at the Rivesaltes Camp (1962–1964). *French Politics, Culture & Society* 31 (3): 21–44.

Mohand Amer, Amar. 2010. La crise du Front de libération nationale de l'été 1962: indépendance et enjeux de pouvoir [The Crisis of the National Liberation Front of Summer 1962: Independence and Power Stakes]. PhD Thesis, Université Paris Diderot.

————. 2014. Les wilayas dans la crise du FLN de l'été 1962. [The *Wilayas* in the FLN Crisis of Summer 1962]. *Insaniyat* 65–66: 105–124. https://doi.org/10.4000/insaniyat.14796.

Mortimer, Mildred. 2018. *Women Fight, Women Write: Texts on the Algerian War*. Charlottesville, VA: University of Virginia Press.

Moumen, Abderahmen. 2010. La notion d'abandon des harkis par les autorités françaises [The Notion of the Abandon of Harkis by the French Authorities]. In *Les Harkis: histoire, mémoire et transmission* [The Harkis: History, Memory and Transmission], ed. Fatima Besnaci-Lancou, Benoit Falaize, and Gilles Manceron, 47–62. Ivry-sur-Seine: Editions de l'atelier.

————. 2011. Violences de fin de guerre. Les massacres des harkis après l'indépendance algérienne (1962–1965) [Violences at the End of War. The Massacres of Harkis After Algerian Independence (1962–1965)]. In *Violence(s) de la préhistoire à nos jours* [Violences from Prehistory to the Present], ed. Marie-Claude Marandet, 331–346. Perpignan: Presses Universitaires de Perpignan. https://books.openedition.org/pupvd/3422. Accessed 1 June 2020.

————. 2012. Housing the 'harkis': Long Term Segregation. Trans. Oliver Waine. Metropolitics.org. https://www.metropolitiques.eu/Housing-the-harkis-long-term.html. Accessed 1 June 2020.

Narayanam, Anndal. 2014. 'Ready to Fight': Veterans of the Algerian War Take the Battle to France, 1958–1974. *Journal of the Western Society for French History* 42. http://hdl.handle.net/2027/spo.0642292.0042.013. Accessed 1 June 2020.

Naylor, Edward. 2013. 'Un âne dans l'ascenseur': Late Colonial Welfare Services and Social Housing in Marseille. *French History* 27 (3): 422–227. https://doi.org/10.1093/fh/crt052.

———, ed. 2018. *France's Modernising Mission: Citizenship, Welfare and the Ends of Empire*. London: Palgrave Macmillan.

Ouerdane, Amar. 1987. La "crise berbériste" de 1949, un conflit à plusieurs faces. [The 'Berberist crisis' of 1949: A Conflict with Many Faces]. *Revue de l'Occident musulman et de la Méditerranée* 44: 35–47. https://www.persee.fr/doc/remmm_0035-1474_1987_num_44_1_2153. Accessed 1 June 2020.

Perego, Elizabeth. 2015. The Veil Or a Brother's Life: French Manipulations of Muslim Women's Images During the Algerian War, 1954–62. *Journal of North African Studies* 20 (3): 349–373. https://doi.org/10.1080/13629387.2015.1013942.

Pervillé, Guy. 2007. La guerre sans nom: appelés et rappelés en Algérie (1992) [The War Without Name: Conscripts and Reservists in Algeria]. http://guy.perville.free.fr/spip/article.php3?id_article=96. Accessed 1 June 2020.

———. 2008. A la mémoire: Charles-Robert Ageron (1923–2008) [In Memory of Charles-Robert Ageron (1923–2008)]. *Outre-mers* 360–361: 373–388. https://www.persee.fr/doc/outre_1631-0438_2008_num_95_360_4804. Accessed 1 June 2020.

Peyroulou, Jean-Pierre. 2008. Setif and Guelma (May 1945). Mass Violence and Resistance – Research Network. https://www.sciencespo.fr/mass-violence-war-massacre-resistance/en/document/setif-and-guelma-may-1945. Accessed 1 June 2020.

Pinoteau, Pascal. 2003. Propagande cinématographique et décolonisation. L'exemple français (1949–1958) [Cinematographic Propaganda and Decolonisation. The French Example]. *Vingtième siècle. Revue d'histoire* 80: 55–69. https://doi.org/10.3917/ving.080.0055.

Prakash, Amit. 2013. Colonial Techniques in the Imperial Capital: The Prefecture of Police and the Surveillance of North Africans in Paris, c. 1925–1970. *French Historical Studies* 36 (3): 479–510. https://doi.org/10.1215/00161071-2141118.

Quemeneur, Tramor. 2011. Refuser l'autorité? Etude des désobéissances de soldats français pendant la Guerre d'Algérie [Reject Authority? A Study of Disobedience by French Soldiers During the Algerian War]. *Outre-mers revue d'histoire* 370–371: 57–66. https://www.persee.fr/doc/outre_1631-0438_2011_num_98_370_4533. Accessed 1 June 2020.

Rahal, Malika. 2004. La place des réformistes dans le mouvement national algérien [The Place of Reformists in the Algerian National Movement]. *Vingtième siècle* 83: 161–171. https://doi.org/10.3917/ving.083.0161.

———. 2010. Les manifestations de mai 1958 en Algérie ou l'impossible expression d'une opinion publique "musulmane" [The Demonstrations of May 1958 in Algeria Or the Impossible Expression of a 'Muslim' Public Opinion]. In *Mai 1958: Le retour du général de Gaulle* [May 1958: The Return of General de Gaulle], ed. Jean-Paul Thomas, Gilles Le Béguec, and Bernard Lachaise, 39–58. Rennes: Presse Universitaires de Rennes.

———. 2013a. A local approach to the UDMA: Local-Level Politics During the Decade of Political Parties, 1946–56. *Journal of North African Studies* 18 (5): 703–724. https://doi.org/10.1080/13629387.2013.849897.

————. 2013b. Algeria: Nonviolent Resistance Against French Colonialism, 1830s–1950s. In *Recovering Nonviolent History: Civil Resistance in Liberation Struggles*, ed. Maciej J. Bartkowski, 107–123. Boulder, CO: Rienner.

————. 2014 [2012]. Ferhat Abbas, de l'assimilation au nationalism. [Ferhat Abbas, from Assimilation to Nationalism]. In *Histoire de l'Algérie à la période coloniale* [History of Algeria During the Colonial Period], ed. Abderrahmane Bouchène, Jean-Pierre Peyroulou, Ouanassa Siari Tengour, and Sylvie Thénault, 443–446. Paris: La Découverte.

————. 2015. 10 février 1943 – Le Manifeste du peuple algérie [10 February 1943 – The Manifesto of the Algerian People]. *Textures du temps*.https://texturesdutemps. hypotheses.org/1458. Accessed 1 June 2020.

————. 2018. *L'UDMA et les UDMISTES: Contribution à l'histoire du nationalisme algérien* [UDMA and Its Members: Contribution to the History of Algerian Nationalism]. Algiers: Barzakh.

Remaoun, Hassan. 1994. Enseignement de l'histoire et conscience nationale [Teaching History and National Consciousness]. *Confluences Méditerranée* 11: 25–32.

Rey Goldzeiguer, Annie. 2002. *Aux Origines de la Guerre d'Algérie 1940–1945. De Mers-el-Kébir aux massacres du Nord Constantinois* [The Origins of the Algerian War 1940–1945. From Mers-el-Kébir to the Massacres in the North Constantine Region]. Paris: La Découverte.

Rigouste, Mathieu. 2017. Algeria's Independence: The Forgotten Protests That Forged a Nation. *Middle East Eye*. https://www.middleeasteye.net/big-story/algerias-independence-forgotten-protests-forged-nation. Accessed 1 June 2020.

Roberts, Hugh. 2004. Sovereignty: The Algerian Case. *Diplomatic History* 28 (4): 595–598. https://doi.org/10.1111/j.1467-7709.2004.00439.x.

Roche, Anne, and Alice Belgacem. 2017. "Je vous le raconte volontiers, parce qu'on ne me l'a jamais demandé": Autobiographies d'appelés en Algérie ['I'll happily tell you about it, because no one ever asked': Autobiographies of Conscripts in Algeria]. *Bulletin de l'AFAS* 43. https://doi.org/10.4000/afas.3027. This article draws on an oral history archive with French soldiers (in French): http://phonotheque. mmsh.huma-num.fr/. Accessed 1 June 2020.

de Rochebrune, Renaud, and Benjamin Stora. 2011. *La Guerre d'Algérie vue par les Algériens. Des origines à la Bataille d'Alger* [The Algerian War Seen by Algerians. From Its Origins to the Battle of Algiers]. Paris: Denoël.

Rousso, Henry. 1991. *The Vichy Syndrome: History and Memory in France Since 1944*. Trans. Arthur Goldhammer. London: Harvard University Press.

Sabeur, Khaled Chérif. 2017. Les tirailleurs sénégalais à travers quelques extraits inédits de poèmes populaires kabyles [Tirailleurs sénégalais in Some Unpublished Extracts of Popular Kabyle Poetry] [Conference Paper]. The Algerian War of Independence: Global and Local Histories, 1954–62 and Beyond. https://oxfordalgeriaconfer-ence2017.files.wordpress.com/2017/05/talks_participants_oxfordalgeriaconfer-ence2017.pdf. Accessed 1 June 2020.

Sacriste, Fabien. 2012. Surveiller et moderniser. Les camps de "regroupement" de ruraux pendant la guerre d'indépendance algérienne [Surveillance and Modernisation. The 'regrouping' Camps of Rural Populations During the Algerian War of Independence]. *Métropolitiques.eu*. https://www.metropolitiques.eu/Surveiller-et-moderniser-Les-camps.html#nh5. Accessed 1 June 2020.

Savarese, Eric. 2002. *L'invention des pieds noirs* [The Invention of the Pieds Noirs]. Biarritz: Séguier.

———. 2006. After the Algerian War: Reconstructing Identity Among the Pieds-noirs. *International Social Science Journal* 189: 457–466. https://doi.org/10.1111/j.1468-2451.2007.00644.x.

Scioldo-Zürcher, Yann. 2010. *Devenir Métropolitain. Politique d'intégration et parcours de rapatriés d'Algérie en métropole (1954–2005)* [Becoming Metropolitan. Integration Policy and Trajectories of Repatriates from Algeria in the Metropole]. Paris: EHESS.

———. 2012. Memory and Influence on the Web: French Colonial Repatriates from 1950 to the Present. *Social Science Information* 51 (4): 475–501. https://doi.org/10.1177/0539018412456917.

———. 2016. The Postcolonial Repatriations of the French of Algeria in 1962: An Emblematic Case of a Public Integration Policy. In *Vertriebene and Pieds-Noirs in Postwar Germany and France: Comparative Perspectives*, ed. Manuel Borutta and Jan Jansen, 95–112. London: Palgrave Macmillan.

Sèbe, Berny. 2010. In the Shadow of the Algerian War: The United States and the Common Organisation of Saharan Regions (OCRS), 1957–62. *Journal of Imperial and Commonwealth History* 38 (2): 303–322. https://doi.org/10.1080/03086531003743999.

Seferdjeli, Ryme. 2004. French 'Reforms' and Muslim Women's Emancipation During the Algerian War. *Journal of North African Studies* 9 (4): 19–61. https://doi.org/10.1080/1362938042000326272.

———. 2005. The French Army and Muslim Women During the Algerian War. *Hawwa* 3 (1): 40–79. https://doi.org/10.1163/1569208053628537.

———. 2012. Rethinking the History of the Mudjahidat During the Algerian War: Competing Voices, Reconstructed Memories and Contrasting Historiographies. *Interventions: International Journal of Postcolonial Studies* 14 (2): 238–255. https://doi.org/10.1080/1369801X.2012.687902.

Sessions, Jennifer. 2011. *By Sword and By Plow: France and the Conquest of Algeria*. Ithaca, NY: Cornell University Press.

Shaev, Brian. 2018. The Algerian War, European Integration, and the Decolonisation of French Socialism. *French Historical Studies* 41 (1): 63–94. https://doi.org/10.1215/00161071-4254619.

Shepard, Todd. 2006. *The Invention of Decolonization. The Algerian War and the Remaking of France*. Ithaca and London: Cornell University Press.

———. 2011. Thinking Between Metropole and Colony: The French Republic, 'Exceptional Promotion' and the 'Integration' of Algerians, 1955–1962. In *The French Colonial Mind. Volume 1: Mental Maps of Empire and Colonial Encounters*, ed. Martin Thomas, 298–232. Lincoln, NE: University of Nebraska.

———. 2015a. 'Of sovereignty': Disputed Archives, 'wholly modern' Archives, and the Post-decolonization French and Algerian Republics, 1962–2012. *The American Historical Review* 120 (3): 869–883. https://doi.org/10.1093/ahr/120.3.869.

———. 2015b. *Voices of Decolonization: A Brief History with Documents*. Boston/New York: Bedford/St Martin's.

———. 2016. The Birth of the Hexagon: 1962 and the Erasure of France's Supranational History. In *Vertriebene and Pieds-Noirs in Postwar Germany and France: Comparative Perspectives*, ed. Manuel Borutta and Jan Jansen, 53–69. Basingstoke: Palgrave Macmillan.

Siari Tengour, Ouanassa. 2014 [2012]. La révolte de 1916 dans les Aurès. [The 1916 Revolt in the Aures]. In *Histoire de l'Algérie à la période coloniale* [History of Algeria

During the Colonial Period], ed. Abderrahmane Bouchène, Jean-Pierre Peyroulou, Ouanassa Siari Tengour, and Sylvie Thénault, 255–260. Paris: La Découverte.

Sidi Moussa, Nedjib. 2014. La révolution au pluriel. Pour une historiographie de la question messaliste [The Revolution in the Plural. For a Historiography of the Messalist Question]. *L'Année du Maghreb* 10: 99–114. https://doi.org/10.4000/anneemaghreb.2048.

———. 2019. *Algérie. Une autre histoire de l'indépendance* [Algeria. Another History of Independence]. Paris: PUF.

Simon, Catherine. 2011 [2009]. *Algérie, les années pieds-rouges. Des rêves de l'indépendance au désenchantement* [Algeria, the Pied-Rouge Years. From Dreams of Independence to Disillusion]. Paris: La Découverte.

Sims, Laura Jeanne. 2016. Rethinking France's 'Memory Wars': Harki Collective Memories, 2003–2010. *French Politics, Culture and Society* 34 (3): 83–104. https://doi.org/10.3167/fpcs.2016.340305.

Sivan, Emmanuel. 1973. 'Slave owner mentality' and Bolshevism: Algerian Communism, 1920–1927. *Asian and African Studies* 9 (2): 154–195.

———. 1976. *Communisme et nationalisme en Algérie 1920–1962* [Communism and Nationalism in Algeria 1920–1962]. Paris: Presses de Sciences Po.

Slyomovics, Susan. 2014. Algerian Women's Būqālah Poetry: Oral Literature, Cultural Politics, and Anti-Colonial Resistance. *Journal of Arabic Literature* 45: 145–186. https://doi.org/10.1163/1570064x-12341283.

Slyomovics, Susan, and Sarah Abrevaya Stein. 2012. Jews and French Colonialism in Algeria: An Introduction. *Journal of North African Studies* 17 (5): 749–755. https://doi.org/10.1080/13629387.2012.723427.

Soufi, Fouad. 2000. Oran, 28 février 1962, 5 juillet 1962. Deux événements pour l'histoire, deux événements pour la mémoire [28 February 1962, 5 July 1962. Two Events for History, Two Events for Memory]. In *La Guerre d'Algérie au miroir des décolonisations françaises: en honneur de Charles-Robert Ageron* [The Algerian War in the Mirror of French Decolonisations: In Honour of Charles-Robert Ageron], 635–676. Paris: SFHOM. A version of this text is available online: https://histoire-coloniale.net/Oran-1962-par-Fouad-Soufi-1-1.html. Accessed 1 June 2020.

Stein, Sarah Abrevaya. 2012. Dividing South from North: French Colonialism, Jews, and the Algerian Sahara. *Journal of North African Studies* 17 (5): 773–792. https://doi.org/10.1080/13629387.2012.723429.

Stoler, Ann Laura. 2002. Racist Visions for the Twentieth Century: On the Cultural Politics of the French Radical Right. In *Relocating Postcolonialism*, ed. David Theo Goldberg and Ato Quayson, 103–121. Oxford: Blackwell.

Stora, Benjamin. 1986. *Messali Hadj (1898–1974): pionnier du nationalisme algérien* [Messali Hadj (1898–1974), Pioneer of Algerian Nationalism]. Paris: L'Harmattan.

———. 1989. L'effet "89" dans les milieux immigrés algériens en France (1920–1960). *Revue des mondes musulmans et de la Méditerranée* 52–53: 229–240. https://www.persee.fr/doc/remmm_0997-1327_1989_num_52_1_2303. Accessed 1 June 2020.

———. 1991. *La Gangrène et l'oubli: la mémoire de la guerre d'Algérie* [Gangrene et Forgetting: The Memory of the Algerian War]. Paris: La Découverte.

———. 1992. *Ils venaient d'Algérie. L'immigration algérienne en France, 1912–1992* [They came from Algeria. Algerian immigration in France, 1912–1992]. Paris: Fayard.

———. 2005. *Les mots de la guerre d'Algérie* [The Words of the Algerian War]. Toulouse: Presse universitaires du Mirail.

————. 2010. *Le Mystère de Gaulle. Son choix pour l'Algérie* [The de Gaulle Mystery. His Choice for Algeria]. Paris: Robert Laffont.

Stora, Benjamin, and Zakya Daoud. 1995. *Ferhat Abbas, une utopie algérienne* [Ferhat Abbas: An Algerian Utopia]. Paris: Denoël.

Suggitt, Kelsey. 2018. Impossible Endings? Reimaging the End of the French Empire in the Sahara, 1951–1962. PhD Thesis, University of Portsmouth.

Suny, Ronald Grigor. 2003. 'Don't paint nationalism red!' National Revolution and Socialist Anti-imperialism. In *Decolonization: Perspectives from Now and Then*, ed. Prasenjit Duara, 176–198. London and New York: Routledge.

Surkis, Judith. 2010. Ethics and Violence: Simone de Beauvoir, Djamila Boupacha, and the Algerian War. *French Politics, Culture and Society* 28 (2): 38–55. https://doi.org/10.3167/fpcs.2010.280204.

Temlali, Yassine. 2015. *La Genèse de la Kabylie: aux origines de l'affirmation berbère en Algérie (1830–1962)* [The Genesis of Kabylia: The Origins of the Berber Affirmation in Algeria (1830–1962)]. Algiers: Barzakh.

Thénault, Sylvie. 2001. *Une drôle de justice: les magistrats dans la guerre d'Algérie* [A Funny Kind of Justice: Magistrates in the Algerian War]. Paris: La Découverte.

————. 2005. Personnel et internes dans les camps français de la guerre d'Algérie: entre stéréotypes coloniaux et combat pour l'indépendance [Personnel and Internees in French Camps During the Algerian War: Between Colonial Stereotypes and the Fight for Independence]. *Politix* 69: 63–81. https://doi.org/10.3917/pox.069.0063.

————. 2008. The OAS in Algiers in 1962: A Story of Terrorist Violence and Its Agents. *Annales. Histoire, Sciences Sociales* 63 (5): 977–1001. https://www.cairn.info/article.php?ID_ARTICLE=ANNA_635_0977. Accessed 1 June 2020.

————. 2012a [2005]. *Histoire de la guerre d'indépendance algérienne* [History of the Algerian War of Independence]. Paris: Flammarion.

————. 2012b. Defending Algerian Nationalists in the Fight for Independence: The Issue of the 'rupture strategy'. *Mouvement Social* 240. https://doi.org/10.3917/lms.240.0121.

Thomas, Martin. 2002. Defending a Lost Cause? France and the United States Vision of Imperial Rule in French North Africa, 1945–1956. *Diplomatic History* 26 (2): 215–130. https://doi.org/10.1111/1467-7709.00308.

————. 2005. Albert Sarraut, French Colonial Development and the Communist Threat, 1919–1930. *Journal of Modern History* 77 (4): 917–955.

————. 2011. Resource War, Civil War, Rights War: Factoring Empire into French North Africa's Second World War. *War in History* 18 (2): 225–248. https://doi.org/10.1177/0968344510394265.

————. 2013a. *Fight Or Flight: Britain, France, and Their Roads from Empire*. Oxford: Oxford University Press.

————. 2013b. Intelligence and the Transition to the Algerian Police State: Reassessing French Colonial Security after the Sétif Uprising, 1945. *Intelligence and National Security* 28 (3): 377–396. https://doi.org/10.1080/02684527.2013.789637.

————. 2015. France and Its Colonial Civil Wars, 1940–1945. In *The Cambridge History of the Second World War: Volume 2, Politics and Ideology*, ed. Richard Bosworth and Joseph Maiolo, 518–604. Cambridge: Cambridge University Press.

Tyre, Stephen. 2006. From Algérie française to France musulmane: Jacques Soustelle and the Myths and Realities of 'Integration', 1955–1962. *French History* 20 (3): 276–296. https://doi.org/10.1093/fh/crl010.

Ulloa, Marie-Pierre. 2007. *Francis Jeanson: A Dissident Intellectual from the French Resistance to the Algerian War*. Trans. Jane Marie Todd. Stanford, CA: Stanford University Press.

Vaïsse, Maurice. 1998. *La Grandeur: Politique Etrangère du Général de Gaulle* [Greatness: The Foreign Policy of General de Gaulle]. Paris: Fayard.

Vaïsse, Maurice, and Jean-Claude Jauffret, eds. 2001. *Militaires et guérrillas dans la guerre d'Algérie* [Soldiers and Guerrillas in the Algerian War]. Brussels: Complexe.

Vautier, René. 1958. *Algérie en flammes* [Algeria in Flames], East Germany: DEFA. Archives numériques du Cinéma Algérien [YouTube channel] https://www.youtube.com/watch?v=fnSrGUDksVo. Accessed 1 June 2020.

Vince, Natalya. 2010. Transgressing Boundaries: Gender, Race, Religion, and 'Françaises Musulmanes' during the Algerian War of Independence. *French Historical Studies* 33 (3): 445–474. https://doi.org/10.1215/00161071-2010-005.

———. 2012. Questioning the Colonial Fracture: The Algerian War as a 'Useful Past' in Contemporary France and Algeria. In *France and the Mediterranean: International Relations, Culture and Politics*, ed. Emmanuel Godin and Natalya Vince, 305–343. Oxford: Peter Lang.

———. 2014. 1962 as Event and Metaphor in Women's Oral Histories in Algeria. Roundtable: The Afterlives of the Algerian Revolution. *JADMAG* 2 (1): 16–18. http://www.jadaliyya.com/Details/29731/1962-As-Event-and-Metaphor-in-Women%E2%80%99s-Oral-Histories-in-Algeria. Accessed 1 June 2020.

———. 2015. *Our Fighting Sisters: Nation, Memory and Gender in Algeria, 1954–2012*. Manchester: Manchester University Press.

Von Bülow, Mathilde. 2007. Myth Or Reality? The Red Hand and French Covert Action in Federal Germany during the Algerian War, 1956–61. *Intelligence and National Security* 22 (6): 787–820. https://doi.org/10.1080/02684520701770626.

Wadowiec, Jaime. 2013. Algerian Women and the Rights of Man: Islam and Gendered Citizenship in French Algeria at the End of Empire. *French Historical Studies* 36 (4): 649–676. https://doi.org/10.1215/00161071-2294910.

Wall, Irvine M. 2001. *France, the United States and the Algerian War*. Berkeley, CA: University of California Press.

Weil, Patrick. 2008. *How to Be French: Nationality in the Making Since 1789*. Trans. Catherine Porter. Durham, NC: Duke University Press.

Welch, Edward, and Joseph McGonagle. 2013. *Contesting Views: The Visual Economy of France and Algeria*. Liverpool: Liverpool University Press.

Westad, Odd Arne. 2006. *The Global Cold War: Third World Interventions and the Making of Our Times*. Cambridge: Cambridge University Press.

Zekkour, Afaf. 2011. Muslim Reformist Networks in the City of Algiers. *Le Mouvement Social* 236: 23–34. https://doi.org/10.3917/lms.236.0023.

Zimmerman, Sarah Jean. 2011. Living Beyond Boundaries: West African Servicemen in French Colonial Conflicts, 1908–1962. PhD Thesis, University of California.

Zoubir, Yahia. 1995. U.S. and Soviet Policies towards France's Struggle with Anticolonial nationalism in North Africa. *Canadian Journal of History/Annales canadiennes d'histoire* 30 (3): 439–466.

INDEX

© The Author(s) 2020

N. Vince, *The Algerian War, The Algerian Revolution*,

https://doi.org/10.1007/978-3-030-54264-1

Printed in Great Britain
by Amazon

38127512R00137